Educating through Art

Dedication

To Peter

Educating through Art

The Steiner School Approach

Floris Books

First published in Swedish as *Filosofens Knapp (The Philosopher's Button)* by Carlsson Bokförlag.
This edition first published in English in 1996 by Floris Books.

Translated from the Swedish by Petal Joan Roberts-Leijon.
Chapter 7 translated by Elisabet Waldenström and revised by Petal Joan Roberts-Leijon.

Joseph Beuys' 'Manifesto' (see Chapter 7) translated by Free International University, 1972.

The translation of this book has been assisted with a grant from the Swedish Council for Research in the Humanities and Social Sciences

British Library CIP Data available

ISBN 0-86315-187-6

Printed in Great Britain
by Cromwell Press, Melksham, Wilts

Contents

Acknowledgments

I am extremely grateful for, and appreciative of, the resources which the Swedish Council for Research in the Humanities and Social Sciences (HSFR) provided for me to carry out this work of research. After almost six years, I still have the feeling that I have made only a tentative start in an exploration which seems to have endless bounds.

I must express my warm gratitude for the kind assistance of all concerned at the Rudolf Steiner Teacher-Training College in Järna and other Steiner schools, where I was readily given access to classes and school events and where time was set aside to answer all my questions. Not least, I much appreciated their understanding of my need to retain independence as an outside researcher, something which is essential for an investigation of this kind. Even after long periods away, on returning I would meet the same helpfulness and willingness to discuss fresh questions which had arisen in my mind, or problems which I needed to air.

Of course, I am myself chiefly responsible for this book. But I should point out that the general direction of my theme and many of the ensuing thoughts and reflections, were influenced by the numerous discussions and meetings I enjoyed over six years of research. It has seemed a great privilege, though at times one hard to manage, to have been offered these opportunities as a researcher.

There are so many people to whom I owe a debt of thanks, that they cannot all be named. Of particular importance, however, were my talks with Arne Klingborg and Walter Liebendörfer on their work in teacher training. Both men made a strong impression through their keenly searching attitude to life and their tremendous generosity and enthusiasm in sharing their wide knowledge and broad outlook.

Conversations with many others were similarly of great value. I would like to mention in particular Inga-Britt Abrahamsson, Pär Ahlbom, Henning Andersen, Erik Asmussen, Wolfgang Brehmer, Birgitta Carlgren, Frans Carlgren, Eleonor Hill-Edwards, Åke Fant, Torgil Holtsmark, Hugo Johansson, Göran Krantz, Dan Lindholm, Johannes Ljungquist, Hans Möller, Sonja Robbert, Karin Ruths-Hoffman, Ingrid

Sahlberg, Hasse Scherlund, Pehr Sällström, Bengt Ulin, Bernt Uno, Erik Westerberg, and last but not least, Reijo Wilenius. In addition, on my many visits over the years — mainly to the Järna Teacher-Training College, but also to the Kristoffer School and once or twice to the Nibble School — I had countless informal encounters with teachers, trainee teachers and others, who allowed me to hear their views of the Waldorf educational system and the role of art in teaching.

I must also express my unbounded gratitude to those who have helped with my manuscript in the final stages. Aant Elzinga and Bengt-Erik Andersson read it in an academic context. Others responded to my requests for help or, out of their own interest, spent time and effort on the undertaking. Here I would mention Gunnar Adler-Karlsson, Urban Dahllöf, Gunnar Eriksson, Nan Fröman, Elisabet Hermodsson, Johan Molander and Margareta Wirmark. Their opinions — supportive as well as critical — have been an important part of the process.

Of importance have also been many summer conversations with Tore Frängsmyr. In tracing literature I was greatly assisted by Birgitta Gustafsson and Dag Kyndel especially, at the library of the Institute for Teacher Training at Uppsala University. I should also like to thank Karin Johannisson for translating some passages from German.

My family has been most affected by my work. Peter has, with a mixture of apprehension and great interest, often wondered what I was really up to. Without the support that he, in spite of everything, offered me, I should probably have abandoned the project. His opinions did not always help to speed up the process, but they served as a constant reminder of how unfamiliar for us today is the way of thinking examined here — which it is easy to forget after working for a long time in an area without outside influence.

And then I have three boys. My discussions over the years with them and their friends have given me a foothold on reality and many ideas from which to find a starting-point.

A.N.

Foreword

The space shuttle 'Challenger' blew up just after take-off on January 28, 1986. Seven people lost their lives, sacrificed to one of the great 'high-tech' projects of our age. Since then, the space agency NASA has run into trouble on several occasions. A recent mishap was the initial problem with the huge Hubble telescope which now orbits our planet, successfully transmitting images of furthest space. Soon after its launch, one of the telescope mirrors proved to have a construction fault. The polished surface deviated a fraction of a millimetre from the point required, but enough to put seriously out of focus the pictures of the stars and distant galaxies being transmitted back to the scientists in their laboratories.

Both these cases remind us of the vulnerability of modern technology. Mere carelessness might have been avoidable; an experienced craftsman would perhaps have discovered the faults in time. But there is now a kind of science based on hierarchy, which has distanced itself from the very Nature it is trying to understand and manipulate.

The physicist Richard Feynman who discovered the fault behind the Challenger disaster, put forward his theory at a press conference in Washington. All he needed was a rubber ring and a glass of ice-cold water. After the ring was dipped into the ice-water, it deformed and took a while to regain its original shape. Deformation at low temperatures, he said, created a leak in a pipe on Challenger where dangerous gases seeped out and then ignited, with the result that the shuttle exploded.

Feynman claimed that he could arrive at this conclusion due to the fact that in his childhood he had not been subjected much to the usual school education. He had taught himself a good deal of science at home, as a game. Since then he had always had a playful attitude to things, thereby retaining an open imagination.

In his analysis of *Laughter* as the releaser of creative imagination, the French scientific philosopher Henri Bergson, writing at the beginning of our century, says:

> Thus we see that art, whether it be a matter of painting, sculpture, poetry or music, has as its sole objective the removal of utilitarian symbols, of conventional and socially acceptable generalizations, in short, the removal of everything which disguises reality from us, so that we can stand face to face with reality itself. It is due to a misunderstanding on this point that the debate between realism and idealism within art has arisen. Art is, to be sure, nothing other than a more direct vision of reality, but this pure perception implies a break with the utilitarian convention, an innate disinterestedness, in particular in the mind or consciousness, in short a kind of immateriality in life itself — that is, what is usually called idealism. Therefore one could very well say, without playing on the meaning of the words, that realism exists in the work of art when idealism exists in the soul, and that it is only through ideality that one can maintain contact with reality.

In fact neither the artist nor the scientist confronts reality with a big 'R'; instead the confrontation takes place through concepts bearing the stamp of the social institutions and the intellectual traditions. There is always a socially constructivist factor. The question here, however, is how limited one might be by these concepts, and what strategies might be found to try and correct that pettiness which is associated with degenerate forms of modern technological culture.

Seen in a larger context, the problem is that between Nature and the scientist today there exists a bureaucratic buffer of decision-makers; moreover, science as a modern institution tends to generate a one-sided rational thinking which deforms our other senses and other dimensions in our intercourse with Nature — among them the artistic and the practical. The same deformation is stamped on our educational systems and the methods which they deploy for passing on knowledge to the next generation. For that reason we should perhaps not be surprised that many of the most eminent natural scientists are those who have defied the normal educational systems. Thanks to this, they retain that freer imagination and playful attitude which is the characteristic of childlike curiosity. This is the same attitude which confronts us in art, although the formal language is of another kind.

In good science, utility, pleasure and criticism are united. In our schools, including the universities, there exists on the other hand a tendency to place rigid utility in the foreground, at the cost of the other two qualities: pleasure and criticism. The bureaucrats' heavy (and rich) hand has contributed to the segregation of the forms of knowledge of art and science — and thereby to a social lobotomy which has spread to the public corners of society.

These problems are under discussion in many places. One important question concerns the possibilities that education has in the interplay between the departure-points of science and art, and their ties with reality already at the educational stage. At present there is a new way of thinking on several points. Hopefully, the changes will not stop at the forms of organization. The dimension of the theory of knowledge is every bit as important.

Since Thomas Kuhn introduced the concept of the paradigm, a growing number of researchers have pointed to important connections between idea and organization behind the terms and conditions of science. How the stuff of knowledge in our social institutions comes into being, is organized and is taught, is not independent of the view of knowledge. In other words, if the organizations are to be remodelled, the theories of knowledge behind the changes must also be examined. This applies to the policies within school and research to an equally high degree. The present book, *Educating through Art,* is a significant contribution to this discussion.

In this work Agnes Nobel takes up an alternative educational tradition — Waldorf education — and much more besides. She traces among other things the epistemological roots of this tradition to Goethe's ideas on Man and Nature. Her portrayal of this alternative is not merely a study in the history of ideas but also has practical value, since she significantly contributes to the expansion of the limits of perception in our present age of reassessment.

Goethe, together with Newton, represents a key reference point in our cultural history. These two have come to stand for complementary ways of approaching Nature and the world around us, from the point of view of an artistic and a classic scientific temperament, respectively. Goethe portrayed the conflict in his epic *Faust.* In addition he challenged the Newtonians on the issue of optics and the theory of colour, wishing to defend the importance of subjective experience as against the objective mathematizing approach to the perception of light as a phenomenon. Newton, and in his extension Mephistopheles, leads humanity towards a high-tech world and towards disaster, while Goethe believes that he himself stands for an alternative which in modern terms would be described as ecological and 'caring.'

The French philosophical scientist, Michel Serres, is a modern thinker who deals with similar themes. He claims that science and technology are founded on a belligerent metaphor — that of humanity's war against nature, with the aim of domination. Serres calls for a *contrat naturel,* a human contract with nature corresponding to that which Rousseau advocated for people in relation to one another, the basis of the modern Constitutional State. Where are the rights of Nature? Should these not be written into our laws along with human rights? The question opens a new branch of ethics/bioethics. The same thinking should be introduced into our modern attempt to establish a sustainable process of global development, which is vital if we are to avoid future catastrophe, whether climatic or environmental.

Regrettably these two approaches, the artistic and the scientific, have come to be disconnected from one another. This is noticeable not least in the currently renewed discussion on C.P. Snow's so-called 'two cultures.' The humanities and artistic education have been rediscovered as a resource in the high-tech community. Business leaders are beginning to argue that a substantial ingredient of education in the humanities should be included in scientific and technical courses, in training for leadership and for politics.

The issues that Agnes Nobel takes up are of great topical interest. She points not only to an alternative system of education designed to keep the mind free from the paralysing injunctions of bureaucracy, but also, as I said before, to its epistemological dimension and to its criticism of civilization. Thereby a vacuum is filled which otherwise could all too easily become the subject of bargain-basement humanism.

The New Age prophets, for example, ignorant of history and steered by the capitalist powers of the market, have adopted the same ideas, but they vulgarize and simplify such things as the ideas of modern quantum physics in their eagerness to find a relationship between their mysticism and science. Agnes Nobel, on the other hand, brings out in her study the criticism of civilization reflected in the stream from Schiller and Goethe. Through bringing Rudolf Steiner's contribution to educational science into focus, she reveals to us several fundamentally important aspects of art as a form of knowledge equal to science.

Aant Elzinga
Professor of Theory of Science and Research
University of Gothenburg

'For, to declare it once and for all, Man plays only when he is, in the full meaning of the word, Man, and is *only wholly Man, when at play.'*

F. Schiller, *On the Aesthetic Education of Man*

'Nur die Fülle führt zur Klarheit
und im Abgrund wohnt die Wahrheit.'

(Only fullness leads to clarity
and in the abyss dwells the truth.)

F. Schiller (Niels Bohr's favourite aphorism)

'Enthusiasm' From the Greek: *en theós* = possessed by a god, inspired.

(Dictionary definition)

INTRODUCTION
The Philosopher's Button

It was with a certain sense of awe that I embarked on this project, which has gone under the working name of 'Art and knowledge — an inquiry with particular reference to the theory and practice of Waldorf education.' It is also with some trepidation that I now present the results of my efforts. I am sure that anyone who has spent time on more thorough studies of anthroposophical literature and anthroposophically-inspired practical activities will understand my feelings.

However, I am not aiming at them first and foremost here. Rather, I have had in mind those who have seen for themselves or who have read about anthroposophical activities — in education, health care, environmental care, architecture, agriculture and so on — and who have been impressed and have wondered about it, but who at the same time feel a wavering scepticism about the theoretical background on which all this is said to rest. Have they perhaps heard some weird notions, tried reading a book on it or seen examples of anthroposophical art, which they neither liked nor understood? That was how I myself began.

That I finally got going, took heart and applied for a research grant for a project of this nature, depended in no small part on the fact that I discovered that Rudolf Steiner — the founder of Waldorf education — actually had a sense of humour. I would never have believed it! This gave me certain assurances. I reasoned that somewhere there was a distant counterbalance to that gnawing impression of odd spiritualism and sectarianism that I had first got. In point of fact, I discovered that Steiner gave a central role precisely to a sense of humour, particularly in contexts which ran the risk of being seen as sentimental. Besides this, he linked humour and play to the area of aesthetics, where they of course belong. At this point my curiosity was really aroused and I began to wonder why this had so completely escaped me — and many others too, I believe. This conflict alone appeared to me to be an exciting phenomenon worth studying in itself.

I mention all this in my Introduction since it is precisely knowing about Steiner's attitude to humour that has helped me in studying this admittedly unusual subject. It has helped me get past the most difficult passages — and I have found quite a few of these! It has helped me to adopt a certain frankness and to continue with conscience intact instead of being simply blocked by things that I found incomprehensible or even sometimes preposterous. On occasion it has helped me to reflect on Swedenborg, Rudbeck, Linnaeus and Strindberg — perhaps the best-known Swedes down the ages — and the strange areas they dared to tackle amongst all those aspects of reality we lightly think we understand.

For a long time I have felt that there lies a danger in higher education and science becoming identified with something serious, formal and difficult, and which the majority of people are not expected to understand. There was an old tradition in Sweden that at the public presentation and defence of a doctoral thesis, a 'Third Opponent' — otherwise known as the Son of Earth *(Terrae filius)* — attended. He was supposed to bring the candidate's thoughts down to earth so that ordinary people could understand them, to give them life, and to act the fool and heckle those in power if he felt like it.[1] Some years back, the function of the Third Opponent was abolished; I think it was a step in the wrong direction. We need more and not less of this kind of play and openness, I believe, in the future. I also believe that fear rather than creativity flourishes in an overblown academic *gravitas.* And the universities often set the fashion in education in any case. Fantasy and play are regarded as legitimate for small children, but what happens further up the educational system? And what happens in teacher training, which is supposed to have a scientific basis?

After many years' experience in higher education, following the debate on culture and sometimes taking part in it, it has struck me how much we fear things with which we feel unfamiliar. Difficult-to-define things such as feelings and values and so-called 'spiritual' qualities in our life arouse anxiety, at times even shaking the earth under our feet, and are usually expunged from the realm of science. But I am afraid that the intellectuals cannot retain their credibility — either here in Sweden or out in the wider world where ways of thinking vary so much — unless they show greater openness towards *different* ways of thinking. In recent years, we see developments which inspire hope. Some of these changes have their roots in the revolutionary rethinking which has resulted from new insights in quantum physics. In addition, a growing understanding for the feminine perspective in research and social development is seen by many as promising hope for the future.

As regards the topic area addressed in this book, we can also detect in many observers a fully justified fear of sectarianism and dogmatism. That danger is implicit wherever a single person or teaching exerts great influence and gathers many critical as well as uncritical followers. One should then be aware of the fact that Rudolf Steiner himself took this very seriously and often emphasized this palpable risk. For instance, it is related that during a walk in the grounds of the Goetheanum, the anthroposophical institution in Switzerland, Steiner asked his companion to stop for a moment while he took a stone out of his boot — otherwise, Steiner feared, everyone in the entire district would be limping the next day.[2]

The central theme in Waldorf education and anthroposophy is the narrowing of the gap between theory and practice. For Steiner, unpractical thinking and thoughtless practice were equally useless as criteria of truth. The whole man must simultaneously take both practice and theory into account. He warns that the issues easily take on an anti-secular theoretical character, and adds somewhat pointedly: *No one can become a great philosopher if he cannot sew a button on his trousers.* The more theoretically a person expresses himself on an issue, the more he must demonstrate practical know-how as a basis for his statements.

How did the German philosophers and scientists of Steiner's day react to the humour and seriousness in a statement of this kind? How do we react today? When I related this story at a seminar at the Centre for Women Researchers and Research on Women at Uppsala University, one of the participants suggested that the phrase ought to be written over the entrance to the University's Main Hall, instead of the present motto: 'Free thinking is great; correct thinking is greater.' An idea perhaps worth thinking about — at least playfully?

During the course of my studies I have found it remarkable how little known is the background to Steiner's educational system (and equally other anthroposophical activities) outside the anthroposophists' own circle, even if this is a fairly large and growing one. It has often struck me that those areas which I have found most interesting, and also most relevant to current scientific-theoretical debate, relate to those areas of Steiner's work operating out of the limelight or completely silenced out of existence. I have also noticed now and again how statements relating to Steiner's ideas, taken completely out of context, turn up in discussions, usually without any wider reference to his theories and the practical work arising from them. In the same way, there is a peculiar silence surrounding the powerful inspiration which Steiner's work has been and continues to be for many leading avant-garde artists.

Considering the great interest in these matters — in Sweden and elsewhere, including now Eastern Europe — it is important that the background be lifted out of the shadows. Without extensive knowledge of the epistemological premises the debate becomes misleading. The practical side can then come to be limited to a mere matter of copying — and in some cases distorting — methods, without the necessary anchoring in the epistemology and deeper human knowledge which is so fundamentally important. Anthroposophists, as well as others with an inquiring nature, would surely welcome the arrival of a freer and better-informed discussion.

My main purpose here has been to try and figure out *why* artistic exercises are accorded such central significance within the context of education. This is a complex matter which goes deeply into the anthroposophical way of thinking and acting. It is about our ability to cross frontiers, and our chances of reacquiring the unity between Art, Science and Religion which has sadly fallen asunder in our culture.

I hope to have the opportunity of writing, more fully than has been possible here, about the many practical experiments being done at Steiner schools in integrating more creative work methods into teaching. Interested readers, however, can acquaint themselves further through Frans Carlgren's and Arne Klingborg's book *Education towards Freedom.*

* * *

In Chapter 1, I discuss why I became interested in the role of art within the context of knowledge. Here, I also set these studies into their wider context of knowledge, as these issues have particularly interested me. This is necessary for readers to be able to orientate themselves from my points of departure and the choices I have made within a vast area, difficult to demarcate. Any reader finding this account superfluous may skip this chapter. Throughout the book I make links between the background which I am here trying to reflect, and events in the present debate around education and culture. Some people regard this as irrelevant to an examination of this nature, while others have found it to be particularly stimulating. I see it as a stage in an attempt at working, more energetically than is usual in research contexts, on coupling the thinking traditions of epistemology to current debates on culture and practical reality today.

I devote Chapter 2 to the special conditions confronting anyone doing research around the bases of Waldorf education. I imagine that my experiences might make it easier for others to tackle the background material for themselves, starting from their own disciplinary background and interests.

In Chapter 3, Rudolf Steiner's own education and upbringing are presented, mostly as he described them himself in his autobiography written towards the end of his life.

Chapter 4 involved the greatest difficulties, but the source material also provided me with the biggest surprises, and captured my interest the most. This section deals with Steiner's research on Goethe and Schiller, which forms the basis of Waldorf education and which is of particular importance when it comes to gaining an insight into why art and one's personal artistic exercises have been assigned such significance.

Chapters 5, 6 and 7 take up educational issues as Rudolf Steiner understood them at the beginning of the twentieth century, and here I demonstrate, too, the connection with later debates on education. I hope it will be clear to the reader how the ideas here are anchored in Steiner's interpretation of Goethe and Schiller, covered in the preceding chapters.

Chapter 8 gives an insight into how Steiner, on the basis of his theories on the development of knowledge and the role of art in that context, proceeded when he started the first Waldorf School in Germany, directly after the end of the First World War.

The book closes with an Epilogue dealing with the role of the creative person when it comes to creating wholeness and an overview, and the role of artistic activity in training our talents for this purpose. In order to achieve this we must train our ability to cross frontiers — not, as now, first and foremost to delimit and to seek contrasts, but rather to strive after complementarity and to unite opposing ways of seeing things. This is an epistemological perspective now becoming the object of growing interest and which, during the period I spent working on this book, has proved to have remarkably strong echoes in work being done on brain research.[3] Here, art and aesthetic development are ascribed a vital but neglected role in the acquisition of knowledge — a view which corresponds directly to what anthroposophists are attempting to achieve within Waldorf education.

> The movements of love have lulled and they sleep
> but their most secret thoughts meet
> as when two colours meet and flow into each other
> on the wet paper in a schoolboy's painting.
>
> *(From a poem by Tomas Tranströmer)*[4]

CHAPTER 1

Background and Points of Departure

In all teaching, there must be something more than a merely mechanical distribution of facts if the teaching is to have life and meaning for students and teachers — and perhaps also if the continuously increasing volume of knowledge is to promote life rather than death in the future.

Small children have the ability to absorb knowledge and get a hold on their surrounding world through their feelings and all their senses. They come to have less and less use for this ability, or opportunity of training it, the further up they advance in the educational system. The higher the system of education, the more theoretical and formalized knowledge is given priority and rewarded in preference to one's own aesthetic and practical experiences. Research on the extent to which this change can be justified is seldom given much attention. Nevertheless research does exist into the role of art and artistic exercises in the matter of training people's sensibility, and which emphasizes this precise aspect as being basic and even necessary for our survival.[1]

My own interest in issues relating to art and knowledge began when I was working in the sixties as a child psychologist at a psychiatric clinic and came into contact mainly with children and young people with school problems. Often the children were unable to adapt to school as they should, according to the adult point of view. General restlessness and concentration difficulties were very common. Failures were particularly obvious in the so-called basic skills subjects — that is to say, subjects which society regarded as most important. Difficulties in reading and writing as well as poor results in mathematics were often part of the problems people sought help for.

When they came to the clinic, I was given the opportunity of meeting the children quietly and in private. It used to amaze me at that time what great inner resources these children proved to have. This was especially noticeable when they were allowed to express themselves artistically — in free play, and in word and picture, when they drew, painted and related things freely. It was then that blocks and inhibitions loosened up, as it were. Here, they dared to give vent to ideas, experiences and knowledge that they had within themselves, but which otherwise they rarely manifested outwardly. Many of them proved to be capable of living, expressive language which one would never have guessed at. Besides which, they also demonstrated on these occasions a remarkable ability to concentrate — provided only they were allowed to occupy themselves with something that really interested them. Ever since that time I have thought about the significance of the artistic element in the theory of knowledge in school teaching. More and more, my interest has extended to the sort of schooling which takes place in universities and colleges.

When I returned to University after six years' practical work, in order to continue my studies in pedagogy, it struck me what a gap there was between the children's own experience of school and the analyses of this which were made from scientific standpoints. They appeared to me to be two separate worlds.

At the social science institutes during the fifties and sixties, interest was primarily trained on very comprehensive macro-analyses with the emphasis on quantity. I experienced the gap between theory and practice as being very large. I found that too little room was given to psychological knowledge touching on the children and the adults, and their qualitative needs.

At that time there was general optimism concerning technological solutions to social problems of all kinds and not least in the area of education. But a precondition here was a mechanical view of man, as well as of society and of nature. One unequivocal expression of this view within schools was, it seemed to me, the virtual explosion in the use of so-called all-purpose textbook series, offering condensed texts in mainly factual prose, while at the same time contact with genuine literature emanating from writers and artists suffered a languishing decline.[2]

In these textbook series the whole educational plan is worked out to the last dot by external experts. One advantage was supposed to be that the schoolbooks were thereby made 'teacher-proof,' as they put it. In other words, they required a minimum of creative personal contribution on the part of the teacher. Another aim was to make them self-instructive for the pupils to work on their own, mostly using 'multiple-choice' where possible answers were limited — often simply 'yes' or 'no.' These schoolbook systems are still being used and comprise a preliminary stage towards programmed teaching using computers.

In expanding cities, with traffic problems and long distances to the countryside, it became all the more necessary for children's education to take place within school walls. There were fewer opportunities for pupils and teachers to start out from reality — from their real surroundings with all their multiplicity and complexity. Instead they had to study in laboratories or classrooms where, with the help of technology, they could listen to 'forest sounds' and 'field sounds' recorded on tape. However, one's own personal sensory experience, with all its qualities, is very hard to replace.

In a highly formalized and textbook-steered education — where, in addition, measurements and tests exercise a controlling effect — it is often assumed that neither teacher nor pupils, in any profound, humanly conscious and varied sense, have a need to influence the educational process themselves. The conscious thinking, feeling and creative person with his own free will and his own sense of responsibility appears all but disconnected from the teaching/learning process in the technical sense. Here the human individuals are not truly participants in the process. Dialogue, movement, the dynamics and the tension which lie in the relationship of person to person, as well as between the individual and a living text or a surrounding reality, are almost entirely eliminated.

How does this affect our human sensibility, our environmental consciousness, our ability to experience insight and our knowledge in a more profound sense? How can knowledge be brought to life in such conditions? Should perhaps art, as a form of understanding, be taken more seriously as a complement to the prevailing scientific and more mechanically coloured way of seeking knowledge about reality? Is it, in the first place, perhaps not so much 'knowledge in school,' which the school debate has been about during recent years, but rather *what* knowledge the schools should develop?

Aesthetics and its role in human education and development is one of the eternal philosophical issues treated throughout the history of ideas, from the time of Plato onwards. To what extent art and the practice of art are significant for the development of knowledge in general — and not merely a matter of entertainment, leisure-time occupation, or the special aesthetic-practical subjects in school — is a question to which neither pedagogical science nor other disciplines have given much prominence. Nevertheless, a certain change in this respect can be discerned during recent years. More and more people recognize the power of art in different contexts. But art, like most things possessing great power, can be used both for good as well as evil. Are perhaps increased demands for objectivity, measurability and scientific proof in a more narrow sense, connected with our experience of how art was abused for propaganda purposes in Nazi Germany?[3] Did this lead to an understandable but excessive objectivizing and technologizing of teaching methods, which also became harmful in its own way? And of course, science, too, was extensively abused by the Nazis. The problems here need to be clarified and analysed from a number of perspectives.

The philosopher John Dewey speaks in his book *Art as Experience* of the aesthetic as a polar opposite to the mechanical. What consequences does this have for the system of education in a culture which, since way back, is still marked in practice by a mechanical picture of the world and a mechanical view of man and knowledge?

The writer, historian and social planner Lewis Mumford has analysed modern social planning and finds it to be largely incompatible with the needs of people. He has also significantly analysed the educational community. He says here that there exists an automatization of knowledge, and holds the view that the prevalent faith in mechanical quantification, without continuous human qualification, makes the whole educational process absurd.

Like many others, he traces the roots of this development to the middle of the seventeenth century, when the experimental method of scientific thinking and its mathematical-physical logic was formulated. The new science sought to reduce all complexities into small, isolated, controllable packages which could be measured exactly. Piece after piece could be added to our knowledge without it being necessary, as it is within an organic system, to work out a comprehensible, all-encompassing pattern, or to unite the pieces into an effective order answering to human needs and aimed at furthering human development.[4]

T.S. Eliot stated that 'not the least significant effect of industrialization is that we become mechanized in our minds, and as a consequence of this we try to equip ourselves with *engineering-like* solutions to problems, which in the main are problems which touch on *life.*'[5]

The futurist scientist Torsten Hägerstrand maintains that 'if one assumes that quality in a really broad sense should be a key word in the future understanding of what is meant by prosperity, then the many cross-connections in life presuppose that that concept be taken seriously in all areas.' He believes, too, that:

> in both research and practice it is necessary to revive the original double meaning of the concept 'art' which previously encompassed both practical skill and works of 'fine culture.' It ought to present itself as a fascinating task to so permeate, by means of research and teaching, the personal philosophy of people with a *new aesthetic keynote* (my italics) that their philosophy would become strong enough to keep narrow rationality, fanaticism and commercial tricks at bay. The Humanities ought to be able to take on significant tasks within the areas of 'a critique of technology and the environment.' More and more people believe that the aesthetic, taken in a broad sense, is the foremost cohesive and moderating force which can be mobilized in our technological age. That thought is an interesting challenge to all those engaged in the business of teaching ...[6]

'Are the natural sciences a means of culture?' the scientist Elias Fries asks, in a popular science essay from the middle of the nineteenth century. He speaks of the risk of our knowledge of nature being passed on too much in the form of generalities and abstractions, and the importance of taking the study of nature 'to heart' — 'if organic nature is ever to be studied with success, love for it must be aroused and upheld in youth.'[7]

How much of this affection are we given in the nature teaching as practised in our schools and universities? With small children there is the possibility of room for it, provided that the teacher is sensitive to its importance. But the further up the educational system we go, the more segregated, specialized and formalized does the treatment become. Scientific facts and information within the humanities and social sciences, are presented as if disconnected from one another as well as from our emotions, needs, conscious thought, actions, and personal responsibilities. Do we really want such a narrow schooling for tomorrow's adults, or should something more, something different be called for? (Already as a sixteen-year old, the artist Pablo Picasso appears to have worked on these questions — see Plate 1.)

Our conceptions of what people need in the scientific-technological society have been continuously secularized and become all the more materialistic, according to the ex-Cambridge philosopher Georg Henrik von Wright. Science in the quantitative sense has grown above and beyond philosophy and art, or has at any rate broken loose as an independent component from the totality of educational life. As a result, that understanding of the whole which is intrinsic to the humanist outlook is under threat of disappearance.[8]

Another philosopher, this time from Finland, Professor Reijo Wilenius, speaks of man as having three basic needs: social, material and immaterial.[9] Is it perhaps these immaterial needs which young people the world over give expression to in their intense interest in music which has developed over the last twenty years — while at the same time, their interest in the subject 'Music' in school is very weak, at any rate here in Sweden?

A growing number of people, scientists among them, stress today the importance of reviewing our narrowly mechanistic view of science and the ensuing picture of the world, a view that has prevailed for several hundred years.[10] It has paved the way for materialistic ways of thinking in a regimented framework. Efforts to achieve more qualitative values with regard to the needs of man and nature, are difficult to combine with what our culture has come to regard as high quality science, as specialized 'big' and 'hard' science based on mathematical considerations is viewed as the primary objective. Similar ideals have been around for a long time within the humanities and social sciences.

In our fascination with the amazing progress achieved by science, more emotional aspects of life, which art for instance stands for, have been pushed into the background. Art then comes to be something apart, belonging to the leisure side of life — or else valuable solely

The cover of Roger Sperry's book with Salvador Dali's Raphaelesque head exploding, *1951.*

for the purpose of investment. Can it rather be said to preserve an indispensable 'keynote' in life? What many people regard as the hallmark of art is its relation to immaterial things — our inner life, our invisible emotions and values, our ability to communicate with the Muses, our intuition, spontaneity and imagination, as well as our ability to synthesize and grasp the whole. Is there perhaps a 'Logic of Poesy' as the philosopher Hans Larsson suggested at the turn of the century?[11] Perhaps it could be a longing for something of this kind which recently made *Dead Poets Society* such a cult film among the young as well as with older people both in the USA and Sweden.[12]

Also of interest in this connection is research touching on the function of the human brain. The cerebral physiologist Roger Sperry points out that in research today the existence of a human inner consciousness is no longer disregarded, as it was for a long time, but that full recognition is now instead attached to it. Sperry also believes that *the educational system has actively contributed* to forming our way of thinking and our skills, by particularly and *too one-sidedly* placing the emphasis on training abstract, mathematical and logical abilities, while complex contexts which encompass a pictorial holistic way of thinking and emotional responses, are not accorded the same cognitive status. The classic neurological doctrine on the dominance of the left half of the brain over the right half is no longer valid, in Sperry's opinion. Both halves of the brain function instead as an *integrated* unit, which is something today's system of education *counteracts,* according to Sperry.[13]

Might it be that the very nature of our system of education leads to our becoming, from a physiological point of view, 'mechanized in the mind' and less capable of grasping whole contexts? Is it thinkable and possible that the modern emphasis on abstract, mathematical and logical functions which have existed for centuries, but have become all the more pronounced, has in some way caused those gifts which we as human beings also have, of seeing complex contexts and making evaluative decisions, to lie fallow and remain undeveloped instead of being practised and trained as an integral part of the process of gaining knowledge?

Albert Einstein is reported to have said that with the atom bomb everything changed, except people's way of thinking. More and more people open themselves today to alternative ways of thinking. Is it possible to find ways of integrating the emotional and ethical aspects in our search for knowledge and truth? If so, that would be far from being a new idea. The true, the right and the beautiful have previously been regarded as a unity in the history of ideas. Why have we in our age distanced ourselves with such force from a more holistic way of thinking?

Another physicist and contemporary of Einstein was the Dane, Niels Bohr. From the 1920s onwards, he devoted more and more of his time to formulating philosophical questions in relation to natural science and the theory of knowledge. He arrived by way of quantum physics

The coat-of-arms of the physicist Niels Bohr's Order of the Elephant, composed from his own guidelines. The text Contraria sunt complementa *means 'Contrasts are complementary.' In the centre,* yin *and* yang, *the two Taoist principles of the universe, between which a continuous exchange must take place in order for a balance to be achieved.*

at his principle of complementarity, which he wished to see as the cornerstone of a new epistemology with universal validity. His idea was that only in the totality could one acquire all possible information about the object, rather than through seeking out differences.[14]

Does the important and stimulating innovation which our age needs perhaps arise in the border area between art and science? This is a question touched on in a supplement to a Swedish government report on 'The Future of Scientific Research.'[15] It is also a central theme underlying and inspiring the approach of Waldorf schools and other anthroposophical activities which are attracting greater and greater attention around the world. (For evidence of this, see Appendices 2 and 3.)

The purpose of the present study is to attempt to understand why anthroposophists strive to let the artistic element become an integrated part of practical daily realities. Why do they attach such significance to art and artistic exercises in the teaching of children and young people, as well as in adult education? Is there any connection between this and the fact that anthroposophists *in deed* accomplish so many things which in other institutions and social organizations rarely get past the formulation of aims, theories and fine words? Is it possible to get closer to an understanding of how and why anthroposophical activities, for so long and so consistently, have been able to get people to participate in and drive projects through to completion which demonstrate both foresight and responsibility in caring for Nature and people? They do not shy away from the great questions of life merely because it is not possible to get at them with the scientific methods we have today. Instead they search for ways to extend the boundaries of science. And this is exactly where they find their most zealous critics.

Two events above all contributed to my interest in the Waldorf system of education. The first occurred at the beginning of the 1960's when on a study visit to one of the homes for the therapeutic education of children with serious mental illnesses, which are part of the Camphill movement. What particularly stuck in my memory from this visit was the natural respect and confidence the adults seemed to adopt towards these children, who appeared so entirely to live in their own private worlds, apparently without any contact with the outside world. Needless to say, the children had their grave handicaps. But for precisely that reason, the adults believed, it was necessary to put in an extra amount of enthusiasm, imagination and feeling for each child, in order to discover how each could be enabled to contribute something of itself, together with others, or in a work task. There did not seem to be the slightest doubt that every one of these children had something extremely valuable to offer within the group. It was up to the staff to use all their feeling, imagination and ability to gain insight, in order to get the child to express what he or she really had to say. Above all, it was through the medium of music that this was supposed to happen. It appeared to me that it must be this obvious confidence in each child — a bit naïvely optimistic, one might think — that was the key to the good care these children, each with their own individual character, could be given.

Other impressions from this same visit came across as peculiar and strange. One instance of this was the dreamlike photograph of Rudolf Steiner which hung in a prominent position in the pale pink assembly hall. As far as I remember, there was something about him that was a little secretive and of which one did not speak. Similarly, I remember that I found it most odd when a very large male member of the staff started to explain eurythmy to us — the special art of movement which they practise here — and also demonstrated some 'floating' movements. However, the little eurythmy performance put on by the handicapped children and youngsters was something I did not find at all difficult to appreciate and understand.

The other event occurred roughly twenty years later. At that time I had heard that the Waldorf system of education, and also other anthroposophical activities, was said to be based wholly and completely on Goethe's work, both as an artist and as a scientist. At that point I did not even know that Goethe had devoted himself to scientific research. This struck me as exciting and I noticed an advertisement in the newspaper for a lecture entitled 'The forms of life in transformation' which was part of a series of lectures called 'Goethe and the science of the organic.' The lectures were held at the Kristoffer School in Stockholm, which is the largest Waldorf school in Sweden. Up until then I had never been there.

The lecturer was Walter Liebendörfer — at that time science teacher at the school and currently in charge of the training-programme for Waldorf teachers in Järna. He posed the question, what would have happened if we had developed a science of the organic — of life — in a different way. With a Darwin Jubilee coming up at that time, the question of evolution had again begun to present itself as more of a puzzle. Sudden alterations of whole systems had been observed and there were no explanations. Liebendörfer said that when the artist Goethe carried out research on Nature, he lived with Nature. He did not wait so much for ideas to arrive from without, but was instead more attentive to an inner force of the imagination which enabled him to grasp 'the *gestalt*-melody' (a biological term) and to feel any dissonances which arose. It was his artistic sense which helped him with this and which caused him to think pictorially. By living in such close proximity to the plant world he could also grasp the conformity to laws within botany resembling that which exists in art. A force of the imagination of this kind, which Goethe possessed in an unusually rich measure, is not cultivated within our educational institutions so that it can be developed into knowledge and lead to scientific research, Liebendörfer said. It is already allowed to grow cold at school. Today, in his opinion, we have achieved a specialization and a theorizing of science which has become a cultural phenomenon with us.

At the end of the lecture he returned to Darwin. He pointed out how Darwin, as a young 28-year old, could describe colours and other experiences of nature with rapture and beautiful words. He read aloud a passage from Darwin's autobiography, written in his old age. Here Darwin calls to mind how, as a young man he enjoyed poems, novels and music, but how he could not stand such things any more. Now the main thing when he read a book was that it should be about beautiful women, and that the whole story should have a happy ending — anything else ought to be made illegal. 'My brain seems to have turned into a machine. Were I given the chance to live my life over again I would read a little poetry every week. Now my brain has atrophied and my emotional life has become weakened,' Darwin confesses.[16] Liebendörfer expressed admiration for the humility and courage required to admit such a thing about one's life.

This lecture was puzzling, but captured my interest in some undefinable way. I felt I had gained new and different impressions to build on, regarding the significance of art as seen from the standpoint of the theory of knowledge.

For me, at that time, having over a period of many years researched questions concerning art and knowledge, it had long been close at hand to take an interest in the Waldorf system of education. But because their particular style of art had made such an alien impression on me, I had not considered studying it more closely. But now I felt I had discovered a way of regarding art from departure-points other than those to which I was accustomed.

Outside the lecture hall one could buy a pocket edition of Rudolf Steiner's exhaustive commentaries to Goethe's scientific works,[17] which Steiner had worked on over a period of fourteen years as a young graduate from the Institute of Technology in Vienna. At that time this was completely new to me. I bought the book out of sheer curiosity and read with great interest, despite the fact that long passages seemed far beyond my ability to grasp. I progressed further and discovered that there was a Swedish lecturer in physics who had published commentaries to Goethe's Theory of Colour, and who had to a great extent started out from Steiner's work on the subject.[18] Likewise, I discovered that a Swedish professor of religious psychology, Hjalmar Sundén, had written a book on Rudolf Steiner.[19] I read these books with great interest and dared after that to tackle several other writings by and also about Steiner.

Important sources of inspiration were also the great book *Education Towards Freedom* by Frans Carlgren and Arne Klingborg and also an investigation into the Kristoffer School which I had earlier read with great interest.[20] The investigation was commissioned by the Swedish National Board of Education, and carried out in 1977 under the leadership of Professor Karl-Georg Ahlström from the Institute of Education at Uppsala University. The investigation affords many glimpses into how the Waldorf school attaches great importance to integrating different art forms into the process of knowledge, and incorporating artistic activities in general, from the first to the twelfth grade. In this investigation, however, they were obliged to leave out the artistic-practical aspects of the teaching methods from the final analysis — an area which the investigators nonetheless found important to examine. Not least, they said that it would be of interest to study the method of teaching science in the Waldorf school. This was what spurred me on to tackle this project.

CHAPTER 2
Researching Steiner — a story in itself

Science and Holism

Researching into Waldorf education and its originator Rudolf Steiner, involves a number of problems calling for a chapter of their own. Whatever one draws attention to in this structure of ideas, one is always confronted with difficulties of language which in fact are impossible to solve. This is inherent in the nature of the subject and has to do with the kind of all-round or holistic thinking required.

To begin with, I would like to relate some of the difficulties I have had during this work. This may be of importance for the readers' judgment of my presentation of the matter, but I also believe that my experiences can help others who want to try to understand this material. Here I shall have to jump ahead of events and give a number of conclusions in advance which perhaps might be thought to belong properly to the final chapter.

Holistic thinking runs like a thread through everything Rudolf Steiner undertakes. He is concerned with the points of union between art, science and religion. Such a quest in itself leads to such a multitude of research problems within each of these three areas, that the problems can appear insurmountable and it can seem naïve even to attempt the undertaking. But at the same time there is also a growing number of prominent academics and writers who point out that modern questions of epistemology have proved far more complicated and impassable than expected. One reads how the need to expand the boundaries of science has evolved in the writings of scientists like Niels Bohr, Jacob Bronowski, Ragnar Granit and Roger Sperry, and the same is also true of an ever-growing number of scientific inquiries.[1]

One can regard Steiner as someone independently persevering, trying to look at things comprehensively while still applying a scientific method of approach. He is seeking not only new interdisciplinary paths *within* the field of natural science, but above all he is also seeking a link between science and the humanities. And he inspires many people not only in theory but *also in practice,* which I find to be the most remarkable aspect (see Appendices 2 and 3). But at the same time it is precisely this which often appears to cause uneasiness. He leaves the field open not only to criticism from specialists, but also to misinterpretation by other commentators.

Steiner based his way of thinking on Goethe. He saw him as *artist and scientist in one and the same person,* and emphasized that Goethe, precisely through this union, was able to give expression to such a virtually religious reverence for life, Nature and humanity. Modern man had something to learn from Goethe on precisely this point.

In Steiner's opinion, however, modern humanity lacks the equipment necessary to embrace this way of thinking and looking at things. Indeed the Goethe scholar Hermann Grimm (son of one of the famous *Fairy Tales* brothers) predicted at the turn of the last century that people would not be able to understand Goethe's scientific research until the year 2000. It is in order to try to equip people better so they can grasp whole contexts that Steiner gradually came to spend an increasing amount of time trying to formulate a different method of teaching in schools as well as a different kind of thinking, to a certain extent, at the university level.

For someone coming from the outside with a traditional research training, and who wishes to study this unconventional way of looking at life, many special problems arise. It becomes clear how the researcher's own personal perspectives, personal view of knowledge and the research method used, take hold of the research process itself and influence what the researcher chooses or does not choose to take an interest in.

It is my impression, too, that many people who look no further have a deeply rooted scepticism coupled to the anxiety that they are dealing with a kind of dogmatic sectarianism. As I have already mentioned, I find such anxiety understandable and even healthy — though not to the extent that it prevents us from approaching the material with an open mind.

I wish to emphasize that I am by no means one of those people who readily absorb either religious writings or esoteric ways of thinking. The case is rather the opposite. But I cherish the idea that there is a religious or spiritual dimension/quality in life for which most people have a basic need, but which they do not find sufficient room for today.

I belong, in addition, to the multitude of people who find it difficult to understand Rudolf Steiner's own style of art, and likewise the typical anthroposophical art which has followed in his footsteps. Now that I have had the opportunity of studying its background and seeing how it is carried out in practice, I look more at the actual practice of the art itself and its way of looking at colours, which lie *behind* these works, rather than at the products as such. The question is rather one of art as a means of *training up talents within us which our systems of education for many years past have not regarded as important.* It is a matter of seeking out ways of reaching a development of knowledge which looks to *the whole person,* which in itself is a prerequisite for the person himself being able to see the *whole, comprehensive context.*

Through these limitations of my own, I imagine that I am fairly typical of quite a good number of people who look at anthroposophy from the outside. My attempts at coming to grips with and interpreting what I have experienced during several years' study should be seen in that perspective. It is possible that my own reserved attitude may make it easier for other sceptical minds to progress in the material. But I am also aware that anyone starting out from completely different points of departure and not encountering the difficulties that I have described here, may find my presentation too limited.

People vary considerably and may therefore be helped by different points of entry to a subject-matter such as this. Some may be captivated by the religious and esoteric aspects of anthroposophy; while for many with a rigorous academic outlook this may be somewhat too 'way out.' It should be possible for the latter, I imagine, to begin with other parts of Steiner's work, which they might never have had a chance of examining, or even knew existed, without an introduction such as this.

This research project has given me the opportunity of spending a good deal of time on trying to penetrate from the outside the fundamental reasons why the Waldorf system of education places such great significance on artistic elements in *all* teaching and for *all* students

After dinner: 'It's crazy still dancing the waltz in our day and age!' — 'They say Picasso has stopped painting in the Cubist manner.' — 'Einstein is still sticking to his Formula.' — 'But one should help the workers, give lectures and so on.' — 'By the by, have you been to hear Rudolf Steiner?' — 'But my dear, you must go to Dombrowski's. The new summer models there — dazzling!'

Cartoon by Karl Arnold from Simplicissimus, 1922. Rudolf Steiner was well-known in various circles in Germany as well as in Sweden.

and teachers, right up to the highest grade of secondary school. In part, I have tried to penetrate Rudolf Steiner's own theories concerning art and knowledge. I have also, by following the training carried out at the Rudolf Steiner Teacher Training College in Järna, observed the extent to which these ideas are today applied in practical teaching. I have been able to follow their work over several, sometimes long, periods at the College. I have had access to whatever teaching and related activities I myself have wished to follow, and have been given the opportunity, during frequent and long sessions with teachers, above all, but also with students, of asking questions and discussing observations and impressions which I have found especially interesting, exciting, peculiar or difficult to understand.

Bihang till Söndagsnumret.

DAGENS NYHETER.

Söndagen den 14 November 1920.

Rudolf Steiner, en modern kulturreformator

Några intryck från antroposofernas högkvarter, Goetheanum i Dornach, som i höst invigts åt andevetenskapen

Den av Rudolf Steiner grundade och ledda antroposofiska rörelsen har på senaste åren vunnit en allt större spridning och tilldragit sig alltmera uppmärksamhet, inte blott i dess egentliga hemland, Schweiz, Tyskland och Österrike, utan även i Skandinavien. Särskilt i höst har denna andevetenskapliga riktning låtit tala om sig i samband med de antroposofiska högskolekurser som hållits i den märkliga byggnaden Goetheanum, i närheten av Basel. En ung svensk deltagare i dessa kurser, hr Bernt Ljungqvist, har i nedanstående artikel meddelat sina intryck därifrån samt tillfogat några konturer ur den ryktbara d:r Steiners liv och verk.

Antroposofiska föreläsningar inom vetenskap, konst och religion

Steiner ogillar känslosvärmeri och andlig osundhet

Goetheanum, en arkitektonisk tillämpning av andevetenskapen

On 14 November 1920, the Swedish daily Dagens Nyheter *devoted the whole front page of its Sunday section to the inauguration of the Goetheanum near Basel in Switzerland. The previous day, the entire front page of the Swedish local newspaper* Upsala *was given over to the same topic.*

I have noticed great interest on the part of students as well as teachers and others for precisely my own questions on the significance of art for the development of knowledge. They ascribe to art a very great role in teaching, and say they believe that it should have an even greater role in the future. At the same time they emphasize how difficult they believe it is to grasp all the issues involved.

I have deliberately refrained from trying to understand or even describe those elements which I have found most difficult to grasp. In practice, I have noticed that those aspects do not play a prominent role unless one wishes them to do so. I have instead thought it was significant and even important to realize how much one can gain from this material — in theory as well as in practice — even without penetrating the whole structure of ideas.

During the first year, I carried out my studies completely on my own, trying to build up my own foundation. I made my own selection of books by and on Rudolf Steiner, which I read. Studying the literature has since then comprised an important part of the whole task. I have usually been obliged to read the books not only once, but several times.

I began my field studies after the end of this preliminary year. The direction of the work was then influenced by what I experienced and shared in contact with people who were active in education and in other practical enterprises connected to anthroposophy.

In all my classroom observations and at lectures, I made very precise — often word-for-word — notes. In interviews, discussions and so on I usually wrote down the content of the conversations directly afterwards.

On a couple of occasions I made my observations over longer periods. During the summer of 1985 I participated as observer at a three-week course for senior grade teachers from Waldorf schools in Scandinavia — which was held at the Teacher Training College in Järna — and was then given the opportunity of following the tough programme from morning to evening, and was similarly able to interview and converse with participating lecturers as well as teachers. I also attended two out of the three weeks of the great Scandinavian Idea and Culture Conference on 'Life-giving Culture' which was held in the summer of 1988 in Södertälje, with special morning seminars at the Rudolf Steiner College. Apart from this I made a great number of visits to the Teacher Training College.

Spiritual Science

Many of the problems which crop up when someone from the outside wishes to attempt to study in this field are, in the first place, of a linguistic nature, and therefore questions of meaning. So-called spiritual dimensions are not easy to grasp. They are above all culturally sensitive matters and are, particularly difficult to broach in a scientific discussion.

Form and content are interwoven in a special way with Steiner, and this is of great significance, I believe, in trying to comprehend those features to which one wishes to draw attention within anthroposophical activities. Thoughts and ideas can then also become even more difficult to transfer from the German language to the languages and cultures of other countries, without important shades of meaning being distorted or lost altogether. Many translations are also greatly lacking in this respect.

So, for instance, the mere use of the word 'spiritual' in the context of what anthroposophists call 'spiritual science' causes many to adopt a sceptical attitude. But the equivalent German *Geisteswissenschaft* also corresponds to what we term 'arts and humanities.'

If one plays with words and translates *Geisteswissenschaft* as 'mind science' instead of 'spiritual science,' then it turns into something quite different. Spiritism is something from which Steiner clearly distances himself. But at the same time I think that what Steiner wants to achieve by drawing attention to the spiritual, has to do with conveying a dimension to science which it presently lacks. By adhering to mere facts and mechanical explanations, one can understand a machine, but never life. To achieve this, another world of ideas is called for. He writes in his memoirs:

> I have often spoken about 'the spirit going forth' from the womb of nature. What then is meant by 'spirit'? Everything that brings forth 'culture' through human thinking, feeling and willing. To speak of some other 'spirit' would at that time have been completely unprofitable. No one would have understood me if I had said that there lay something as a basis for that which expresses itself as 'spirit' in human

> beings and in nature, which was neither spirit nor nature but a perfect unity comprising both parts.[2]

It is this he later on ventures to explain, and which then becomes increasingly difficult to follow. But is it perhaps also precisely this difficult undertaking which stimulates so many people to put so much time and effort into trying to comprehend his way of thinking on this topic?

The historian of ideas Sven-Eric Liedman writes that if one wishes:

> to learn something about present traditions of research in the humanities, one should take one's point of departure from the conflicts in the nineteenth century in Sweden surrounding 'the spiritual sciences.' These conflicts have now for the most part sunk into the subconscious and therefore cause a great deal of disarray in research work. It is important to bring them back into the light.[3]

According to Liedman, one can speak of two main sides to the controversy. The one — the part now dominating the social sciences including education — took its ideals and point of departure from rationalism:

> All science (and in the main, all other human activity as well) must be rational. Rationalism had come to its foremost expression in natural science and in particular in Newton's mechanics. Newton's theory was precise and made it possible to perform exact calculations and predictions. Why should the same excellent qualities not be inherent in theories of man and society?

Statistics were seen as opening the way to a whole new kind of mechanics. In this precise social science, individual variations are of no consequence, except for artists and writers.

Gradually a transformation took place in which specialization took a leap forward:

> A good scientist should not make *ex officio* declarations concerning God, ethics or politics — things which scientists

> previously travelled from country to country giving speeches on. A good scientist should keep to the subject to which he was designated.

This limitation in the areas of competence implied an enormous transformation. Here it is a matter of a very complicated process which Liedman thinks that we can study most simply by following certain linguistic changes which now arose. From the first half of the nineteenth century onwards, the word 'science' had already, in English and French, come to mean simply 'the science of nature,' whereas the German word *Wissenschaft* also encompassed the Arts. Wilhelm Dilthey's *Geisteswissenschaften* was, according to him, a translation of John Stuart Mill's 'moral sciences.' Today, the German word *Wissenschaften* retains the sense of 'science,' while *Geisteswissenschaften* now refers to the humanities, and social science has acquired other kinds of term. In the following presentation I mainly use the term 'spiritual science' since it is the translation commonly used in the literature I have studied.

Questions concerning the relationship spirit-nature, as well as the connection between the humanities and the natural sciences, have fallen into the shadows in scientific contexts, whether of natural science, the humanities or social science. Nor have philosophical questions concerning the relationship between art and knowledge been given a prominent place in the scientific-theoretical discussion for a long time. During the 1970s and 80s however a noticeable shift of interest back to this type of cultural problem has occurred.

With Steiner, as with the Russian artist Wassily Kandinsky, who has shown himself to be greatly influenced by Steiner, there is a close relationship between the spiritual and art. Both treat these questions in relation to the predominant scientific theory (see Chapter 5, and Plates 2 and 3). The same is true of the artist Joseph Beuys, a key figure on the European art scene, who was similarly inspired by Steiner in his ideas regarding the role of art in society (see Chapter 7).

Many of Steiner's writings must be read time and time again — chewed over, as he says himself. The reader must keep up with him the whole time and actively interpret the text. He also makes a comparison with how one reads meditational writings. In the preface to his book *Theosophy,* Steiner gives the following advice:

> This book cannot be read in the same way one usually reads books in our time. In certain respects the reader must *work to assimilate* each page, indeed, many a clause. This is something I have deliberately striven after, as only in this way can the book become to the reader what it ought to be. The person who merely reads through it has not read it at all. Its truths must be experienced. Only in this way does spiritual science have any value.[4]

In the preface to another of his books, *Occult Science: An Outline,* Steiner declares that he quite deliberately avoids writing in a popular fashion. Instead he wants a certain mental effort on the part of the reader so that the latter can digest the contents. In this way the very act of reading his books constitutes the beginning of a spiritual schooling:

> Since the calm, contemplative mental effort which becomes necessary when reading this writing, strengthens the powers of the soul and thereby puts the reader into a state where he can approach the spiritual world.[5]

Steiner's language can appear heavy, tough, elaborate and full of repetitions. Is it coincidental that it has certain similarities with the writing style of the Swedish visionary, Emanuel Swedenborg?[6]

The Swedish author Walter Ljungkvist has the idea that because reading Steiner's writings demands such mental activity, the reader's ability and will to persist grows.[7] Perhaps this is partly why reading these writings becomes of great importance to many — not least to teachers. Here, the reader is not underestimated.

Reading Steiner is perhaps to some degree reminiscent of reading Schiller. Since Schiller's twenty-seven *Letters on the Aesthetic Education of Man* make up one of the pillars of the Waldorf educational system, it is interesting to see how Schiller himself begins his fifteenth letter:

> I come closer and closer to that goal towards which I lead you on a less than pleasurable path. Deem it worthwhile to accompany me yet a few steps farther, so shall an even freer

> horizon open itself and a happy insight perhaps repay the exertions of the way.[8]

For my own part I have found that it can often also be a matter of not becoming blocked when confronted with passages in Steiner's writing which seem incomprehensible on a first reading. I have in such cases skipped that section instead and gone on in the text. Sometimes, I have then found that I understood a great deal more when I returned to reading that passage on a later occasion.

My way of reading is reminiscent of how one proceeds when solving crossword puzzles. The difficult part, not infrequently, may lie in accepting the fact that certain passages do not appear to be solvable — at any rate not by me right at that moment. Of course the crossword puzzle can be badly constructed, but it can also be due to limitations in my own abilities.

It appears to be a very individual matter what attitude one adopts when reading Steiner. Some people hold the opinion that he was in a rare way open to both an Eastern and a more Western way of thinking and that this is instrumental in his coming to interest many Russian intellectuals and artists (see Chapter 6). Other people adhere to the idea that the feminine side of man — *anima* — is supposed to be specially prominent in Steiner and to be responsible for his special ability to embrace different ways of looking at things and different perspectives on life.

Forty books, six thousand lectures

I often get the impression that people are sceptical or ignorant about what Steiner stood for. This is in itself highly understandable, considering the time-consuming work involved in familiarizing oneself with his vast works. Apart from some forty-odd books, there are numerous articles and six thousand lectures besides, which were mostly taken down in shorthand and published in printed form in various editions. Of these, only three hundred were intended for public reading, while the rest were aimed at anthroposophists or others already well-versed in anthroposophical trains of thought. It is most likely that the very printing of the latter type of lecture has to a large extent been responsible for quotations — difficult to grasp and taken out of context — becoming the starting-point for discussions which on occasion could become very animated.

Steiner gave lectures in Germany and in various European countries. Amongst these were several lecture tours in Scandinavia from 1910 onwards up to the First World War in 1914. In Berlin he gave series of public lectures each winter in the Berlin Architektenhaus during the years 1903-1918.

Steiner himself was against having his lectures printed, partly because they were intended for verbal presentation, but also because it was impossible for him to find time to check the shorthand versions of his lectures which others had made. This is an important point to take into consideration when judging his work. It is clear from his autobiography (see Appendix 1) that he would have preferred most of all not to have the lectures written down. But more and more people interested in his ideas demanded that they be printed. And so publication of the lectures eventually came about in spite of everything.

Throughout this work I have taken pains as far as possible to present only quotations taken from Steiner's own books, or from lectures which he had edited himself before publication. Certain parts of Chapter 8, however, are exceptions to this rule, since his methodological ideas on teaching are only to be found in his lectures on education and in his courses for teachers. I have here and there cited fairly long quotations from his books, in order to give readers the opportunity of forming their own impression of his style of writing. Thereby they can gain a more authentic idea of the content than if I myself tried to reformulate Steiner's own presentation where subtle semantic differences might be of great importance. At this point it must however be mentioned that some misunderstandings can also arise from the fact that the quotes are taken from existing translations, which not infrequently fall short of the mark.

Steiner spoke without a script and took pains to adjust his presentation to the audience he had in front of him. He is careful with linguistic nuances, which, he himself says, are instrumental in his often presenting the same things with several different turns of phrase. This also contributes to his language on occasion becoming long-winded, especially when it appears in print.

At first I was ignorant of how much there was written, and how much is still being published on enterprises and ideas with anthroposophical connections. The majority of books are published in Germany by anthroposophic publishers. But even mainstream European publishers such as Rowohlt and Fischer Verlag publish pocket editions of works by and on Rudolf Steiner and on various anthroposophically inspired ventures. Fischer Verlag, for instance, have published a special pocket-book series called *Perspektiven der Anthroposophie,* which in 1986 numbered sixty-one titles.

In 1961 — a hundred years after the birth of Rudolf Steiner — the publication was begun of an edition of his collected works — *Gesamtausgabe (GA).* Three hundred and fifty four volumes have been published up to 1990. Subject and name indices are often missing in these volumes though, which makes research difficult. On the other hand, there are three comprehensive volumes with a general outline of the collection, where Part 1 is a bibliographical summary, Part 2 contains a terminological index and index of personal names, and Part 3 is a summary of the contents of the various volumes.[9] Large parts of the collection have now been published in pocket editions and translated into many languages. Altogether there are probably several hundred volumes available in Swedish and English today.[10]

For my own part I have made my selection of literature from accounts that others from widely different fields have given of Steiner, accounts that have often led me down my own path of reading. It is amazing how many people, mainly in letters or discussions/interviews, acknowledge that they have been inspired by Steiner in more or less fundamental ways.

Sheer lunacy or great genius

I have found it helpful to read how other people declare their ambivalence *vis-à-vis* Steiner. This is true for instance of the Russian author Andrei Belyi, but also of many other Russian authors, as well as the American writer Saul Bellow.[11]

One particularly illuminating and interesting example is writer Edith Södergran.[12] Here some of the difficulties the reader and research-scholar confronts are clearly demonstrated. She writes in a letter to Hagar Olsson:

> When I got Steiner's book in my hands, I regarded him with great suspicion. I continued to do so for quite a long time. (You, best of all, know my aversion towards supersensible ideas.) But now I have battled through to the acceptance that this is the truth.
> (6 January, 1920)

And a few months later:

> 'The Spiritual Leadership of Mankind' was the first thing by Steiner I laid hands on. At that time it appeared to me to be sheer lunacy. Now I have reduced my opinion by at least 70 per cent of what I held to be madness. (13 July, 1920)

A few sentences further on in the same letter, she writes about the mystery dramas which Steiner had written:

> The dramas demonstrate his genius with ease, and after reading them one understands the great genius in the other books. Since I became acquainted with Steiner I have not done anything else than study him. Have laid everything else to one side, regarding it as a waste of time.

Nevertheless, she is tortured by the fact that she does not understand him wholly and completely:

> Each time I take out his portrait I feel a strong sense of antipathy, suspicions awaken within me. And these suspicions hurt me deeply for his sake. This phenomenon of my reluctance crops up every time, and I cannot explain it to myself. Did you have any similar experience when you saw him in the flesh? (17 June, 1921).

She also wrote somewhere that it was impossible to be without Steiner one single day. If she had not written with such an exhilarating nimbleness and audaciousness, one would many a time find her reactions, if anything, to be morbidly overstrung. For this reason it is important in this context to also mention what her close woman friend

Hagar Olsson has to say on this matter. She points out that certain of Edith's declarations:

> can seduce many a person into these false speculations on her standing on the edge of mental illness and such like, which a self-satisfied world so willingly falls back on when faced with such a phenomenon as a person of genius. Edith could be as fantastic as you please, but she never lost her balance, her critical clarity was always there as a regulator, as was her sense of humour. Edith's sense of humour is a story in itself, it pops up everywhere in the letters, many a time so subtle and disguised that anyone not knowing her well could have a hard time spotting it.

Gunnar Tideström also points out how easy it is to misjudge Edith Södergran's poetry, and think that it is of a dreamy nature consisting of pictures of the imagination, when in actual fact they are of the most tangible reality. She 'gives a dreamlike appearance to reality.' In Tideström's opinion, what caught her attention in Anthroposophy was not the complicated theories, but the central religious outlook, the experience of the divine essence of reality. He stresses too that she herself has said that it was her feeling for Nature that had led her to mysticism. During the last years of her life she also liked to read Goethe. And 'she has ladled up ideas and rules for living and famous dictums out of Goethe's works more than out of any other writer's production,' Tideström writes.

Another interesting description of Steiner is found in the Slavonic scholar Magnus Ljunggren's thesis on the Russian author Andrei Belyi, 'The Dream of Rebirth' (1982). In a later article, 'The Decade of Anthroposophy in Russia,' Ljunggren discusses how the philosopher Nikolai Berdyaev feels deep ambivalence towards 'spiritual science,' which both attracts and repels him, and observes that this ambivalent attitude towards Steiner is found to a greater or lesser degree in all the Russian Symbolists, including Belyi, in the decade up to 1917.

Ljunggren stresses here too how Steiner came to break with Theosophy and its Indian-Buddhist centricity and wanted instead to give back a Western anchorage to esotericism. In this connection Steiner came to show a particular interest in Russia, lying as it does on the borderline between Eastern and Western cultures and styles of thinking.

His broadmindedness towards contrasts and opposites is central, I believe, to fathoming his complex personality. His charisma as a speaker undoubtedly made an impact on his audience but their impressions differ vastly. The humorous, cheerful and spiritual traits which emerge in descriptions given by close colleagues, associates and friends, contrast starkly with the evidence of many others. In the same way we gain the impression of a vivid play of opposites if we compare the reportedly bubbling humour of his conversation, noticeable even to some extent in his lectures and autobiography, with the lack of humour in his principal writings and books. But precisely therein, he himself might have said, lies the essence of the comical. Someone who lacks a sense of opposites and contrasts does not have a sense of humour either, he writes in 1890 in an essay 'On the Comical and its Connection with Art and Life.' Irony, comic satire such as parody and travesty have no other purpose than to make people laugh by juxtaposing the paradoxical aspect of an event with its opposite. Steiner wishes here to show the idea of the comical as a form of the aesthetic.[13]

Steiner turned now and then against the anthroposophists' sentimentalism. Andrei Belyi recounts a story of some woodcarvers from the Goetheanum building site who were upset that some people wanted to build private houses near to the building. They could not accept the fact that people might hang out their washing on washing-lines around the cultural temple. Steiner explained to them that in that case they had misunderstood the object of the Goetheanum — to unite the temple with life. It was merely an expression of sentimentality to want to cut off the temple from daily life. Belyi thinks that he also said: 'There should be nappies flapping on a line right here.'

Rudolf Steiner was the chairman of a club for young people — Die Kommenden — started by the young poet Ludwig Jacobowski in Berlin at the turn of the century. Stefan Zweig describes the atmosphere at these meetings:

> Here were crowded together the most heterogeneous

> elements, poets and architects, snobs and journalists, young girls who spent their time on handicrafts and sculpture, Russian students and blonde Scandinavians who wanted to perfect their German. Germany itself had representatives present from all parts of the country, heavily-built Westphalians, honest Bavarians, Silesian Jews: all these people cast themselves without reservation into the wildest discussions. Now and again poems or dramas were read aloud, but the main thing for everyone was getting to know each other. In the midst of these young people, who purposely behaved as Bohemian as possible, sat, as touching as a Santa Claus, an old grey-bearded man, respected and loved by all, since he was a real poet and a real Bohemian: Peter Hille ...

When faced with Steiner as a person, Zweig, like many other people, is puzzled. He did not stand out as a particularly impressive leader type, but he was captivating. The breadth of his scholarship, according to Zweig, was astounding:

> In his dark eyes there resided a hypnotic power and I could listen to him better and more critically when I did not look at him, since his ascetically lean face, marked by spiritual suffering, was well suited to appearing convincing, not only to women ... I always returned home from his lectures and even from many a rewarding private conversation simultaneously enraptured and somewhat dejected.[14]

Steiner's complex character and multi-faceted work bothered many people at that time, as indeed they do today. The difficulty in surveying — let alone in fully understanding — all his work, increases the feeling of uncertainty. With some people this anxiety took the most atrocious forms of expression. During his lifetime he was the target of odious persecution campaigns and threats against his life, and all anthroposophical activities were banned by the Nazis.

As a researcher in this field one often comes across statements that various people have made about Steiner, which one would very much like to look into further.[15] Both Ellen Key and Selma Lagerlöf, two other very influential Swedish writers, showed interest in Steiner's achievements. The latter writes in a letter:

> The man is certainly a highly remarkable phenomenon which one should try to take seriously. He preaches a couple of doctrines in which I have believed for a long time, for example, that it is not acceptable in our time to come and proffer a religion full of unproven miracles, but that religion must be a science which can be proved. It is no longer a question of believing but of *knowing*. Further, that one acquires knowledge concerning the spiritual world through a firm, conscious, systematic form of thought. One should not sit like a dreaming mystic, but exert one's whole ability to think to ultimately arrive at seeing that world which is otherwise hidden from us. All this is of course true and right and everything about him inspires confidence, and is wisdom without charlatanism. In a few years' time his teachings will be preached from the pulpits.[16]

These ideas on religion and science which Selma Lagerlöf propounds here, are controversial. The points of tension which are associated with this field of research are also reflected here.

Allow me also to quote the following lines from Goethe which Steiner often used to cite and which he took up in a series of lectures:

Wer Wissenschaft und Kunst besitzt,
hat auch Religion;
Wer jene Beiden nicht besitzt,
der habe Religion.
W. von Goethe, 'Zahme Xenien'

He who possesses Science and Art
has Religion too;
He who does not possess these two,
may he have Religion.[17]

Perhaps something of an 'artist's soul' is also called for, in order to be able to expand the limits of knowledge. Can it perhaps be a 'tacit knowledge,' which can be read between the lines and which we have lost our ability to see, on account of the multitude of facts and statistics and informative texts to which we have grown accustomed in schools and universities, as well as in many professional situations? Perhaps a more 'meditative seeking for the truth' is *also* called for which our culture and our educational institutions discourage rather than encourage by looking more towards limitations in, and differences between, art, science and religion, rather than to what brings them together.

Considering the growing interest in various countries for 'alternative culture,' I find it remarkable that Steiner's work has remained so relatively unknown in scientific circles. There is also a very palpable dilemma, both in Germany and in Sweden, that the more the general public take notice of alternative solutions, the more people become anxious on behalf of science or religious belief.

Making the unknown background to anthroposophy and its applications more widely and better known, seems to me to be the only viable approach if one wishes to achieve a more all-round and in-depth analysis in the future. My own contribution, which I here present, represents such an attempt.

> 'Every sentence I say must be understood not as an affirmation, but as a question.'
>
> Niels Bohr[18]

CHAPTER 3
Rudolf Steiner's Education and Upbringing

Childhood and school

Rudolf Steiner was born in 1861 in Kraljevec, which then stood in Hungary, but is now part of Croatia, and died in 1925 in Dornach, near Basel in Switzerland. He moved many times during his life and, as a result, gained experience of different central-European *milieux.*

His father was a railway station inspector, serving at a number of minor railway stations in an era when the railway was still a great new experience for many people. He changed his job location several times during his son's childhood, sometimes to make it easier for him to go to school.

In the autobiography that Steiner wrote from his sickbed during the last year of his life, he describes the beautiful mountain landscape and life in the small railway community where he lived together with his family from his second to his eighth year. Here, the railway passed directly outside the house, and not only his own but also the whole village's interest was largely directed towards the railway traffic. Steiner writes:

> I think it has been of great importance for my life that I spent my childhood in such an environment. Living like this, my interest was drawn early on towards mechanics. I know that this interest threatened all the time to get the upper hand of my senses, which were drawn towards the beautiful and grandiose Nature where the trains time and time again disappeared into the distance, subjected to the laws of mechanics.[1]

As a little boy he was keenly interested in how the railway worked. He taught himself telegraphy on the station telegraph, and he came into contact with the laws of electricity by following and closely observing the work at a railway station.

His father was anxious for him to learn to read and write early on, and he was sent to the village school when he had reached school age:

> The schoolteacher was an elderly man who found it a bothersome task keeping school. I for my part also found it a bothersome task to go to his school. He often came home to us, together with his wife and little son. And the latter was, to my way of thinking at that time, a real good-for-nothing. I got it into my head that anyone with such a good-for-nothing for a son could not possibly have anything to teach anybody else.[2]

Fairly soon the father himself took over his son's education, but with him too the boy failed to take any real interest in the things that adults thought he ought to learn:

> I was obliged to sit for hours by his side in his office and read and write, while he himself in the meantime did his office work ... I was interested in what my father was writing and wanted to do the same as he did. In that way I learned a great deal of things. But the things he regarded as being necessary for my education I found irrelevant. On the other hand, in a child's way, I grew familiar with everything appropriate to everyday life. The routine at the railway station and everything that was associated with it aroused my interest. But in particular, it was everything that had to do with the laws of nature and their manifestations that attracted me. When I wrote, I did so only because I had to, and I even did it as fast as I could, in order to quickly fill a page. Then, you see, I got to sprinkle sand over what I had written, the same way my father used to do. I was fascinated by seeing how quickly the ink dried and the mixture that then formed. I examined with my fingers time and time again which letters had dried and which had not. My curiosity was too great, and therefore, as often as not, I touched the letters too soon. My writing exercises as a result took on

> an appearance which my father did not approve of. But he took it in his stride and punished me merely by often calling me an incorrigibly careless boy. — But that was not the only result of my writing exercises. More than the formation of the letters, I was interested in the appearance of the fountain-pen. If I took my father's paper-knife, I could make physical studies of the elasticity of the pen by pushing the knife into the slit on the nib. Needless to say, I bent the spring of the slit back into position afterwards, but the appearance of my writing suffered as a result.[3]

When Steiner was around the age of eight, the family moved to a small place called Neudörfl in Hungary, close to the border with Austria. Here again he felt that he had not much particular use for the education he received in school. The school consisted of one single schoolroom where five classes with boys and girls were taught simultaneously:

> While the boys at my bench-row were supposed to write a story about King Arprad, the youngest pupils stood out front at the blackboard where the letters 'i' and 'u' had been chalked up. It was regrettably impossible to do anything other than sit idly and let one's hands write down the words almost mechanically.[4]

He writes that he was a meditative boy who had a number of unanswered questions on his mind, and he thinks that this contributed to the fact that he became fairly lonely in his childhood.

One event now led to a turning-point in his life. He did not write about this in his autobiography, but described it elsewhere. A relative living nearby committed suicide. With this event he became aware of a previously unknown and invisible world — the life of the soul *(Leben in der Seele)* in which not only the outer trees and the outer mountains communicate, but also a world behind these.

From this point on he differentiates between 'things one can see' and 'things one cannot see.' And now the problem which came to occupy him for the rest of his life arose, namely how to prove the existence of this invisible world, as easily as one can prove the existence of the world of which one is aware through the medium of one's senses.[5]

Steiner felt he found proof of this in the world of geometry.

> Soon after starting school at Neudörfl, I discovered a geometry book in his (the assistant teacher's) room. I was on such a good footing with this teacher that I was able without any problem to borrow the book for a while. I got stuck into it with great enthusiasm. For weeks at a time I was completely taken up with congruence and resemblances between triangles, quadrangles and polygons; I puzzled over the question where parallel lines really cross, and Pythagoras' theorem held me spellbound.
>
> It accorded me the greatest satisfaction that purely inner pictures of the mind, and forms without any impressions taken from the outer senses, could feed my imagination. It gave me comfort and dissipated the mood the unanswered questions put me in. To be able to grasp something on a purely spiritual level gave me a sensation of happiness. I know that it was through geometry that I first understood what happiness was.
>
> I see in my relationship to geometry the first foundation of that view which has gradually developed within me. It was already there more or less unawares in me in my childhood, and took on a definite and completely conscious form when I was about twenty years old. I said to myself: Objects and events which can be observed by the senses exist in space. But in the same way as this space exists outside the individual, so there is a kind of inner space inside the soul which is the scene of action for spiritual beings and events. In my mind I saw revelations of a spiritual world and inner pictures which people make for themselves of things. It appeared to me to be as if geometry were a form of knowledge, superficially created by man himself, but yet with a significance which was completely independent of him. As a child I could naturally not formulate it completely clearly, but I felt that in the same way as it was with geometry, one must carry knowledge of the

> spiritual world within one. I was as equally convinced of the reality of the spiritual world as I was of the reality of the sensory world. But I needed a kind of justification for this assumption. I wanted to be able to say to myself that one's experience of the spiritual world was as little an illusion as one's experience of the sensory world. In geometry, I told myself, one really *is allowed* to know something which the soul experiences solely by virtue of its own power. In this feeling I found my justification for speaking of the spiritual world I experienced, in the same way as I spoke of the physical world. And I did speak of it that way. My mental pictures were of two kinds: I differentiated between things that were 'seen' and things that were 'not seen.' This, though as yet undefined, played an important role in my inner life, even before my eighth year.
>
> I relate these things truthfully, although people who look for evidence that can justify their calling anthroposophy fantastic will perhaps conclude that since I was inclined to the fantastic already as a child, it is no wonder that later I evolved a fantastic view of the world.
>
> But it is just because I know that later when I described the spiritual world I did so according to the inner necessity of the facts themselves, and not according to any personal inclinations, I can look back quite objectively to the childish and awkward way I justified to myself, by means of geometry, that I had to speak of a world 'one does not see.'
>
> To this I have only to add that I loved to live in that world. I would have felt the sense-world as spiritual darkness around me, had the former not received light from that other world.
>
> By means of his geometry book, the assistant teacher at Neudörfl provided me with a confirmation of the spiritual world which at that time I needed.[6]

Steiner had much reason to thank this teacher, who lent him his geometry book, even if he did not learn anything from him during lessons at school. It was the same teacher who came to initiate Steiner into the world of art. He played the violin and the piano himself, and

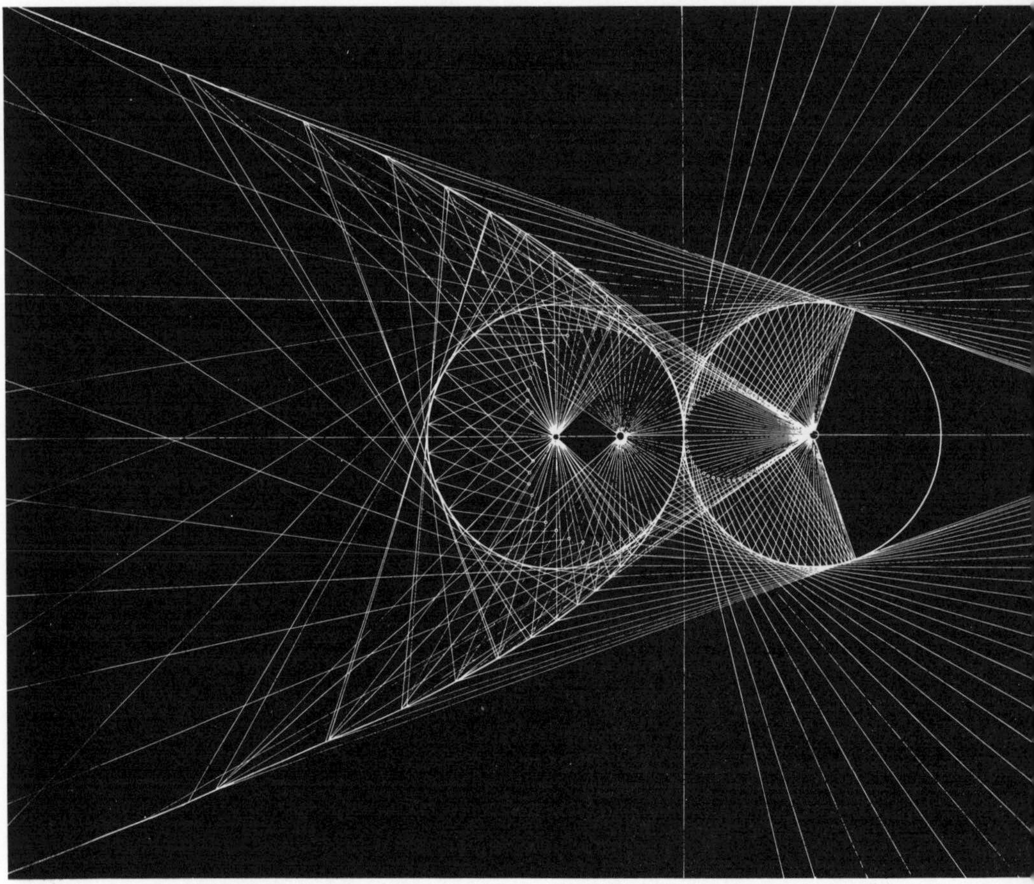

A geometrical construction by Class II. 'Through geometry we can learn to see with the aid of thought. If we wish to arrive at that stage, we must however wean ourselves from the idea, for example, of the dot as a pin-prick, the line as a rod, the parallel as a pair of railway lines, and so on. First when we have endeavoured to achieve a way of imagining things completely "free of the senses" can we rise to that plane where the true geometrical visualization can be played out.' (From Education Towards Freedom *by Frans Carlgren and Arne Klingborg.)*

was a diligent draughtsman. As often as he could Steiner took himself off to the teacher's house where he was given the opportunity of drawing with charcoal under his guidance, as well as of copying pictures and portraits.

Steiner also writes about the impression made on him at this time by Hungarian gypsy music. During his youth he took every chance he could to develop his understanding of music. He experienced the world of tones in itself as an important part of reality, and the music was of revolutionary significance to him, he writes, in his efforts to obtain a more secure basis for spiritual experiences.[7]

The assistant teacher at the school was at the same time organist in the church, as well as its verger, and he was in charge of the mass vestments and other church inventories. The schoolboys were obliged to perform choir service at masses and funerals and Steiner writes that:

> [the] ceremonial inherent in the Latin language and ritual appealed to my child's mind ... From my childhood in Neudörfl I have a vivid memory of how the ritual in connection with the music, in a very suggestive fashion, called forth the enigmas of life. The instruction the priest gave us on the Bible and the Catechism had far less effect on my spiritual life than the effect he, as practitioner of the ritual, had, in being a link between the sensible and the spiritual world. All this was already from the beginning not only an outer form for me, but a profound experience. This was all the more so because the subject was not mentioned in my home. I lived as it were still in the mood of the church service also in everyday life at home. I lived in my normal social surroundings without taking part in them. I was aware of them, but my thoughts and feelings really belonged to the other world. I can assert, however, that I was not at all a day-dreamer, but as a matter of course adapted myself to all the practical conditions of life.[8]

Everything that happened in the village school was connected with the nearby church. There was a priest with a very strong personality who also came to mean a great deal to Steiner. He had once come to the school, and in the teacher's small room had gathered together some of the more mature pupils, amongst whom he counted Steiner. The priest had himself made a large drawing which he unfolded for them. Using it as a model, he explained the Copernican system of the world for the children.

> He spoke very vividly about the movement of the earth

> around the sun, about the turning of the axis, the inclination of the earth's axis, about summer and winter and about the zones of the earth. I became completely captivated by the subject, copied the drawing and was later on given an extra lesson by the priest on the eclipses of the sun and moon. From this occasion all my thirst for knowledge was directed towards this subject.[9]

Another observation from his childhood, which Steiner remembered and related in his autobiography, gives a background to the weight he would later place on pictorial seeing and pictorial thinking in educational contexts as a whole. He points out that as a child he

> ... had a completely different attitude to reading as opposed to writing. In my boyhood years I read cursorily without noticing the words, dived immediately into the pictures, concepts and ideas so that the act of reading in itself did nothing to develop my sense for the orthographical (correct spelling) or the grammatical aspects of the written word. On the other hand, I endeavoured when I wrote, to capture the word-pictures in terms of sound, such as I understood them from my dialect. It was therefore only with the greatest difficulty that I gained command of the written language, while already from the beginning I had found it very easy to read.[10]

Yet another adult who came to mean a great deal to Steiner during this period was a peripatetic doctor who occasionally visited the little village and also Steiner's parental home, where he was looked upon as a somewhat eccentric character. Through him, Steiner heard for the first time about Lessing, Goethe and Schiller. Such writers were unknown in Steiner's home and 'thus it happened that a whole new world opened itself to me.' This doctor willingly spent time on the boy and they used to walk together back and forth at the railway station, discussing German literature. The doctor did so, 'not in a lecturing tone of voice, but in an enthusiastic fashion,' Steiner writes.[11]

Time passed, and the question arose of the boy's secondary

education which his father decided should be aimed towards future employment on the railway. The boy, then around eleven years old, was therefore required to undergo an entrance exam for the junior secondary school, which he passed with excellent marks. But yet again, in the new school, which lay in the small town Wiener-Neustadt, he found that what took place there left him relatively unconcerned. He points out that he felt a strong need for people who could be examples to him, but that he lacked such persons, at least during the first two years at the secondary school.

He carried out studies on his own and, during this period, put in much effort into reading by himself an article which the headmaster had written in the school's annual report, on 'The force of attraction regarded as the effect of movement.' In this there was also a reference to a book by the same headmaster, which Steiner saved up enough money to buy. The book was called *The General Movement of Matter as the Basic Cause of All Natural Phenomena.* As an eleven-year-old, he says, he could of course scarcely understand anything of the content, since its starting point was higher mathematics. But he still had a feeling that it would be of great importance to him if he could achieve some understanding of these things. He therefore battled on through both the article and the book, reading them again and again. He thought he understood one or other point and he established a bridge of thought between the theories of the construction of the world which he had previously heard from the village priest, and the things the headmaster wrote about here. He did not feel at all inclined to share the headmaster's point of view, but he still did what he could in order to understand the way he thought. He also took every opportunity to find other books on mathematics and physics.

Later on he had different teachers in mathematics, physics and geometry whom he all admired highly for their teaching which he felt was a model of order and clarity. He says he was influenced by these teachers when 'the questions of the enigmatic natural phenomena arose in [his] childish awareness.'[12]

In due time he also began his studies in chemistry, and thereby gained 'a number of new enigmas alongside the old,' as he puts it. The chemistry teacher's method of teaching consisted almost entirely of experiments:

From the chemistry workbook of a Waldorf pupil in Class 11.

> He did not talk much but let the natural phenomena speak for themselves ... It gave one the impression that this was a man who was used to looking with an investigative eye at the phenomena of Nature, and thereafter to retain the visual impressions he had experienced.[13]

During this period Kant also came into his world of thought. At that time he knew nothing at all about Kant or the opinions held of this philosopher by others. He happened to go past a bookshop window where he saw Kant's *Critique of Pure Reason,* and then did everything in his power to buy this book as fast as possible. He became gripped by an enormous interest in Kant's thought and says that in his childish way he tried to understand through Kant's writings to what extent human common sense can gain real insight into the essence of things.

He was often hindered, however, from being able to spend as much time as he would have liked on this book. Three hours journeying to school, an interminable amount of homework and so on, contributed to:

> ... there scarcely being any time over to read *Critique of Pure Reason.* But I found a way out. In the history classes, the lessons were organized so that the teacher gave the appearance of holding a lecture, while he in point of fact read everything up out of a book. We were then supposed, for each lesson, to learn from our own book what we in this way had heard during the lessons. I thought to myself that reading what was in the book was something I had to do at home in any case. I gained no benefit from the teacher's 'lecture.' It did not do me the slightest good to listen to what he read up. I then took separate pages out of Kant's little book, taped them into the history book which I had lying in front of me during the lesson, and then read Kant while the 'history lesson' was delivered from the teacher's desk. Naturally, it was a great crime against school discipline, but it did not disturb anyone and subtracted so little from what was required of me, that that year I gained the mark 'passed with great distinction' in history.
>
> During my holidays I continued eagerly reading Kant. I probably read many pages more than twenty times in a row. I wanted to form an idea of the relationship between man's thinking and nature's creative forces.
>
> My feelings facing the prospect of this brainwork were affected by two things. Firstly I wanted to develop my own thinking so that each thought would be fully lucid and clear, and that no emotion should influence it in any direction.

> Secondly, I wanted to achieve harmony between this thinking and religion. Religious knowledge also at that time claimed my interest in the highest degree. In this particular subject, we had quite excellent textbooks. With true dedication, I culled knowledge from these books on dogmatics and symbolism, ecclesiastical history, and on the meaning of the ritual. I entered vigorously into these subjects. But my relationship to them was determined by the fact that the spiritual world was part of my world-philosophy. These subjects touched me so strongly expressly because I felt that man, by means of knowledge, could reach through to the spiritual or supersensible. I know quite definitely that my reverence for the spiritual was by no means diminished as a result of my attitude to knowledge.[14]

He read a lot on his own, alongside his schoolwork in most subjects. Through the impressions he then formed, it became quite difficult for him to accept the teaching given in the school. But he nevertheless tried very hard to assimilate it, by trying, on his own, to make the subjects come alive with the help of what he had discovered through his reading outside school hours.[15]

He had a strained relationship with his German teacher, who was irritated by his long essays. When he came to read Greek and Latin poetry translations at school, he noticed how much of the character pertaining to Greek and Latin art was lost in the translation. He then went out and bought textbooks and read courses on both these subjects by himself — apparently in such an effective way that he managed a few years later to give extra lessons to pupils in these subjects, too.

During the summer months of 1879, between the junior secondary school and his later college studies, he spent all his time on philosophical studies. Above all, he studied Fichte's theory of science at that time, but he also continued his studies of Kant. By so doing he wished to establish firm grounds on which to base his own thinking, but he also points out how completely uncritical he was at that time as regards Kant. He then felt it his duty to search out the truth through philosophy, and worked 'all the more consciously on clothing the immediate *outlook* I had on the spiritual world in *thoughts.*'[16]

All these studies still did not stop him from occupying himself as

Rudolf Steiner at the age of eighteen.

well with practical matters and developing certain skills. As an example of this, he relates how during the summer holiday between the fifth and sixth class he taught himself bookbinding so that he could himself bind his textbooks (an experience which may have contributed to the fact that great store is set on bookbinding and handicrafts in general within the Waldorf system of education). During the same summer holiday he also taught himself shorthand. Other practical occupations mentioned are that he was obliged to help tend a small garden that the family had been allotted, with fruit trees and a potato patch. It was he too who took on the chore of doing the shopping in the village in his spare time.[17]

According to his own account, he seems, in spite of these comprehensive interests and many occupations, to have also found time to make friends. He writes:

> I have always been a sociable person. By virtue of this, already during my schooldays in Wiener-Neustadt and later on in Vienna, I had many friends. My opinions rarely agreed with those of my friends, but that never stopped

there being a sincerity and a strong sense of mutual respect in our friendship.[18]

Studies in Vienna

Judging from Steiner's own later portrayal of his boyhood and youth, it was an unusually meditative, independent young man with a thirst for knowledge who, at the age of eighteen, matriculated at the Institute of Technology in Vienna. The year was 1879 and he came to stay on in Vienna until 1890. Here he experienced the prelude to that turn-of-the-century Vienna which is today the object of great interest as the hotbed of modernism and new ways of thought and creativity in both arts and sciences.[19] But he himself would come to follow paths of his own.

Steiner matriculated at the Institute of Technology with the purpose of reading mathematics, natural history and chemistry. But it was by no means only scientific studies that he pursued. The teaching at the Institute appears to have contained rich opportunities for more general studies, with many bridges between science/technology, on the one hand, and the humanities and social science on the other, between which such a cultural gap is still manifest today.

Judging from Steiner's own account, it would nevertheless appear that he was relatively alone in really taking advantage of the rich options for making interdisciplinary studies which were available at the Institute. In a series of lectures on the central points of the social issue and the consequences for a system of general education, which Steiner held many years later, in May and June 1919, he spoke of how vital it was that 'a certain nucleus of education [should] be the same for people from all classes ... whether they work with the mind or the hand,' something which up to then had scarcely been taken into consideration. However, he stresses that in this respect things had been even worse when he, in his youth, was a student at the Institute of Technology in Vienna. To be sure, there were, he says, 'opportunities for also taking up something universal alongside one's professional studies.' But the students seem to have absconded from these lectures, and Steiner, who was extremely anxious to be allowed to follow these lectures says that:

> [he] always had to drag somebody along with [him], since provided at least two persons were present the lecture had to be given. But one could only keep them going by dragging along another person; it was nearly always someone new every time.[20]

During his time at the Institute, as previously at school, the differing personalities of the various teachers played a large part in what Steiner gained from their teaching. Many of the teachers he met here were themselves prominent cultural personalities and authors of important books used as essential course literature. He emphasizes in his autobiography what a strong impression it made on him to be now able to hear philosophy from the mouth of the philosophers themselves and not merely, as previously, through their books. Of course he was there to read science, but he says that he felt it his duty to search for the truth through philosophy and he was convinced that science would not give him anything, unless he had a sound philosophical ground on which to support his experiences.[21]

Of particularly great importance to Steiner was Karl Julius Schröer, who taught German literature at the Institute of Technology. He became captivated at once by Schröer's lectures on Goethe and Schiller. It was now he first became inspired to read Goethe's *Faust.* Schröer had published the first part of *Faust* and was in the process of publishing the second part, with commentaries. Schröer's ambition in doing so, Steiner writes, was primarily to overcome the false evaluation which had taken root in intellectual circles, that the second part of *Faust* was supposed to be a weak poetic work from the hand of the ageing Goethe.[22]

Steiner became friendly with Schröer, and often visited him in his home. Long discussions on *Faust* were carried on there — discussions which later on came to have decisive significance for Steiner's continued life.

It was for him a 'profound spiritual experience,' Steiner writes, to observe what a great difference there was between the various personalities of the teachers, and to notice that their ideas did not completely agree with each other. He could be as equally highly impressed by the 'strictly systematic aesthetics-theorist' Robert Zimmermann's lectures and his book on *Aesthetics as the Science of Form or Design,* as he was by Schröer's intuitive nature, where a certain contempt for the systematic could be discerned. He took a great interest studying the differences between the two.

This is what Steiner writes on Schröer's method of presentation:

> He never systematized his thoughts. He thought and spoke from a quite special intuition. He held the greatest possible reverence for the art of expressing oneself in words. This was most likely the reason he never improvized his lectures. He needed to write them down in peace and quiet in order to be satisfied with his way of converting his thoughts into spoken words. He then read up what he had written with great and ardent feeling.[23]

A completely different type of teacher, who similarly fascinated Steiner, was the philosophy teacher Franz Brentano. In contrast to Schröer, he was the perfect logician:

> Each idea was perfectly clear, deduced from a great number of other ideas. These ideas were formulated with the greatest logical scholarliness. But I had the feeling that his thinking had nothing to do with his own personal experiences in life, it was foreign to reality.[24]

In the centre of Steiner's thinking lay problems concerning the relationship between theory and reality. He returns again and again to his having seen the spiritual world as a reality ever since his childhood, which the people around him could not understand and did not wish to hear of.

> Some people began, at the most, to talk of spiritism. But then it was I who would not listen. I found it distasteful to approach the spiritual in such a manner.[25]

He did not, however, need to be completely alone with these ideas during his days at the Institute. He writes:

But it then happened that I made the acquaintance of a simple man of the people. Every day he travelled on the same train as myself to Vienna. He gathered medicinal herbs in the country and sold them to the chemist shop in Vienna. We became friends. With him, it was possible to talk about the spiritual world as with a person who had personal experience of it. He was a deeply devout person. He had no schooling at all. Certainly, he had read many books on mysticism, but in his speech he was completely unaffected by what he had read there. The things he said bared a spiritual life which in itself bore a completely elementary, creative wisdom. It soon became clear that he read books simply for the reason that he wanted confirmation from others of what he knew himself. But that did not satisfy him. It was as if his personality were merely a mouthpiece for the spiritual content which was trying to speak from concealed worlds. When I was together with him I could gain a profound insight into the secrets of nature. On his back he carried a bunch of medicinal herbs, and in his heart the experiences which he had won on the most inner essence of nature, when he had gathered these herbs. Sometimes when I walked on Wiener Alleegasse with this 'initiate,' some third person might join us, and would smile covertly. This was not so surprising, as his way of expressing himself was not so easy to understand directly. One first had to learn his 'spiritual dialect,' as it were. I did not understand him either, at first. But from the first moment of our acquaintance I felt the deepest sympathy for him. And it gradually came to feel as if I were together with a soul from very ancient days, who furnished me with instinctive knowledge from prehistoric times, unaffected by civilization, science and the prevailing outlook on the world.

If one takes the concept 'to learn' in its conventional sense, one might say that it was not possible to learn anything from this man. But if one had oneself experienced a spiritual world, one could gain deep insight into it through this man, who was securely anchored in that world.

Apart from this, he was a man who was distant from all

> connotations of over-enthusiasm. When one came to his home, one found oneself in the circle of the most down-to-earth, simple family. Above the door to his house was written: 'All things rest in the hands of God.' And one was entertained in the same way as the other villagers. I always had to drink coffee there, not in a cup, but in a mug, which probably held a whole litre. To eat with the coffee, I was offered a piece of bread of gigantic proportions. Neither did the villagers regard the man as a romantic. His way of life never gave rise to any ridicule amongst them at all. He also had a healthy sense of humour, and knew how, on every occasion, to talk with old or young in such a way as to delight them. There, nobody laughed up their sleeves, as those who walked beside us on Wiener Alleegasse did, and who for the most part saw something highly peculiar in him.
>
> Even though our ways have parted, this man stood very close to my heart. He is to be found again in my mystery plays, in the guise of Felix Balde.[26]

In his description of this man, one can get an idea of how Steiner looks at the ability to experience a spiritual dimension of reality, and what significance such an ability can have for our way of developing knowledge. He points to how our ability in this respect has altered from the old days to the present. Today, he seems to think, we must first learn a new language — a 'spiritual dialect,' to be at all able to understand what it is all about.

For Steiner, it was obvious that each person has his own spiritual individuality, of which the corporeal and the physical worlds are only an outer manifestation.

> I realized that many people felt a conflict between sensory knowing, and thinking. For me, thinking was in itself perception of the kind that experiences give, and not of the kind that come to one from outside.[27]

Steiner became accustomed at an early stage to keeping such ideas to himself, since he observed that such ideas offended people. But he sensed early on that man, through the path of knowledge, could get through to the spiritual or supersensory — and not merely to what we can see and understand with our senses, and he came later on to write many books on the subject.

Steiner was more familiar with, felt closer relation with, and also reverence for, the spiritual world which he saw in his inner eye. He had even, during the whole of his childhood and youth, found it difficult to find the way to the outside world via his senses.

> I have always found it difficult to remember the external data it was necessary to assimilate in, for example, the area of science. I have to perpetually look at a natural object to learn what it is called, to which class it belongs purely scientifically, and so on. I can probably say that the material world for me had something shadow-like about it, something like a picture. It went past my soul or mind as pictures, while my connection with the spiritual, throughout, had a genuine character of reality.[28]

He claims to have felt this already as a child. But he experienced it most strongly at the beginning of the nineties when he had passed his finals at the Institute of Technology and, as a researcher at the Goethe-Schiller Institute in Weimar, was working on the publication of Goethe's scientific writings. Hegel's method of presenting the reality of thought was close to his, during this period, and it came to mean a lot to him. But at the same time as he saw Hegel as the greatest thinker of the new age, he was repelled by Hegel's disbelief in a concrete or tangible spiritual world.[29]

During his student days, Steiner was obliged to keep all these ideas at a distance:

> I have to say, that I did not let my insight into the spiritual affect in a detrimental way my studies in the science subjects, as they were designed at that time. I devoted myself to the classes and had only in the background a hopefulness that I might one day be able to see a connection between science and the spiritual world.[30]

Steiner had matriculated at the Institute of Technology in order to study the natural science subjects. The scholarship he had won was only renewed if he continuously passed his examinations in these subjects. He succeeded in these studies, despite the fact that his enormous thirst for knowledge led him, alongside the obligatory classes, to follow classes at other faculties — such as the Faculty of Medicine.

Since Steiner had previously occupied himself a great deal with differential and integral arithmetic and also analytic geometry, he could be absent from many mathematics lectures without losing the train of thought. Mathematics had also its great importance for Steiner as the foundation of his whole search for knowledge:

> Mathematics has a system of ideas and concepts which are obtained independent of all external sensory perception. And yet, I told myself continually, one comes via these ideas and concepts close to the reality of the senses and finds the conformity to law in that reality. Through mathematics, one learns to understand the world, and yet one must, in order to do so, first derive mathematics out of the mind of man.[31]

Yet another teacher whom Steiner held in great esteem was Edmund Reitlinger. He taught physics and showed proof of a universal way of thinking which Steiner admired.

> From the historical way of regarding the physical problems, he always went on further to general, historical-cultural perspectives. Indeed, purely general philosophical ideas also came forward in his science lectures. He analysed such things as optimism and pessimism, and spoke most stirringly about the justification in working out scientific hypotheses.[32]

Reitlinger was at the same time a supporter of the purely inductive method of research, and Newton characterized for him the high point of physics research. Through the mechanical theories of heat and wave-length pertaining to the phenomena of light and electricity, he came into studies on the theory of knowledge in his lectures. Steiner's way of describing the, then prevailing understanding of these things, and placing it in relation to his own way of thinking, is important for an understanding of the problems he wrestled with, and why he found it so difficult to make himself understood.

> The physical external world was understood in those days to be a process of movement in matter. Sensory perceptions stood forth merely as subjective experiences and as merely the effects of the process of movement on the human senses.
>
> The processes of movement in matter are played out in space, and when these come into contact with man's sense of heat, he experiences a sensation of heat. Outside man exist the wave movements of the air; if these come into contact with the nerve of sight, the sensation of light and colour arises in man.
>
> This outlook met me everywhere. It caused me tremendous difficulties in my thinking, since it disregarded the spiritual in the objective external world. It was clear to me that if the phenomena of Nature led to such assumptions, one could not arrive at these assumptions through a spiritual outlook. I realized how misleading such assumptions were for the philosophical direction, which at that time was strongly influenced by science. Nor was I mature enough to decide to replace the prevailing way of thought with my own way of thinking, if only privately. Precisely this gave rise to sore conflicts in my mind. I had to continually keep my over-simple criticism down and await a period when further sources of knowledge and methods would give me greater security.[33]

And Steiner continued searching on his own. It was now that he came into contact with Schiller's *Letters on the Aesthetic Education of Man,* which a few years later would come to be very significant for the first book Steiner published in 1886: *A Theory of Knowledge Based on Goethe's World Conception* (see Chapter 2 here).

The *Letters* are extremely inaccessible as regards both their form and content — a fact that has probably contributed to their neglect. Steiner was immediately stimulated by the content of these Letters. He returns to the ideas in them again and again in various connections throughout his life. Through these Letters he felt already as a young man that he gained a more secure basis when it came to more closely approaching a theory on the interplay between the external, material, visible world of the senses and the inner, invisible world of the spirit — a question which had occupied him ever since his childhood and which always remained central to his thinking. It is not a book which one assimilates once and for all. It is rather a book of meditation and a book which ought to follow each teacher in his professional work, Steiner believes.[34] Much later, Herbert Read was also to accord the *Letters* a similar importance.

Experiences as private tutor

To those experiences during his youth which may have contributed to Steiner's later educational work, also belong the frequent teaching and tutoring he engaged in alongside his own studies.

From 1875, when he was only 14 years old, he gave private tuition to children of various Ages. He continued with this right up until he left his studies at the Institute in Vienna and moved in 1890 to Weimar to begin his employment as researcher at the Goethe-Schiller Institute.

Since he had already proved to be a clever pupil at school, he was encouraged by his teachers to give extra lessons to weaker classmates and to children in lower grades. In this way he could also help his parents to finance his studies. He had a lot to thank this extra tuition for:

> By teaching what I had learned, I saw the relationships more clearly in a way. I cannot put it in any other way, than that I only took in the knowledge I picked up at school as in a dream. On the other hand I was wide awake when it was a matter of things I had to wrestle with, or things I acquired from some spiritual benefactor as the doctor in Wiener-Neustadt. The things that flickered by like pictures in a dream in the schoolteaching differed considerably from the things I absorbed in a wide-awake and fully conscious

mental state. The fact that I had to make my knowledge living for the extra lessons helped me to digest what I had taken in in a half-awake state.

Through my extra tuition I was already obliged at an early stage to devote myself to practical psychology. My pupils gave me insight into the questions of the mental development of man.[35]

And he writes later:

The spiritual development of many people during their childhood and youth was then woven together with my own development. I have observed how differently the male and female sexes mature to face life. Apart from teaching boys and young men, it was namely my lot also to teach a number of girls.[36]

Above all during his study years at the Institute of Technology in Vienna, Steiner was forced for financial reasons to spend a lot of time giving extra tuition. Fate decreed, he says, that he should be designated an altogether special task in the field of education. The way Steiner in his own words portrays the task he here took upon himself sheds light on the pedagogical thinking which forty years later would come to practical expression:

I was recommended as private tutor to a family with four boys. To three of them I was to give preparatory tuition for the primary school, and later, help with their homework from the grammar school. The fourth boy, who was around ten years old, was handed over for me to take complete charge of his education. He was his parents,' in particular his mother's, problem child. When I came to them, he had scarcely learned the most rudimentary elements in reading, writing and arithmetic. He was looked upon as so abnormal in his physical and mental development that his family doubted he could be educated. His thinking was slow and sluggish. Even the tiniest spiritual effort caused him to get a headache, lowered his vitality, made him pale and put him in a mental state, which made us all worry.

After I had come to know the boy, I came to the conclusion that an education adapted to his physical and mental organism must awaken his slumbering talents to life. I therefore proposed to the parents that they hand over his education to me. The boy's mother demonstrated her trust in me by accepting the proposal, and I could thereupon take on this special task of education.

I was forced to find the way to a soul which at that time existed in a kind of dormant state, but which in the end must gain dominance over the functions of the body. First I had to, as it were, incorporate the soul with the body. I was convinced that the boy had great spiritual gifts even if they lay hidden. It made my task feel profoundly important. The boy soon began to show me warm affection. That had the effect of my merely being with him rousing his dormant mental abilities to life. For his teaching, I had to think out special methods. For every extra fifteen minutes his lesson took, departing from the fixed amount of time, his general condition was negatively affected. The boy had very great difficulties in finding any relationship to many subjects.

The task of taking on his education became a rich source of knowledge for me. Thanks to the teaching technique which I was obliged to apply, I gained an insight into the interplay between spiritual-mental and physical aspects of man. It was now I completed my real studies in physiology and psychology. I realized that education and teaching must be an art which has its grounds in real human knowledge. I was forced to work under strictly economical principles. Often I had to prepare myself for two whole hours for a half-hour lesson, in order to be able to present the teaching material in such a way that I, in the shortest possible time and with the least possible strain on the boy's spiritual and bodily forces, could achieve maximum performance. The sequence of the subjects had to be carefully contemplated and the whole daily timetable professionally planned. With satisfaction, I noted that the boy, within the space of two

> years, had caught up with the primary school teaching, and therefore could pass the entrance exam to the grammar school. His health had also improved considerably. The hydrocephalic condition he suffered from was receding with great speed. I could therefore propose to the parents that they send the boy to an ordinary school. I felt that it was necessary for his personal development to be with other boys. I was private tutor to the family for several years, and spent a great deal of time then on this boy, who, for his school attendance, was wholly and completely dependent on his work at home being continued in the spirit in which it had been commenced. I was given occasion at that time, as previously mentioned, to broaden my knowledge of Greek and Latin, since I had to give extra tuition, at grammar-school level, in these subjects too, to another one of the boys in the family.
>
> I am grateful that fate gave me such conditions of life. Through them, I gained such a living knowledge of man as I could not have acquired in any other way.
>
> My protégé went through grammar school, and I followed his progress right up to the penultimate class. He had then come so far that he did not need me any more. After passing his education certificate examination, he went on to the faculty of medicine, became a doctor, and fell as such, victim to the Great War.[37]

Fred Poeppig writes in his biography of Steiner, in regard to the education of this boy, that it was characteristic of Steiner that he here worked out a method completely on his own, without turning to text-books and established theory. He starts out from the living phenomenon, which in itself holds the solutions to the problem, when it is examined in a spiritual fashion. What Steiner understood, intuitively at first, was that it was important to bring about an affectionate relationship with the child, so that merely being with him could make dormant mental forces begin to awaken within the boy. After that it was a matter of being able to get the material through to the boy by means of strict doses in a concentrated form, which called for very intensive preparation if it were to be successful.[38]

For six years Steiner was tied to this family, where he experienced a warm family fellowship which he valued highly. He relates stories of things both humorous and serious that happened in all sorts of contexts.

> Before I came into this family, I had not had many opportunities of participating in the usual games and gambols of children. This was how it came to pass that my 'playtime' did not occur until I had turned twenty. Then I was also obliged to learn the games, since I was supposed to lead them. I did so with the greatest pleasure. I even believe that I have not played less in my life than other people. The only difference is that what one generally has stopped doing in that respect at the age of ten, I caught up on between the ages of 23 to 24.[39]

Simultaneous with his social life and his direct educational activities with the children, he also spent time on studying the theory of knowledge. During this period he acquainted himself with the philosophy of Eduard von Hartmann and in particular his theory of knowledge.

> I spent many late nights at Attersee, the family's summerhouse, after leaving the boys to themselves once we had admired the stars at night from the balcony of the house, studying *The Phenomenology of Moral Consciousness* and *The Religious Consciousness of Mankind and its Stages of Development.* While I read these writings, I won all the greater certainty in respect of my own viewpoints on the theory of knowledge.[40]

Being together with these boys surely gave Steiner many experiences which contributed much to his later work on education and, perhaps even more, to his approach to therapeutic education.

Steiner later carried on an extremely comprehensive teaching activity, to which I shall return. Apart from the work which was associated with the first Waldorf School, which was started in 1919 in Stuttgart, he acted as teacher and lecturer in widely different connections. During a four-year period, 1899-1904, he was tied as a teacher to the Workers' Educational Institute in Berlin (see Chapter 5). Later on, his lecturing activities — first in Germany, but then increasingly throughout Europe — came to take on enormous proportions.

A summary

'... not in a lecturing tone of voice, but in an enthusiastic fashion'

I have here given an extended account of the memories of his childhood and schooling which Rudolf Steiner gave expression to in his autobiography, because they provide an important insight for understanding of his later work in education.

His portrayals of his childhood differ from what he otherwise published in book form, as far as I have been able to discover. He does not stick so rigidly to his unwillingness to write about personal things here, which perhaps adds to these descriptions being accessible in a different way despite the content, revolving around spiritual matters and great existential issues of a normally not easily assimilated nature. Do perhaps the issues also gain a greater nearness and concreteness for many people just because they derive from a child? Here, too, that humour shines through on occasion, to which Steiner attaches central importance in serious contexts as well — a subject on which he wrote an article entitled, 'On humour and its connection with art and life.'[41] This humour is otherwise difficult to find trace of in his rather serious presentations, even though it is often present in his lectures on education, and above all, is often referred to by his friends and particularly by teachers at the first Waldorf school. Taken as a whole, his portrayal of his childhood is a valuable complement to the other conflicting impressions one gains of him as a person. The things which come out here agree best with those sides of him which are highlighted by people closer to him.

In spite of the profound issues of life which his childhood experiences also revolve around, and the fact that some of these most certainly are later readjustments made by the adult, the impression is that it is a child's thoughts and experiences which are being described. Certainly, we are dealing here with a very special child. But we know through research, literary portrayals and our own experience of children, that children do wonder about such things — especially as four year olds, according to textbooks on developmental psychology. But what happens at school, and further on up the system of education? Do we seriously reckon with children's individual thought-processes? The schooling that society provides children with is based on points of departure other than those required by the children to be able to develop the talents and aptitudes each child has within himself to grow as man, in Steiner's opinion. This is an important starting-point for the reformation of the educational system which he as an adult would come to recommend.

Steiner describes how as a little boy he contemplated the spiritual dimension of life in their relation to everyday and practical duties. Thus he is fascinated for instance by the railway and other technical inventions, at the same time as these very things give rise to aesthetic and ethical questions in his mind. He is afraid that his great interest in practical and mechanical problems sometimes threatens to dominate over feeling and his experience of the beauty of Nature. He perceived early on in his, as he says, childishly clumsy way, the spiritual as a reality in the same way as the external, material sensory world. He believed already as a small child in the possibility of finding a bridge between spirit and Nature and that it must be possible to extend the limits of knowledge which his era had set up.

He believed that school-teaching was too exclusively concerned with visible and measurable objects and facts, all presented in a lecturing manner, and did not concern itself with spiritual, 'hidden knowledge,' as it might be termed today.[42] He was himself passionately interested in both sides of life, and not least in how they seemed to interact with one another.

It was in connection with geometry studies on his own that he first observed that it was possible to grasp something purely spiritually. This he found comforting, and said that for the first time he understood what happiness meant. Mathematics, too, captivated him in a special way at that time, because it was concerned with concepts, obtained independently of external sensory perceptions and which yet gave such tangible knowledge of the world.

Early on, he was as equally assured of the reality of the spiritual world as he was of the sensory world, something which he believed that the Western world in particular had lost its understanding of, and which he therefore came to spend the rest of his life trying to demonstrate (compare Emanuel Swedenborg). The fierce resistance which he met throughout his life on this point he had already noticed as a child and kept therefore all his ideas on spiritual things to himself.

These childhood experiences should help us to understand why Steiner came to put such emphasis on a different kind of human knowledge, which found expression especially in his pedagogical and therapeutic-educational work. He was critical of his contemporaries' too one-sided empirical science as applied to psychology and education. In order to reach the spiritual side and the inner invisible aspect of man, as well as of life as a whole, something else and something more were required.

Throughout his life, he retained his early scientific and technological interests, as well as a great admiration for the practical progress made by science. He chose to pursue his own higher education at an institute of technology. He also held the view that it was important to have the option of advancing within those areas of knowledge which are closest to the humanities — and within the sphere of philosophy as well as religion.

It was these interdisciplinary viewpoints which he later attempted to realize in founding the university for spiritual science in Dornach — the Goetheanum — which today still represents the world centre of the anthroposophical movement.

From his description it is clear, too, what a strong impression the differences between adults made on him. These were adults he came into contact with outside school — often friends of the family. The one who made the greatest impression on him was a completely unschooled man. These experiences and observations may similarly have contributed to his later coming to place such a great emphasis on adults as examples and authorities for children in their upbringing and education. He even seems to be quite stimulated by the contrasts in others' points of view — for example, the differences between his teachers, some of them systematic thinkers or logicians, others more intuitive types, seem to act rather as a driving force, adding to his excitement and inspiring him in his own thinking.

Of importance to his educational work were also his youthful experiences as a tutor, teaching classmates at school and in private tuition. As regards his own schooling, he says he took in knowledge in a half-awake, dreamlike state, but that he on the other hand was wide awake when he had, in practice, to present the content to his pupils during the extra lessons. When he was forced to struggle to acquire knowledge on his own in order to pass it on in concentrated form to someone else in practice, his own mental activity also woke up. Do perhaps such early experiences comprise the best possible seedbed for later fruitful efforts in the sphere of education?

One particularly important experience was when he as a young student over a period of many years was given the responsibility of educating a physically and mentally backward boy. The work that this involved contributed to his further understanding of the close connection between the physical and the spiritual, and to his sense in particular for the significance of this connection in achieving good results as a teacher and also as a doctor. He is grateful for the living human knowledge which he gained by teaching this handicapped boy, and does not believe that he would have been able to assimilate such a deep sense for the connection between the physical and the spiritual in another way. It was now, he writes, that he came to realize that teaching must be an art with its base in a profound knowledge of man, which in itself must mean an openness *also* towards spiritual dimensions in life.

Steiner was already as a child prepared to spend a great deal of time and effort on trying to understand literature which was not easily absorbed, and on reading difficult texts again and again, something that he perhaps therefore found natural to also expect of those who read his own texts, as well as in reading as a whole. In a similar way, this is a possible background to why the Waldorf system of education avoids working with programmed textbooks, and shuns so-called 'general purpose' ready-made teaching systems. On the contrary, a central idea seems to be that the student, as well as the teacher, should work independently with the topics, so that they can be grasped and assimilated with one's own thinking. Such a command of the material is necessary for a teacher if, from out of her own inner being and in an inspiring way, she is to be able to pass on knowledge to her students. To do so an artistic dimension is required, which each teacher must provide. *'Schwung, Schwung, Wärme, Wärme!'* was how Steiner used to urge teachers in the first Waldorf School to show warmth and animation in their teaching.[43] Teaching should not be a matter of the teacher, *from without,* in a 'lecturing tone of voice,' imparting knowledge in the form of facts and information. The aim should rather be to mediate knowledge 'in an enthusiastic fashion,' so that the spirit and the creative ability which exists *within* every teacher as well as *within* every student can be developed and have free room to play. But more on that in the next chapter, where we examine the fundamental influence of Goethe on Steiner's work.

CHAPTER 4
Goethe — the Basis of Waldorf Education

Steiner's research into Goethe

Many who are well acquainted with Goethe's enormous influence as a poet and as a cultural personality have never heard of the extensive scientific research which he engaged in for the greater part of his life. Goethe himself is said to have accorded this work even greater importance than his literary achievements, which he considered someone else could have done just as well.[1]

Furthermore, among those familiar with Waldorf education, many do not realize the extent to which — like diverse other activities of Steiner – it was influenced by Goethe's research method and the view of nature and the world to which Goethe gave expression through *both* his poetry and his research.

There are many reasons why the scientific side of Goethe's work has been so neglected, together with the fact that Steiner's research in this area has received so little notice. Goethe saw with great unease the direction which the scientific research of his time was taking. He reacted against the mechanical way of seeing things where man as an active subject was relegated to distant observer. He dared to question the methods of science and thereby to a certain extent its foremost exponent, Newton. It is quite understandable that the scientific community of his time found it hard to take such criticism really seriously, from a non-specialist and a poet to boot. Perhaps, too, the simple, forthright and non-academic language in which the criticism was presented made Goethe's views all the more unacceptable in certain quarters?

To analyse Goethe's contribution as a scientific thinker and relate this to the cultural climate of his time is a huge task which does not fit into the present context. Many scholars since Goethe's days, even in our own time, have returned to Goethe's scientific writings in an

J.W. von Goethe 1749–1832. Drawing of 1817, by Jaegermann.

attempt to understand their deeper meaning. In the shadow of the Second World War, for example, several leading atomic physicists suggested that a closer study of Goethe's view of science would help to re-assess the unwelcome traits in our high-technological civilization. Did Goethe have a point in his defence of the subjective value of quality in scientific contexts and even in the increasingly mathematical abstractions of physics research? (See below, p.139.)

Steiner came to spend the first fourteen years of his adult life on research into Goethe's scientific theories. In 1883, as a twenty-one year old newly graduated from Vienna's Institute of Technology, he was given the job of participating in a German national edition of Goethe's collected works — the so-called Kürschner Edition.[2] Academic specialists were responsible for editing and interpreting different sections of Goethe's life and work. In 1888 Steiner was also invited to become a colleague at the Goethe-Schiller Archives in Weimar, where the renowned *Sophienausgabe* of Goethe's collected works were published.[3] Here the task was to revise a number of formerly unknown and scientifically valuable manuscripts which Goethe's grandson had left in his will to the Grand Duchess Sophie of Saxony. The work was carried out in collaboration with the foremost Goethe specialists in Germany. That Steiner, after many years' work on Goethe's scientific works, and having published and lectured on the subject, was given this even more qualified job shows that the scientific research community had great confidence in his work up to then as a Goethe researcher.

For the first seven years Steiner's work was carried out in Vienna. After being engaged at the Goethe-Schiller Archives, he moved to Weimar. In his autobiography he says that he took a lively part in the cultural life there. However, in the long run he was not specially happy at the Archives, where he felt that his own ideas ran the risk of becoming completely rigid under the influence of the 'philological method' which was employed there.[4]

It was his teacher at the Institute of Technology, the Goethe researcher Julius Schröer, who originally recommended Steiner for this research work. During their many long discussions together, he had had the opportunity of seeing Steiner's suitability for the task. But Schröer knew very well, too, how sceptical many scientists of the day were regarding the scientific side of Goethe's work, and it is possible that it may have been difficult to find anyone willing to take on the risky job.

Both Goethe's basic material as well as Steiner's commentaries, are extensive and deal with some of the most difficult issues in science. Goethe himself never made any epistemological analysis of his research — such things were not in his line, according to Steiner — which makes their interpretation a sensitive and often uncertain matter. Sometimes it is difficult for the reader to discern which are Goethe's own ideas and which are Steiner's.

Steiner, himself a scientist with a great admiration for the progress of science, nonetheless felt sympathy with Goethe's critique of the weaknesses in science. It was fitting then that he should become the first to address the task of penetrating this work in its entirety and presenting it to the public together with comprehensive introductions and commentaries.

From the very beginning, Steiner was well aware of the difficulties of this 'honourable task.'[5] Towards the end of his life, he wrote in his autobiography how seriously he saw the task:

> For me this job meant that I must make my own position clear on the one side *vis-à-vis* science, on the other *vis-à-vis* Goethe's whole general view of the world. Since I was now to present to the public such an exposition, I had to finalize in a way my personal struggle thus far to acquire my own general view of the world.[6]

According to Steiner, Goethe was a great pioneer and far from being the dilettante in science which many people considered him. At a very early stage, Steiner noticed how odd it was that Goethe's contemporaries could grant his literary work such importance, while completely underrating his scientific research. Steiner found that both sides of Goethe's work are intimately related and together comprise an unusually high achievement. Above all *Faust,* but also most of Goethe's literary and scientific works, are saturated with his view of knowledge and Nature. But Goethe's contemporaries did not realize this. Many do not see it today either, because of our own view of knowledge and the method we use to seek knowledge, in which art and science are isolated from each other instead of being regarded as an integrated whole.

Steiner's first book was published in 1886. Steiner had soon become aware, he writes:

> [that there] ... existed no epistemology for Goethe's kind of research. This induced me to sketch one out. I wrote my *Theory of Knowledge Based on Goethe's World-Conception* from an inner need, before I got going on the following volumes of Goethe's scientific writings.[7]

This book was published later as an appendix to Steiner's section of the Kürschner Edition.

The preface to the second edition, written towards the end of Steiner's life, reveals how the ideas he formulated about Goethe in his younger years remained with him. He writes that the book still made up:

> ... the epistemological foundation and justification of all that which I have later said and published ... What I had

> sketched a long time ago in this little publication as being the theory of knowledge according to the Goethean world conception, appears to be to be just as necessary to say today as it was forty years ago.[8]

The same importance is still accorded to the book by anthroposophists today.

In 1888 Steiner gave a lecture to the Vienna Goethe Association entitled *'Goethe als Vater einer neuen Ästhetik'* (Goethe as the Founder of a New Science of Aesthetics). When this lecture was published in a second edition twenty years later, in the foreword he rebutted those who claimed that over the years he had changed his ideas. He explains how this is not in fact the case at all, but that what he had said here stands out as a sound foundation for the anthroposophical teachings which he later developed. Indeed, it even seems to him that the anthroposophical conception of things is particularly suited to contributing to an understanding of Goethe's ideas.[9]

At the end of the Weimar period, in 1897, he published, independent of the Sophie edition, his own summarizing book on Goethe entitled *Goethe's World View.* In an epilogue to a reprint in 1918, Steiner refutes critics who claimed that the writing really did not give any picture of Goethe's general philosophy of life, as the title purported, only of his perception of nature. Steiner pointed out that even if the book appeared to deal almost exclusively with Goethe's ideas on nature, the criticism is still not justified. Steiner believed that in his book he had shown precisely how Goethe's ideas on nature are intimately associated with the whole of his philosophy. He suggested that Goethe's view of nature itself was the point of departure for his way of thinking of the whole, and this likewise influenced his standpoint on psychological, historical and other ideas. In Steiner's opinion, what is expressed in Goethe's idea of nature is precisely a philosophy and not merely a perception of nature.[10] He even believed that Goethe arrived in principle at a fundamental position which had as great a significance for the science of organic life as Galileo's basic theses had had for the inorganic. Steiner regarded it as his task to lay the ground for an understanding of these principles. He says too that he would be delighted if others could follow him and develop this work further.

During these fourteen Goethe years, Steiner began to display his very great capacity for work, his interests at this time by no means focussed solely on researching Goethe. While in Weimar, between 1890–97, he published a great number of writings. In 1891 his doctoral thesis on philosophy appeared, entitled 'The Basic Issue of Epistemology with Particular Regard to Fichte's Doctrine of Science. Prolegomena to the Philosophical Consciousness's Understanding of Itself.' The main content was reworked the same year into a book entitled *Truth and Science. Prelude to a Philosophy of Freedom.* Then, in 1894, came *The Philosophy of Freedom. Basic Lines of a Modern Philosophy. Spiritual Observational Conclusions in Accordance with the Scientific Method.* This book, regarded as one of Steiner's central works, represents for many readers a text which is extremely difficult to get through. It seems likely that many of those interested in anthroposophy and recommended to read it, have given up at this point.

In the same year he wrote an introduction to an edition of the collected works of Arthur Schopenhauer, and a little later on, in 1895 there appeared *Friedrich Nietzsche, ein Kämpfer gegen seiner Zeit' (Friedrich Nietzsche, a Fighter against his Own Times.)* In 1897 he was the author of an introduction to selected works of Jean Paul. Apart from this, during this period he gave a huge number of lectures on various subjects.

In this chapter, I will go on to consider those aspects of Goethe's work that contribute most to Steiner's ideas on art and knowledge. My sources here are in the first place Steiner's own works, in particular the three books already mentioned: *A Theory of Knowledge Based on Goethe's World-Conception, with particular reference to Schiller; Goethe's World View* and *Goethean Science* (commentaries to the Kürschner edition of Goethe's collected works). Except in certain cases, I have not been able to approach Goethe's own writings here. Nor with regard to Steiner have I been able to make a comprehensive analysis of the literature concerning his studies on Goethe, since these studies permeate and influence most of his books and articles and his thousands of lectures. Of great value for my theme has also been the Swedish edition of *Goethe's Theory of Colour* with commentary by the physicist Pehr Sällström in collaboration with the artist Arne Klingborg. Sällström acknowledges the invaluable assistance given by

Rudolf Steiner's commentaries in the Kürschner Edition. He also points out how he noticed more and more clearly:

> how thoroughly well-informed and pertinent Steiner's interpretation is of the method and theory of knowledge which has found expression in Goethe's scientific writings. To him, too, the honour is due of being the first person who really understood and pointed out the momentous value of this long misunderstood side of Goethe's many-faceted life's work.[11]

My studies on Goethe as the basis of Waldorf education have become far more extensive than I had first intended. During the course of my research it came as a surprise to discover how central this, largely unknown, material is to our context. I have therefore found it imperative to try to reveal this background, within considerable limitations. It seems quite clear that, without an insight into this background, one lacks the prerequisites for understanding the theory of knowledge lying behind Waldorf education and other anthroposophical activities.

My presentation is somewhat speculative in character and is therefore in no way to be regarded as final. Here, it is chiefly my endeavour to try to present the issues in such a way as to make it easier for others to form their own questions from their own differing points of departure. I therefore aim to offer a *starting point* rather than a definitive research conclusion.

Goethe and Schiller

I begin by examining Goethe's and Schiller's influence on the view of man and knowledge within the Waldorf system of education. It is evident here that there was much in Steiner's character and early experiences which made him particularly suited, unlike his contemporaries, to understanding Goethe's scientific research. The more I have tried to understand the perception of art within Waldorf education, the more essential I have found Steiner's interpretations of Goethe's and Schiller's works. There is certainly much in this material which

The Goethe-Schiller statue outside the Theatre in Weimar.

appears at first alien to our time and thinking. But the longer I have spent on the undertaking, the more I have come to wonder if it really is so alien to us.

In the introduction to his first book *A Theory of Knowledge,* Steiner explains how Goethe's and Schiller's contributions to the scientific debate were disregarded by the philosophers of their time. And yet he says that Goethe is unthinkable without Kant, Fichte, Schelling or Hegel.[12] In Steiner's opinion, philosophy and science in Goethe's time existed in grand isolation from general cultural life and this was damaging to its development. Commenting in a new edition of the book published forty years later, he writes that this earlier statement no longer appeared justified in the world of Nietzsche and Einstein. Nevertheless, his *motives* for making the judgment were still valid.[13]

In hardly any other period in history had philosophy been less popular than during Steiner's own lifetime, he writes, though paradoxically people longed more and more for a philosophy of the world, life and morals. Philosophy should, instead of isolating itself, go hand in hand with cultural development in its entirety. Philosophy must also satisfy the spirit, and should not 'seek its welfare in an artificial seclusion and supercilious isolation from all other spiritual life.' Its proponents must address the great issues concerning humanity if people are to take an interest in philosophy. For this to happen philosophers must not merely clarify their relationship to our classic thinkers and writers — philosophy must also seek in them the seed to its own development; it must be imbued with the same spirit which pervades our culture. Instead of returning to such a high degree to Kant, philosophy should also immerse itself in Goethe's and Schiller's scientific works — then it will once more be in a position to play a role in cultural life.

Granted, Goethe was no philosopher, unlike Schiller. But a deep philosophical insight lay behind the basis for Goethe's views on nature and thereby on the world, even if this does not find expression in the form of fixed scientific theses. Neither Goethe's nor Schiller's poetical works are thinkable without their underlying philosophy, and their philosophical disposition is for the two men an important element of their artistic creativity. By making the connection to Goethe and Schiller it should be possible to 'jerk philosophy from its rostrum of isolation and incorporate it with the rest of cultural development,' Steiner believed.[14]

Both in *A Theory of Knowledge* and later too in his commentaries on *Goethe's Scientific Works,* Steiner stresses that the scientists of his time often approach Goethe in the wrong way. They turn back on the threshold because their own thinking is so different and they are therefore unable to approach Goethe's thinking without presuppositions. Neither the literary scholars, the psychologists, the aesthetes, the philosophers nor the scientists of the day have the basic knowledge and the openness demanded. Instead of viewing Goethe *as a whole,* they see him *either* as a poet *or* as a scientist. In Steiner's opinion this error derives from the fact that the prevailing philosophy set up predefined boundaries concerning our acquisition of knowledge and understanding of the world.

Goethe, as far as his own search for the truth went, was not happy with current philosophical assumptions. The Platonic differentiation between idea and physical experience which was prevalent here went against Goethe's nature. For Goethe idea and reality — like thought and physical experience — spirit and Nature, were perpetually interwoven with each other:

> A world of ideas which does not penetrate Nature, its coming into being and its demise, which does not call forth its being and its growing, is for him (Goethe) a fragile web of thought. To spend time unravelling logical thought without an anchor in the true life and creativity of nature, appears to him to be fruitless. For he feels himself to have coalesced deeply with Nature. He regards himself as a living part of Nature. That which arises in his soul, Nature, in his opinion, has caused to rise up within him. Man must not stand in a corner and believe that he can spin a structure of ideas by himself which will have anything to say on the essence of things. He must perpetually allow the stream of world events to flow through him. Then he will come to sense that the world of ideas is no more than Nature's creative and working force. He will come to not want to stand above things in order to meditate on them, but he will come to delve into their depths and bring out whatever lives and works there.
>
> It was in such a context that Goethe saw his own artist's nature. With the same necessity as a flower blooms, he felt his poetic works emanate from his very self.[15]

The questions concerning Nature and spirit, outer and inner reality, thought and physical experience, which so occupied both Goethe and Schiller, were also main issues for Steiner. In particular it is Schiller's *Letters on the Aesthetic Education of Man* and his ideas on how each person should be brought up to be able to experience a wholeness in life, in the way Goethe did, which Steiner takes as a foundation for his educational activities. Perhaps it was significant that it was in connection with the practical task of teaching a handicapped boy that

Steiner first came into contact with Schiller and began to attach importance to his ideas. (See Chapter 3.)

A friendship developed between Goethe and Schiller for which it is hard to find a parallel in the history of letters. They met for the first time in 1794 and saw one another after that often daily, sometimes eating their evening meals together. They spurred each other on and each developed through the other.[16]

The prelude to their friendship was a lecture on science which they had both attended together. Afterwards they happened to get together and discussed on the content of the lecture. Both of them are then said to have commented on how disjointedly Nature was looked upon in the lecture and that nowhere was there a trace to be found of that *Geist* — spirit — which lives in Nature. And Goethe mentioned that he called precisely this cohesive, spiritual principle, which exists in all plants, the *Urpflanze* or 'archetypal plant.' He described to Schiller how he imagined it to be and how clearly he could see in his mind how each plant in itself expressed something real, something living. Schiller then at once realized the idealistic nature of the 'archetypal plant' and said that it did not have anything to do with reality. He is reported then to have said: 'Yes, but that is not an experience, that is an idea,' upon which Goethe replied: 'It sounds very pleasing that I should have ideas, without being aware of the fact or even seeing them with my own eyes.' This spurred Goethe on afterwards to think over the relationship between that which he called 'type' and the empirical reality. With that, according to Steiner, he had arrived at a problem which is one of the most significant within any human research: the problem of the connection between idea and reality, thinking and physical experience — that problem which Goethe's scientific research would continue to revolve around.[17]

Goethe and Schiller, as well as Steiner, considered that science had turned away from such difficult but vital issues. It is precisely Goethe's inclination to unite ideality and reality and to sense that both spirit and Nature are something real — of which his 'archetypal plant' is an example — that makes parts of his work so difficult to grasp for highly educated and scientifically schooled readers.

On the aesthetic education of Man

During this period of friendship with Goethe, Schiller wrote his *Letters on the Aesthetic Education of Man.* Written as a series of letters to the Duke of Augustenburg, these comprise a comprehensive thesis on the significance of art and creativity in human development. Goethe and Schiller had discussed the problems together and the contents of the letters are to a large extent based on Goethe's ideas and on Goethe as a human being, according to Steiner.

Schiller's letters were published in 1794. The following year Goethe published an allegorical fairy story, *The Tale of the Green Snake and the Beautiful Lily.* The tale aroused uncertainty within the German cultural Establishment and they did not know how to interpret it. Steiner was the first to say that the same content was portrayed here in fairy-tale form as that dealt with in Schiller's letters. Whereas Schiller uses an abstract philosophical method of presentation, Goethe's language is pictorially visual: 'his ideas are not abstract thoughts but living pictures, which are formed in a way similar to thoughts in the mind.'[18]

If we are to try and understand Goethe's thinking on art and science, developed in close friendship with Schiller, then we must start from Schiller's *Letters on the Aesthetic Education of Man.* Here those problems are discussed which Steiner considers the most important for the future, namely how we can arrive at a better understanding of the importance of the spiritual dimension in our material physical world. We should be able to extend our limits of understanding considerably were we to intensify our thinking and allow this to include spiritual realities. It should even be possible, Steiner thought, to achieve understanding with the same clarity as we find in mathematical understanding. Such thoughts were undoubtedly incompatible with the scientific thinking of his day but by no means totally new in the history of ideas. Clear roots were to be found in the tradition reflected in the writings of the fifteenth century theologian, philosopher and mathematician Nicholas of Cusa.

According to Steiner, Schiller's *Letters* are among the most significant writings in the field of aesthetics, but they have been disregarded by the 'systematizing aesthetes' who have not found them sufficiently scientific. And in educational life, which Steiner thought should be completely pervaded with the ideas expressed in the *Letters,* there is no real trace of them. Here the highest educational ideals are presented in a way which ought to make the book a people's book. The content ought to permeate every reader, especially in higher education. But the contents are hard to grasp. The right effect is not produced merely by reading and studying the book; instead it should follow a person throughout his whole life, like a book of meditation, he says in a lecture he gave in Berlin one hundred years after Schiller's death.[19]

Nor have the Letters become easier to read with the passing of time! The opposite is closer to the truth. Is it perhaps because the Letters are hopelessly old-fashioned and mostly an expression of German speculative thinking of the most indigestible sort?

Yet the art historian and social philosopher, Herbert Read (1893–1968) declared to a Unesco gathering in 1953, that these *Letters* are 'without comparison [the] most profound which have ever been written on education.'[20] According to Read, their neglect can be explained by the fact that they came into being at an unhappy time when Europe was entering an era of technical discovery and industrial expansion which required a type of education directly opposed to what Schiller recommends. The very concept of 'living form,' central to Schiller's philosophy, is diametrically opposed to the dead forms of machine products and industrial organization. The apostles of profitability of the period were not inclined to take seriously a recommendation to develop the playful instincts of people. A philosopher who in a work on education tried to get people to see that man is man only when he is creating, as in play, must at that time have been regarded as a lunatic, according to Read.[21]

What then are the *Letters* about, by Steiner's interpretation? I shall try to summarize Steiner's account of the main themes in the lecture he gave in 1888 to the Vienna Goethe Association, later printed under the title *Goethe as the Founder of a New Science of Aesthetics,* and also in his 1905 talk, 'Schiller and our Times.' In addition, the Letters are frequently mentioned in his autobiography.[22]

Schiller's aesthetics

Schiller believed that man is torn between two basic urges: *Stofftrieb* and *Formtrieb. Stofftrieb* expresses our need to remain open to the inflowing outer world. We absorb a rich content of inflowing perceptions but we are unable to have any determining influence ourselves on their nature. Here everything happens with a categorical necessity. What we discern is determined from the outside; in this respect we are often unfree, we must quite simply obey the laws of natural necessity. The other basic urge — *Formtrieb* — brings law and order into the confused chaos of the content of these perceptions. As a result of its work a system is set up in the things experienced. But neither are we free here, says Schiller, because in this work reason is subject to the unalterable laws of logic.

It is in a third world — between the sensory and the formal, the world of physical experience and the world of idea — where the material and the formal are no longer separated but are interwoven with one another, that we ourselves can alter reality at will. This is the world of art. And the urge which lies as a ground for art is the basic urge for play — *Spieltrieb.*

Schiller — the poet of freedom — sees in art man's free playing on a higher level and calls out ecstatically: 'Man is only man when he is at play ... and he only plays when he is man in the full sense of the word.' Schiller regards the child's playing as analogous to art. In his play man is free to put real objects from the outside world into contexts which give him satisfaction. He can here achieve changes himself not only in accordance with the law of logical necessity — the formal objectivity — but also from subjective, sensuously experienced needs. In this way the person playing stamps his subjectivity onto reality and gives subjectivity in turn objective validity. In play nature is elevated to spirit and spirit descends to nature — the natural is spiritual, the spiritual natural.

If we are ever going to be able to bring about a reconciliation between reality and the scientific idea, mere physical experience will not be enough. A third factor must enter in, first created by ourselves. Here, living form springs into existence. This necessary third realm between soul and reason is the world of art and the world of the aesthetic mood or frame of mind. Art is the divine and necessary part of the world and man himself must implant art into the world. It is this that is the artist's elevated religious task, according to Goethe.[23]

It is this uniquely human, creative capacity which, in Steiner's opinion, distinguishes Goethe. It originates in a concept of nature and art, or a philosophy, which gives both his poetry and his research such a profound and universal significance. But *each and every* person has the aptitude for a creative ability and it is when it comes to training this aptitude that educational theory displays such great negligence, according to Steiner.

The aesthetes cannot understand the independent significance of art. Aesthetics should begin with an examination of the sense of pleasure, which of course is an aesthetic phenomenon. The pleasure we experience when looking at a work of art is in no way inferior to a purely intellectual sense of pleasure which we experience when regarding the purely spiritual. It is an outright debasement when art is merely given the task of being entertaining. What then is it that gives us such a sense of satisfaction when faced with the world of idea? No more than inner heavenly peace and the feeling of perfection which it conceals within itself. No resistance and no distrust arises because it is something endless in itself. Everything which makes this picture perfect is incorporated within the picture itself. It is first through art and beauty that we can get through to and discover secret and hidden laws of nature.

The following is a selection of quotations from Goethe which Steiner cites in lectures or writings on art and knowledge:

> Beauty is a manifestation of secret laws of nature, which without art would have remained eternally obscured.
>
> Art is the free continuation of the natural processes.
>
> The dignity of art appears perhaps most eminently in music, since music lacks material substance which must be discounted. It is wholly and completely form and content, and elevates and refines all it expresses.

It is in the third realm — the world of art — spanning *Stofftrieb* and *Formtrieb* that man is fully man and free. He acts here not by being compelled to do so but by laws he derives from himself, with no other motive for his actions than his own insight.

According to Steiner in *A Theory of Knowledge,* Schiller also debated these issues with Kant, who based his standpoint on the law of duty. He considered that the law of morals would be debased if it were dependent on human subjectivity. In his opinion man acts morally only when he excludes all subjective motives and bows completely to the majesty of duty. But Schiller saw in this view a debasement of human nature. Could our humanity really be so bad that, in order to be moral, it was obliged to set aside entirely its own motives! In contrast, Schiller's and Goethe's philosophy only recognize the point of view expressed by Steiner himself as: *The point of departure for human action is to be sought in man himself.*[24] (My italics.)

But Schiller also begins with Kant's examination of the kind of delight we experience when we look at beautiful works of art. According to Kant, this experience is completely different from any other. That sense of pleasure has nothing to do with being the owner of the object, with its existence. It is not attached to the object itself at all, only to the idea of the object. While the need for purpose, for usefulness creates an immediate urge to transform the idea into reality, we are, as regards beauty, satisfied with the picture alone. But beauty is appropriate to its purpose in the inner sense — without serving any outer purpose. If we discern a natural object or a product produced by human technology, then our reason will come and demand usefulness and purpose, and its possible application. But when it is a matter of beauty, the phrase 'for what purpose' is incorporated in the object itself and there is no need to involve reason. And this is where Schiller comes in, Steiner believed. And he does so by introducing the idea of freedom into the range of ideas:

> The essence of play consists here of being a matter of real objects whose relationships are altered in any way whatsoever. By this change of reality the law of logical necessity is not determinative, such as when we, for example, construct a machine where we must follow the laws of reason exactly, but here a subjective need is wholly and completely fulfilled. The person playing puts the objects

> into a context which gives him pleasure; he in no way imposes compulsion on himself.[25]

In this way the person playing stamps his subjectivity onto reality and he endows this (the subjectivity) in turn with objective validity. Now the separate effects of two basic urges have ceased; they have flowed together into one, and have thereby become free: That which is natural is spiritual, that which is spiritual is natural.[26]

In *The Philosophy of Freedom* Steiner writes that it is when the spiritual and sensible are woven together that man becomes free, and only when man is free, creative and artistic does he desire and is able to act morally and out of love. In this concept there are clear traces of Schiller.[27] In the foreword to the same book Steiner points to Schiller's two ways of seeking for the truth — *both* out in life and within the heart of man. In particular the latter method needs promoting in our time. 'We do not any longer want solely to *believe;* we want to *know.* Belief demands the acknowledgement of truths which we cannot wholly and completely penetrate.' A knowing which only bases itself on blind faith on testimony coming from the outside, cannot involve any satisfaction, instead the knowing must *also* originate from the inner life of the personality. We do not wish to have a knowledge which:

> once and for all has been rigidified into academic rules preserved in manuals valid for all time. Each one of us regards himself as entitled to start out from his latest immediate experiences, and from there advance to an understanding of the whole universe. We strive after certain knowledge, but each one of us should strive in his own way.[28]

Our scientific doctrines should no longer adopt such a form that their acknowledgement appears to be something entirely compulsory. None of us, Steiner says, would wish to give a scientific publication a title such as Fichte once did: *A Clear and Explicit Account for the Greater Reading Public on the Real Nature of the Latest Philosophy. An Attempt to Force the Reader into Understanding.* In our day and age no one should be *forced* into understanding. We demand neither acknowledgement nor agreement of those people who are not impelled to a view out of a special, individual need. Nor do we nowadays wish to stuff information into the still immature person, into the child. Instead, we seek to develop the child's capabilities so that it no longer needs to be forced into understanding but has the desire to understand.

> All science would be merely a satisfaction of vain curiosity, if it did not strive to elevate *the existential value of the human character* ... Learning is of value only through its contribution to the *comprehensive* development of the *whole* of human nature. Science must be used for human objectives if it is to stand in the service of life. One must be in a position of continuously experiencing things *(erlebend)* in relation to *the idea; otherwise* one falls into slavery under the idea.[29]

A summary

If I were to attempt a short summary of what Steiner, starting from Schiller and Goethe, sees as important in the aesthetic education of man, I would stress the following main points. Certain observations here originate from pedagogical lectures where Steiner often took up Schiller's *Letters.*[30]

The student as well as teacher must be in a position of continuously experiencing as well as creating the knowledge and the material with which he comes into contact. Without such an inner effort, and the formative, shaping aspects which it involves, no real insight is achieved — no knowledge of life in its full extent. A process of learning which consists only of a mechanical, passive repetition of facts, laws, concepts, and so on, without the possibility of these being actively experienced inside every teacher's and every student's own person, results in the mere deposition of dead knowledge, and the process is not able to produce a picture which can have any importance for that person's development of knowledge and understanding, in turn leading to action. By introducing a creative, artistic element into the process of knowledge, the material can be given a concrete living form and thereby the interplay and unity between form and content, as between Nature and spirit, the inner and the outer, can also be experienced by the person.

It is in art and in play that man is free and creative. It is first here that he is man and is able to grasp this unity between the outer world and his own inner world, something which traditional teaching and the whole system of education works against rather than facilitates (compare pedagogy which is sometimes defined as non-play).

This talent for creativity exists not only in artists but also in *each and every* person, and it is this that Steiner, following Schiller, particularly adheres to in his educational theory. If the individual's talents are not encouraged to grow, and if he is not trained continuously in the active creation of knowledge, but is given all his information on both organic and inorganic material through the educational system and following a mechanical view of knowledge, the individual will lose faith in his own part in the thinking process and he will be unable to form an idea of integration and will only see splintered fragments. He will then also lose his sensitivity to the wonderful, the inexplicable in life. Such things as relate to the reverence and love of life, humanity and Nature, merely become words without any substance. And all this clearly leads to consequences for his will-power and his actions and for those priorities he will come to make later on in life. In this way an artistic element is firmly coupled to man's whole attitude to life and his will to take an active part in it and to shape it. An artistic element is thereby of fundamental educational significance, according to Steiner's way of looking at the matter.

However, according to Steiner, it is not only within school education that these ideas are important. For *every adult* in our time — whether in agriculture, health care, teaching, economics or other profession — it is important that our education contains more free play (even if often fairly serious) and *also that* continuous practical artistic exercises should make up a part of our life and development. This would be the best guarantee of producing in the future more free-thinking, responsible, sensitive and creative people and of our being able gradually to correct the imbalance between science and art which has arisen in our civilization ever since the Renaissance. Artistic exercises have, then, a central significance for the individual, as they have for social life.

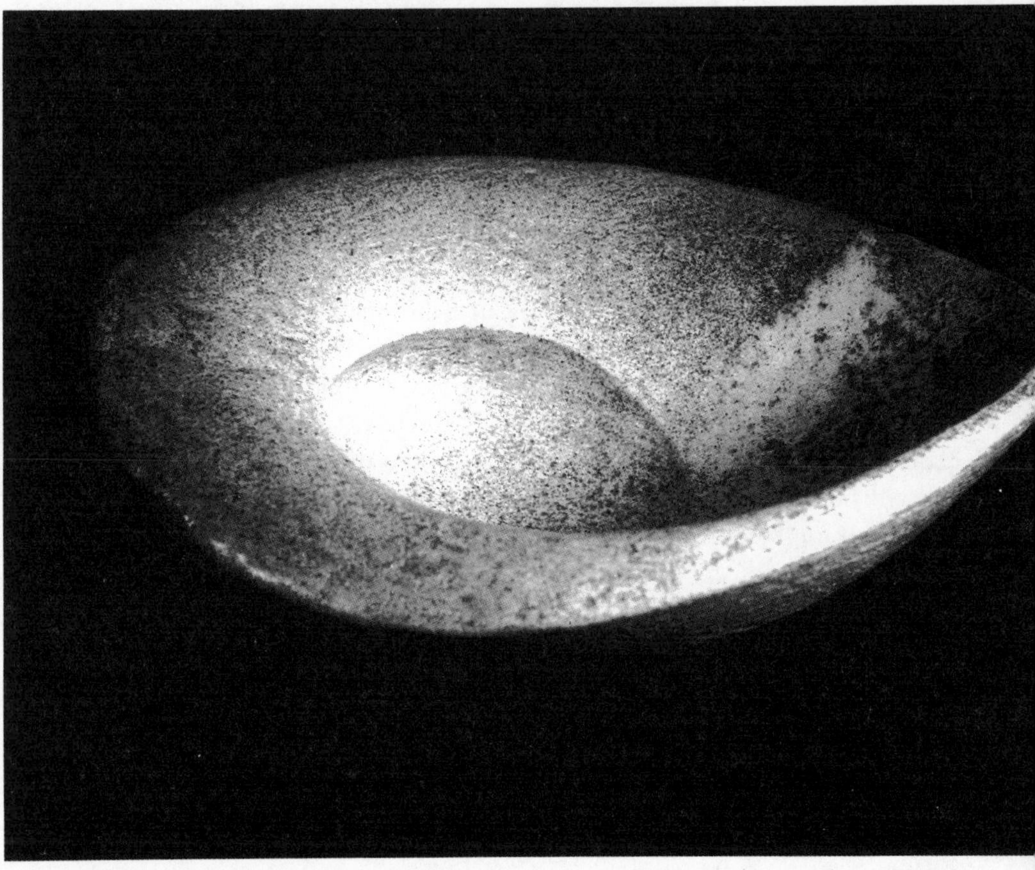

Meeting between inner-outer in the work of Marta Harrison, artist and ceramics teacher at a Waldorf School.

According to the artist and Waldorf teacher, Arne Klingborg, the *Letters* are about the development of society — of achieving an ethic and aesthetic state by nurturing the individual's talents in order to produce responsible actions. At a conference in Stockholm in October 1990, I heard him explain his ideas. The conference was aimed 'at all those interested in how companies, authorities and organizations can be developed into environments where people's creativity and desire to work may grow and flower.' Arne Klingborg spoke before a large group of people from business and institutions. Amongst other things he referred to Herbert Read's book *Education through Art* written in the middle of the Second World War. Witnessing the catastrophic destruction all around, Read believes that a new frame of mind and a new relation to moral life must be developed.

Klingborg described how, during a visit to Stockholm in 1960, he asked Read if he had had much response to his book, and got the reply: No, it has already been forgotten — I think that you are probably the only ones who have listened to it. He was very pessimistic and sad. Granted, there were a number of courses held here and there, but the *issue* itself — the social issue — nobody listened to that. The confidence in art, and the confidence that in *each and every* person there resides an artist — or at least the aptitude for art — was missing.

Klingborg himself speaks of how modern man himself must be morally productive and that in order to achieve this it is not sufficient to institute mere commands and laws. He calls for a spiritual awareness and morals which should become a spontaneous act of will and that it is here that an aesthetic upbringing becomes an important means to this end. One possible way of cultivating ethics is through art. Through art man can learn that he can develop himself and that he can become free, that is, can become productive. In the process of production, it is not a matter of only changing a substance but also of changing oneself. After that, man can regain his dignity. Intellectualism is not enough. Nor is propaganda. Man must become active himself and this frame of mind must come about by means of the schools. Health, playfulness, production are key concepts to which Klingborg here attempts to give living form for our time — setting out from his own artist's soul, and with inspiration from both Schiller, Steiner and Read.

In every person there are seeds which with care can be developed, but without care they wither and are no longer able to grow, Klingborg believes. He tells of how when William Morris (in England at the end of the nineteenth century) spoke to workers, he noticed that the seeds, the stimuli, had already been destroyed. This is a burning educational issue, which Ellen Key also realized. But in order to achieve this it is essential that education becomes an art, in the same way that our relationship to life must become an art. It was an impulse towards this kind of renewal that Rudolf Steiner attempted to give, in Klingborg's view.

Goethe — artist and scientist

A new outlook on the 'organic'

In his autobiography Rudolf Steiner wrote that the mode of thinking of his day seemed to him suitable only for forming ideas on inorganic Nature. He considered this way of thinking insufficient for the true understanding of organic Nature. And it is in this perspective that he found Goethe's research so unique and important.[31]

According to Steiner, Goethe's greatness was due to his being a poet and a scientist in one and the same person. But his contemporaries could or would never see the connection. And Steiner thinks that from such a perspective it is impossible to understand either side of Goethe. Goethe would not have been able to write his literary works without the insights of his comprehensive and systematic nature studies. Nor would he have been able to arrive at the pioneering aspects of his scientific activities without the artistic qualities he possessed. Steiner thinks that every single opinion expressed by Goethe can only spring from the totality of his genius and that science can never arrive at an understanding of his deep comprehension of Nature as long as it fails to view him both as poet and scientist.[32]

By this yardstick the tens of thousands of literary analyses published to date on the poetical works of Goethe — not least on *Faust,* his epic on the theme of knowledge — fall far short of the mark.

Certainly, scientists have acknowledged that Goethe made important discoveries — above all concerning the principle of metamorphosis within botany, the discovery of the premaxillary bone, plus other results of his meticulous morphological studies. But according to Steiner these discoveries, regarded as significant by the scientific community, are really the least important. The most important thing, but also the most difficult to understand, was what they ignored — namely the *method* Goethe used to study reality and obtain his results.

And the results he obtains are, according to Steiner, due to the fact that he uses intuition as an investigative principle, something which science hardly encourages.[33]

Time after time in his lectures and books, Steiner returns to this theme. Indeed, his whole life's work was spent on getting people to reflect on how we have lost our former ability to unite science, art and religion — our ability to comprehend life in its entirety and not merely break it down into parts, which we then find difficult to put together again into a living whole.

An image which Steiner often returns to — and which we also find in Goethe — is that man can no longer read the 'book of Nature' and in particular not the 'book' on human nature. Even Goethe himself was forced to apply himself to a long and laborious 'spelling-out,' as he describes it. He says in a letter what inexpressibly wonderful joy he felt when the 'spelling-out' suddenly passed over into his being able to read Nature.[34]

The science of our day does not involve reading in a real sense — says Steiner — but can be regarded rather as a 'spelling-out.' This is especially destructive in the area of education if the teacher has been only given 'spelled-out knowledge' on children, without progressing further from this basic knowledge to a full comprehension of the entire nature of the growing child. Training up this kind of sensitivity when faced with the child is necessary if the teacher is to be able to get a grip on his teaching. The teacher must then form his own idea on what the children really do and do not assimilate — to what extent the material is living and can continue to live on in the children, or whether the material is merely absorbed as something dead and without real meaning either for the child right at that moment or for his development of knowledge in general. Modern psychology and pedagogy do not apply themselves to this problem and the research findings are therefore of no real help to trainee teachers.

This method of thinking appears unscientific and mostly mystical to a modern reader. Steiner finds it quite natural if we should feel alien to this, since we have acquired other viewpoints through the education we have been given and have thereby lost the conditions required and the sensitivity necessary for understanding these kinds of context.

To regard Goethe as being far too unscientific, as being as bad a philosopher as he was a good poet, is to completely misjudge Goethe's nature, says Steiner. He writes that:

> Nowhere in the modern age did that inner security, harmonious completeness and sense of reality in relation to the world seem to me to be as fully represented as in Goethe.[35]

Goethe acquainted himself thoroughly with the scientific thinking of his time, and had close contact with many leading scientists. He regarded contemporary science as an important part of his own outlook on the world and view of Nature. But what he learned caused him unease and made him look critically at the direction that science had taken. This became the motivation for his own research on Nature.

It is a short step for Steiner to take, who in his own thinking had arrived at the same conclusion, to become particularly interested in this side of Goethe. He explains that he saw it as his mission to attempt to bring attention to the most important things Goethe wanted to say, things which were often misunderstood.

In the introductory section of the Kürschner edition of Goethe's scientific writings, Steiner emphasizes that one of the most distinguishing aspects of Goethe's thinking in the area of science is that it is not a matter of discovering new facts, but a matter of looking at Nature in a certain way and of thereby *opening new points of outlook.* It is true that Goethe made a whole series of great and exceptional discoveries. But as the basis for all these discoveries we must look to Goethe's sublime way of looking at Nature. And the most brilliant discovery, which puts everything else in the shade and which we must 'grasp with the eye,' is in this case his teachings on the nature of the organism. It was the idea of wholeness which was the all-encompassing thing with Goethe. In his research he did not concentrate one-sidedly on the object itself but above all on objects set into their whole context and also on the connecting link between the observer and the object of his study.

In the same introduction Steiner writes that the methods adopted by science prior to Goethe in investigating organic life must also lead to misinterpretations since they did not pay attention to the organism in its entirety. They examined the organism only in its parts and their composition and looked only at external characteristics. That this is deficient can be noticed only when we understand the organism as a whole, since the parts in isolation do not bear their explanatory principles within themselves. They can only be explained if one takes their nature of wholeness into account, since it is the *wholeness* which gives them their essence, their significance and their importance. Only by striving harder to proceed from an idea of wholeness can science avoid making serious mistakes. It was first after Goethe had revealed this nature of wholeness that he understood what was wrong with scientific statements; they could not be reconciled with his notion of the nature of life, but directly contradicted it. If he wished to proceed further along his road he was obliged to remove such prejudices.

Steiner also points to the importance of the reader not regarding Goethe's aims from the start as unattainable. If one is ever to arrive at an understanding of Goethe's way of looking at Nature, one must remain open to the issues, with no prior assumptions, something which in the end will be rewarding, Steiner believes.[36]

His optimism in this respect is remarkable. To understand Goethe's thinking — which in this case means in Steiner's version — is by no means easy. Perhaps there are new and different prerequisites in our day to accomplish this?

In spite of the difficulties there are many who have tackled these ideas. I can here name only a few.

The sociologist and literary historian Georg Lukacs stresses in his book on Goethe's *Faust* that Goethe turns against contemporary science in order to find a new path, and thinks that:

> both Faust and Goethe long for a philosophy of Nature which will lead to full realization of and insight into the dynamics of Nature, a philosophy which goes beyond the merely contemplative, the lifelessly objective and which will lead knowledge of Nature out of its isolation from active human life.[37]

The philosopher Georg Henrik von Wright, who during recent years has figured greatly in debates on the theory of science in Sweden and Finland, writes about Goethe in his book, *Tanke och förkunnelse (Thought and Promulgation).* He stresses Goethe's wide participation in social, political and economic realities and how his active enterprises over a period of many years within these fields, in combination with his works on science comprise a background for what he as poet gives form to in *Faust.* Von Wright also compares Goethe's scientific activities with another artist's activities within the domain of philosophy — namely Tolstoy. He stresses that their works, of course, are not 'exact' in the same sense that Darwin's or Mendel's theories were. But yet he feels that all those scientists who see the wider perspective of their particular discipline need to compare their own views with those of these artists, and that they can be inspired to a deeper realization of their standpoint, to self-criticism and to a reassessment of accepted truths and values.[38]

In 'Goethe as the sage' (1957) T.S. Eliot ponders why, after many years of an unsympathetic attitude to Goethe, more and more he has been captivated by his extensive, but difficult to survey, works. He too considers how the fact that he is both poet and scientist influences his work, and reflects on the great resistance Goethe met in his day precisely because of this.[39]

Metamorphosis — the eternal transformation of life

The summit of Goethe's teachings on the metamorphosis of plants is not the discovery of specific facts relating to the leaf, the calyx, the corolla, and so on. What really matters is his brilliant exposure of the underlying 'archetype' — the ideal construction — with its laws of formation flowing through and acting on an organic whole *(aus sich heraus* — 'from one's inner life and outwards'). The greatness in this idea of transformation can only be realized when it is thought about and when one attempts to make it a living concept in one's own mind. We then become aware that it is the nature of the plant itself translated into idea which lives in our spirit just as it does in the object; we then notice too that we bring an organism to life down to its smallest part when imagining it in one's mind, not as an inert, isolated object but as something developing and coming into being. It is only when idea and reality give life to each other in this way that we arrive at 'wholeness.'[40]

As far as I understand, it is here that the individual observer's own inner creative thoughts and feelings, his artistic aptitude, must be applied if knowledge of the natural phenomena is to become as complete as possible in the way Goethe and Steiner meant. And teaching can be said to be an art in that it is this kind of method of acquiring knowledge that the teachers must apply, both in order to gain a real knowledge of man for themselves as a basis for their teaching, and also in order to be able to pass on a more complete knowledge and understanding of life and a sensitivity to Nature to their pupils.

Goethe's doctrine of metamorphosis is perhaps the most central and innovative result he arrived at through his researches on nature. That plants grow and are transformed through a process which alternately involves expansion and contraction is an idea deeply rooted in him. The seed is the most concentrated, compact stage of the plant. After this stage an expansion takes place in the leaves, following which the vital forces again contract into the calyx of the flower and the bud which, by expanding, forms the corolla of the flower, by contracting, into the stamina and pistils, by expanding, into the fruit, upon which all the vital forces of the plant again hide themselves away in the most contracted state, the seed.

Organic Nature can only be understood in its making, in its process of development. The organism comprises the movement in itself — 'coming from inside it reshapes itself perpetually, transforms itself, creates metamorphoses.' It is in no sense a mechanical way of looking at things; there is an underlying, higher principle that Goethe wants to get at. He does not fix and arrange events one after the other, or make summaries of what he has arrived at, but it is rather the passages between various events and the process as a whole that his method is identifying. Goethe does not reckon with any constant or definitely fixed element — everything floats in continuous movement and constitutes the mobile life of Nature.[41]

Since the essence of this idea of metamorphosis coordinates with formative forces which are visually apprehended and which depend on spatial sizes, one probably understands these laws most easily by making a drawing of the process, according to Steiner, who quotes Goethe:

> 'As I did not see any way of preserving this remarkable thing, I got the idea of making a very precise drawing of it, through which I achieved an even greater insight into the basic concept of metamorphosis.'[42]

The idea that organisms grow and are transformed rhythmically, through a process alternately involving expansion and contraction, is also deeply rooted in Steiner's educational theory and practice. This refers to the child's growth in a physical as well as a spiritual sense, as well as implying an attitude towards everything from the planning of the teaching during one school day — the planning and shaping of the teaching material — to the formation of the school's architecture. Everything should reflect the perpetual transformation of life for man.

Goethe's interest in botanical studies became particularly manifest after his arrival in Weimar when Duke Karl August gave him a garden there in 1776. Goethe became interested early on in the writings of Linnaeus, which shows how seriously he took his endeavours in science. Goethe did not however immediately understand the significance Linnaeus would come to have on his own outlook on Nature.

Linnaeus' endeavours were above all concerned with a systematic method of knowledge of the plant kingdom. In order to be able to recognize each plant and put it into its right place in the system, it was necessary to note aspects which *separated* the plants from one another. In this way Linnaeus and his disciples came to attach particular importance to *external* characteristics such as size, number, position and so on, of the particular organs. The plants were in this way linearly arranged in the same way as one might arrange a whole number of inorganic phenomena where there was no need to consider the internal nature of the plant — the inner necessary relation.

Such a way of looking at things could not satisfy Goethe who said:

> That which he — Linnaeus — tried to keep apart by force, must, so the innermost part of my being told me, strive towards unification.[43]

Steiner also points out the limitations that the study of plants would have as a result of Linnaeus' and his disciples' method. The ideal was to seek out the differences between particular plants. In this way the most insignificant characteristics could be used to identify new species and subspecies. If one happened upon some unexpected diversion from the arbitrary characteristic of the species, there was no need to explain this diversion from the starting-point of this very characteristic. Instead, one quite simply identified a new species.[44] Steiner writes that Goethe wished to make an observation of the different plant forms in order to discover and acknowledge *(erkennen)* the common aspects residing within them. He — the artist in him — wanted above all to know what it is that makes all these formations, these configurations, into plants, while Linnaeus had satisfied himself with describing the different plant forms and placing them next to each other in a fixed order.[45]

Only after Goethe had acquired more time to himself in order to think and make his own observations in Nature, did Linnaeus become more useful to him. He then discovered in Linnaeus the explanation of many details which led him further in his work on combinations.[46]

Linnaeus fulfilled the first task that thinking (interpreting) has to fulfil, namely, discrimination and the creation of concepts with sharply defined boundaries. Here Goethe started out from Linnaeus' studies. But he was not satisfied with that. Instead, he proceeded further and then fulfilled the second task of thinking, which is to summarize the particular concepts created, using Linnaeus' method, into a unitary whole.

This stage is often missing in scientific research and the development of knowledge. It is regarded as lying beyond the range of human ability. But it is at this particular point that man's artistic aptitude and his own creative thinking come into play.

At about the same time as Goethe first made acquaintance with Linnaeus, he also came into contact with the botanical studies of Rousseau. In Goethe's World View Steiner points out that Goethe found in Rousseau a more naïve relationship to the plant world than he had found with Linnaeus.[47] Goethe thinks that Rousseau in his 'Botanical Letters to a Lady' shows proof of an exemplary method of teaching Nature in both a professional and a warm-hearted way and believes that these letters comprise an appendix to the educational novel *Emile.* Steiner makes the comment that one thing Goethe and Rousseau have in common is that they do not take an interest in plants primarily for scientific reasons but from universal motives.[48]

The ability to look beyond boundaries — from multiplicity to totality — Steiner felt was one of the most significant aspects of Goethe's life and work. It was the artist in him which gave him this ability. The ancient mystics had also had this way of approaching

A sketch by Goethe showing how the stem is developed out of segments and leaves. To the right: a segment with its leaf. In the middle: the segment's development. To the left: contraction, i.e. the stem-leaf's contraction into the calyx. (From The Metamorphosis of Plants.)

The leaves from a smooth sow thistle (Soleraceus) *placed in the same order they have on the stem.*

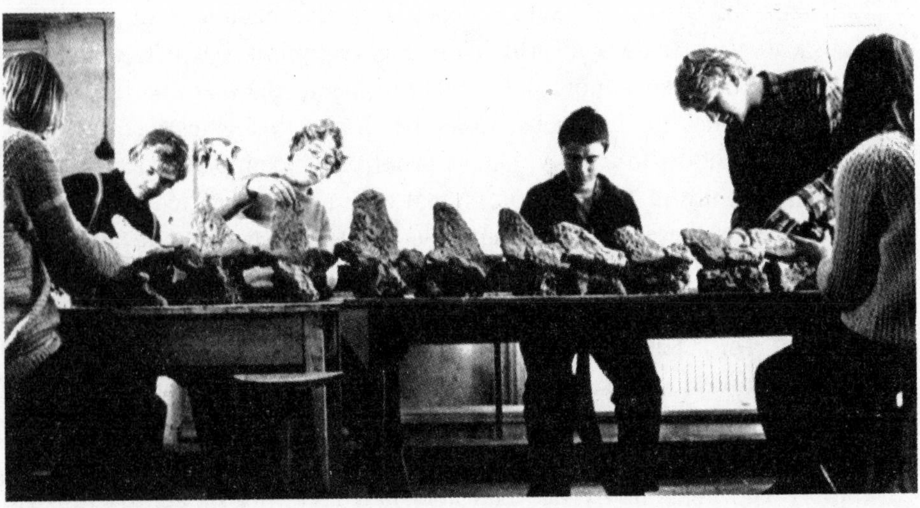

Vertebrae. Artistic group-work at the Rudolf Steiner College in Järna.

objects in the surrounding world, but neither the philosophers nor the scientists of Goethe's day had any trained sensitivity to this — amongst them such ideas were more likely to be regarded as something suspect. (See also 'Beyond the limits of science,' on p.163.)

The spiritual band of union

It is the concept of 'life' itself which is difficult or impossible to encompass and grasp with the measurements of science. Science has failed to develop a theory of the organic, and therefore, instead of searching out new ways of approaching it, excludes the concept of life in its deep, intrinsic sense. Goethe, on the other hand, was spurred on in his research to try and capture the very innermost core of the life of an organism. He fastened particularly on to the most inaccessible parts of life, which scientists of other periods had avoided both because of their inaccessibility and from a general fear of speculation and metaphysics.

According to Steiner, Goethe believed that man has lost an understanding of the living organism which he had previously had, namely that its exterior is subject to an *inner principle,* and that the whole acts within each organ. All exterior phenomena can for a time be observed even after life has been destroyed. But when we look at a dead organism, it is in point of fact no longer an organism. The principle which pervaded all the separate parts has disappeared.

Goethe attached decisive importance to the fact that the scientists of his day to such a large extent only studied limited parts and then often through the microscope. 'Observation which destroys life in order to gain knowledge on life, Goethe, at an early stage, sets against a higher possibility and a higher need,' Steiner wrote.

Steiner relates how Goethe in 1770 wrote about a butterfly, which when it is caught in a net trembles and struggles so that the most beautiful colours are rubbed off, and eventually it lies stiff and lifeless. But the body is not the whole creature. Yet another part belongs to it — the principle of life itself!

Goethe expresses this idea in *Faust,* where Mephistopheles says to the student:

Wer will was Lebendiges erkennen und beschreiben,
sucht erst den Geist herauszutreiben;
Dann hat er die Teile in seiner Hand,
Fehlt, leider! nur das geistige Band.
(Should living thing be researchèd and marked out,
then must the spirit first be driven out,
thereon one has the parts in one's own hand
but alas, not the spirit's uniting band!)

In these words, as far as I understand, is portrayed in poetical form the main spirit both of Goethe's aspirations in the field of science, and of Steiner's later anthroposophical aspirations following in Goethe's footsteps.

But Goethe did not stop at this negative view, Steiner explains:

> He developed it further, and then arrived at the idea of the entity, the essence, through which each separate part makes the other parts live — one principle pervades all the separate parts, the whole acts in all the organs.
>
> *Wie alles sich zum Ganzen webt*
> *Eins in dem andren wirkt und lebt.*
> (Into the whole how all things blend,
> Each in the other working, living!)
>
> and in *Satyros* [Act 4]:
>
> *Wie im Unding das Urding erquoll*
> *Lichtsmacht durch die Nacht scholl,*
> *Durchdrang die Tiefen der Wesen all,*
> *Das aufkeimte Begehrungsschwall*
> *Und die Elemente sich erschlossen,*
> *Mit Hunger ineinander ergossen.*
> *Alldurchdringend, alldurchdrungen ...*
>
> *Und auf und ab sich rollend ging*
> *Das all und ein und ewig Ding,*
> *Immer verändert, immer beständig.*

(How from nothing the primal thing arose,
How power of light through the night did ring,
Imbuing the depths of the beings all;
Thus welled up desiring's surge.
And the elements disclosed themselves,
With hunger into one another poured,
All-imbuing, all-imbued.)

> This way of looking at the world and the whole universe, which 'borders on the mystical,' represents however merely a passing episode in Goethe's development and resolves soon enough into a healthier and more objective conception of things.[49]

We shall return to this healthy conception in due course.

The important point with Goethe according to Steiner, is that he shows that if we are to be capable of coming closer to understanding that which is life, then we must realize that such knowledge must also encompass a spiritual dimension — something which man can only get at himself, in his capacity as a creative, artistic, *whole* man.

This disregard for the spiritual cohesive 'band or bond' in life jarred fundamentally against both Goethe's and Steiner's view of life — its organic as well as its inorganic parts. Both came to challenge the very heart of the scientific view which had been prevalent ever since Descartes, and which had later found confirmation in the doctrines of Haeckel and Darwin.

We may note, however, that Darwin in his autobiographical notes writes that if there is anything in his life he has regretted, it is that he had not spent more time on art and spiritual things — what he calls 'higher aesthetic values:

> The loss of these things is a loss of happiness, and it is perhaps also harmful to the intellect and, which is more credible, to the moral character through its weakening of the emotional life.[50]

It is worth investigating what part Goethe's scientific writings played in the German debate on organic life. In Sven-Eric Liedman's

M.C. Escher (1956): 'The band of union.'

comprehensive *German Debates on Organic Life, 1795–1845,* one is struck by the fact that Goethe's name really does not appear at all. The preface says that it is above all the lack of a biologically directed debate on the nature of organic life that the dissertation is aimed at compensating. But such a debate, Liedman writes:

> ... would probably not merely be interesting in itself, but should also throw a certain amount of light on other lines of development during the same period. Terms such as 'organic' and 'inorganic' played an exceptional part in political, aesthetic and religious conceptual worlds too. In this dissertation I have concentrated on the biological matters, but I trust, of course, that this specialization will not have led to distortion.[51]

According to Rudolf Steiner's way of looking at the issues of knowledge, such specialization would certainly amount to distortion. And Goethe should have been given a central position in a review of the German debate on organic life, precisely because of his unique striving not to fragment but to tackle the problems on a broader plane.

But Goethe has long been ignored in publications on the history of ideas and science. Another example of this neglect is Gunnar Eriksson's eminently readable popular edition of his work on Elias Fries, *The World of Romanticism Reflected in Nineteenth Century Swedish Science* (1969). Considering the very strong influences from German science which are accounted for here, and Goethe's central position in German cultural life, it would appear that a connection here could be extremely interesting and fruitful. Eriksson stresses how difficult it is to summarize the nature of Romanticism, and this would seem to summarize exactly the problems Goethe deals with. Eriksson notes too, that 'the scholars have mostly fastened on to the literature of Romanticism, but disregarded its strong connections with science.' Yet while acknowledging the fact that the man of science within the Romantic tradition has suffered undeserved neglect, Eriksson finds the negligence understandable since 'the scientific results of Romanticism have only in rare instances survived to our day.'

He mentions the Romantic natural philosophers and how these were united in their belief of the primacy of life and their scepticism towards the mechanistic view. At one point he notes that 'they were attracted and fascinated by the great fundamental idea: that Nature, the object of all natural researchers' interest and love, should gain a new dignity, a deeper meaning than that which many, both Christian and materialistic thinkers alike, had wished to give it.'[52] And in his portrayal of the botanist Bishop Agardh, Eriksson emphasizes that he:

> had kept perhaps the most positive characteristic of the Neo-romantics: the characteristic of daring to behold the totality, allowing the gaze to break through the most immediate, material destitution and look another, often truer, existence in the eye.[53]

In this connection we also recall how Elias Fries in the nineteenth century wrote about an early love of nature being a necessary basis for scientific studies, as well as the need, as he puts it, for taking the studies of nature 'to heart.'[54]

A growing number of people today would wish, like the Romantics, for a broader vision in science. Many would surely like there to be greater room for 'love' and 'dignity' and deep interest for the primacy of life in the science faculties of our universities and colleges. The fact that scientific attempts to tackle these problems have not survived to today is perhaps only to be expected — rationally speaking. Such attitudes do not accord with the idea of science which we have been taught. But perhaps a new vision is on the way. Nowadays, it should not be regarded solely as romanticism to adopt a more philosophical and ethical way of regarding Nature and the role of man in the context of Nature.

It would appear to be the search for 'the spiritual, harmonizing bond,' in Goethe's sense which Steiner calls for, especially in our Western civilization, and which, towards the end of his life, he worked at introducing into university-level studies. In his opinion, this can only happen by striving to find ways of bringing art, science and religion closer to each other.

Judgment through observation

It is the totality (the idea) that determines, and therefore it is not enough to take into consideration just what can be apprehended by the senses. Mere observation is not sufficient; we must *also* go outside the world of the senses in order to be able to encompass the unity and the whole. In order to be able to understand organic, living nature in this way, we need a special ability, which Goethe calls 'the power of judgment through observation' *(anschauende Urteilskraft).* The spiritual is an active force in this kind of interpretation and in it we must also acknowledge intuition as a scientific principle, according to Steiner.[55] An organism can only be understood intuitively and intuition means that we acknowledge the ideal (the totality) as such — *'aus sich heraus'* (from one's inner life and outwards).[56]

Goethe was highly influenced here by Spinoza who, together with Shakespeare and Linnaeus, exerted the greatest influence on him.

Spinoza speaks of three ways of achieving knowledge, where the highest way comprises *scientia intuitiva,* intuitive knowledge, and it is this which Goethe aimed for. With Spinoza, God is the same as the idealistic content of the world — the driving, the supporting, the all-bearing principle. Goethe saw God in Nature and Nature in God.[57]

Merely *observing* is the most barren thing that can be conceived of, and it only acquires content first through the act of thinking. 'Our thinking is the interpreter that explains the dumb-show of experience.'[58] From the outside we only acquire the empty shape. That the content of reality is only the mirror-image of the content of our soul is clearly proven by the fact that the person who has a rich spiritual life sees a thousand things which say nothing to the spiritually impoverished person, says Steiner.

This reverence for Nature and life; a feeling for the wonder of life and the sensation of happiness which the experience of this gives, is something that systems of education generally counteract rather than train in people, and this makes for disastrous consequences. This is the fundamental reason for Steiner's development of a system of education where much thought is given to integrating this spiritual dimension.

The basic delusion of modern science is that it regards the very perception of the senses as something finite. And probably only positivism is consistent in this respect, quite simply rebutting every step above and beyond perception, according to Steiner. But he also says that in almost every science efforts in the same direction can be observed.

> One belittles thinking, if one deprives it of its ability, in itself, to perceive things which are inaccessible to the senses. In reality, apart from the qualities of the senses, there must exist yet another factor, which is understood by thinking. Thinking is a human organ, which is designated to observe something higher than what the senses can provide. That side of reality is accessible to thinking, of which a merely sentient nature would never experience anything. It is not there for the purpose of ruminating on sensory aspects, but to penetrate that which is concealed from the sentient nature. Sensory perception provides only *one* side of reality. The *other* side is the understanding of the world achieved through thinking.

As adults, Steiner believes, we must fulfil two tasks with our thinking: the first, to create concepts with sharply defined contours; the second, to summarize into a unified whole the individual concepts which have thus been created. In the first case it is a matter of segregation, and, in the second case, unification. For a long time the task of science has been sought only in a meticulous segregation of things. Discrimination is the business of *the intellect* and it is a necessary first stage in every higher science — after all, definite, clearly constructed concepts are a must before we can look for a harmony between them. But we must not remain still before this discrimination. Getting beyond this point is the business of *reason.* It has to do with allowing the concepts created by the intellect to merge with each other. Discrimination is something which has been artificially established, and it is a necessary thoroughfare for our search for knowledge, but it is not the end of our search. The person who understands reality only through the intellect distances himself from it and only establishes an artificial quantification which has nothing to do with the nature of reality. The intellect distances itself from Nature, loses from view the 'spiritual bond' uniting the separate parts of reality.

Discussing Goethe's theory of knowledge in the Kürschner edition, Steiner formulates this in the following way: Distancing oneself from the *immediate* sensory world is characteristic of Goethe's opinion of what real knowledge is. The immediately given is experience. In *erkennen* (the search for knowledge) meanwhile, we create an image of the immediately given which contains decidedly *more* than the senses can provide, which nevertheless are the conveyors of all experience. In Goethe's method of acquiring knowledge of Nature, we must not get stuck on facts — it is in the very act of processing knowledge that something intrinsically higher is concealed. The idea is not the content of subjective thinking, but the result of research.[59]

We are dissatisfied when faced with visible reality, but are on the other hand satisfied when faced with envisaged reality. The visible reality stands out as finite, it is simply there without our having contributed anything to it. That is why we feel as if we were standing in front of a foreign entity which we have not produced ourselves. We can only encompass (understand) something when we know how it has come into being. An idea does not present itself to me as a finite image in the way sensory observations do. I must participate myself in its coming into existence. The idea becomes the end of a process. I must follow the subject myself through each step of its coming into existence.[60]

But Goethe was also aware of the risks involved in this. In his paper 'Experiment as mediator between object and subject' Goethe writes about the many lurking dangers to be watched out for if experience and human judgment are to be fruitfully combined:

> 'One can therefore not guard oneself enough against jumping to conclusions on experiments. For, in the passage from experience to judgment, from knowledge to application, it is as though one were travelling through a mountain pass where all the enemies of man lie in wait: fanciful imagination, impatience, rashness, self-satisfaction, rigidity, formalism, preconceived ideas, convenience, thoughtlessness, capriciousness and whatever the whole troop with its retinue might be called, all lying in ambush and overpowering unexpectedly both the energetic man of the world, and the calm observer, who might be thought to be insured against all passions.'[61]

Thinking versus accumulating

'We are informed about everything, but we know nothing,' says the author Saul Bellow.[62] This, I imagine, Waldorf teachers would agree with and see as related to the fact that we are not trained to think for ourselves, or to be creative in acquiring knowledge, which is a premise for our ability to understand anything.

To summarize Steiner's position, empirical science — science based on practical experience — is today wandering irresolutely in a world of experiences. This sensory world appears to us as confused and variegated because we do not have the energy to penetrate through to the centre. When we set things right through thinking, we see more than others do — *we see with the eyes of the soul or spirit.* But *the act of thinking* must govern our observations in a way that nature dictates. This cannot be achieved if scientists have lost faith in the power of thinking, which they have done today by not probing sufficiently *into the depths.* Instead, they spend their time endlessly accumulating observations without having the courage to compose them into a scientific understanding of reality. At the same time, the German philosophy of idealism is accused of being unscientific because it had the courage to do just that.

The great enigmas in life are thought to be unsolvable. The only thing regarded as possible is to systematize the evidence gained from practical experience. But in doing so, it is forgotten that a rejection of thinking and an insistence on sensory experience do not, at bottom, differ from blind faith in religion. The Church, too, presents far too many ready-made truths which we are merely required to believe in. It is not necessary to make the effort to think for oneself, nor to probe deeper into the meaning itself. It is not necessary to make the effort of testing the truth for oneself, using one's own capabilities. But *man must himself point out the direction of travel.* The only thing worthy of man is that he should himself search for the truth and here neither experience nor vision (taken separately) can guide him.

Man must himself be creative and take responsibility for his thoughts — only then is he fully man, according to Schiller. In this respect one could say that Steiner himself practises what he preaches. It cannot be denied that he possessed an unusually high degree of courage in composing his observations into a scientific understanding of reality, as he saw it, as well as creating practical activities coupled to this understanding.

Steiner also believes that the object of thinking is ideas. That is what Goethe arrived at through his discussions with Schiller. Man's true communion is to make room for ideas in reality and that is what creative man — the artist within each person — is capable of. Thinking has the same significance *vis-à-vis* ideas as the eye has for light, and the ear for sound — thinking is the organ of comprehension.

Looked at in this way, it becomes possible to unite two things which are regarded today as incompatible, namely empirical method and idealism as scientific world-philosophy (objective idealism). Today it is believed that if one acknowledges empirical method, it follows that one must reject idealism. This is completely wrong. This conclusion is arrived at when it is believed that the senses only convey such contacts between things as can be referred back to mechanical laws. But there are other, equally objective, aspects of reality, which are not considered because they cannot be referred back to mechanical laws.

The only satisfactory comprehension of reality is therefore empirical method coupled with idealistic research. It is a question of idealism, but not of some hazy, dreamlike unity of things; instead it is an idealism where the concrete idealistic content is sought for in reality and is acquired by experience to the same extent as the exacting research methods of today seek to specify the factual content.

The philosopher Eduard von Hartmann also rejects the purely mechanical comprehension of Nature, as he does a dogmatic Darwinism which adheres to external aspects, searching instead for the concrete idea using empirical-inductive methods. Steiner says that his own view diverges from Hartmann's only on the question of pessimism. That dissatisfaction in the world outweighs satisfaction Steiner sees as being man's good fortune. We should stop striving to be happy and should instead search out the meaning of our lives by unselfishly fulfilling the idealistic tasks which our reason prescribes. Steiner asks, what does this mean except that we seek our happiness merely in restless action? Only he who acts unselfishly, without seeking any reward for his pains, fulfils his mission. It is foolish to want to be repaid for one's deeds; there is no real/true payment. The only possible driving force for our actions is love. Only by acting out of love does one act morally *(sittlich).* The idea must be our guiding star in science, and love in our actions.

Goethe has morality arise from man's world of idea. Neither external, objective norms, nor mere instincts drive moral action; instead it is the ideas, clear in themselves, through which the active, creative man, out of his own inner self, gives himself direction. He does not follow them out of a sense of duty, as he would have been obliged to do with objective norms. Nor by being forced to do so, as one follows one's urges and instincts. But he serves them out of love. He loves them as one loves a child. He wants to bring about their realization and adjusts himself in accordance with them because they are a part of his own being. Idea is the guiding principle and *love* the driving force in Goethe's ethics. For him, 'duty is when one loves that which one commands oneself to do.'[63]

Action in accordance with Goethe's ethics is *free* action because man is not dependent on anything except his own ideas. And he is not answerable to anyone besides himself. There are no general laws on what is right or wrong. Ethical actions are, after all, a product of what is valid within the individual — an outlet for individual intentions. One general law of nature applicable to all peoples and all ages is an absurdity *(ein Unding)*. Such things come and go with peoples and ages and even with individuals. Individuality is always the determining measure. Ethics, like all other sciences, is a theory of existence *(eine Lehre vom Seienden)*.

We seek the heart of existence in man himself. No one can visualize a dogmatic truth for man, no one can impel him through action. *He is sufficient unto himself, must create all through himself.*[64]

These ideas, as well as the following ones, seem to agree with Schiller's idea of the creative human being, discussed in the previous chapter. Our ethic is something artistic which each human being creates for himself.

Things speak to us, and our inner self speaks when we observe things. These two languages derive from the same original entity and the task of man is to achieve an understanding between the two. That constitutes what is known as knowledge, *Erkenntnis.*[65] And this and nothing else is sought by the person who understands the needs of human nature. To him who does not succeed in achieving this understanding, things in the external world remain alien. He cannot hear the voice of the nature of things in his inner self. He therefore presumes that this nature behind things is concealed. But things remain only external things as long as we merely observe them. When we think of them they cease to be outside us. We fuse with their inner essence. For man, the contrast between objective external perception and the subjective internal world of thought only subsists as long as he does not acknowledge the mutual connections between these worlds. The human inner world is the inner world of Nature.

It makes no difference here that different people have different ideas about things. The purpose of the universe and of the nature of existence does not lie in what the external world can provide, but in what lives and takes place in the human spirit. This is why Goethe notes with dismay that the natural scientists wish to penetrate the inner world of Nature with instruments and objective experiments, since:

> ... man in himself — as long as he uses his common sense, is the greatest and most exact physical apparatus there is, and it is precisely this that is the greatest misfortune of new physics, that the experiments have, so to say, been distanced from man, and people only see Nature in what artificial

> instruments show, indeed, by means of them they wish to limit and prove what Nature can achieve.[66]

What is a string, and all its mechanical divisions, in comparison with the musician's ear?

Man must allow things to speak from their spirit if he would learn to know their nature. This is nothing mystical. Only by starting out from himself can man judge the world. Man must think in an anthropomorphic way. In the most simple statements one speaks anthropomorphically, for example 'One body collides with another.' All physical explanations are disguised anthropomorphisms. One humanizes Nature when one explains it. One puts into it the inner experiences of man. But these subjective experiences are the innermost nature of things and one can therefore not say that man does not acknowledge the objective truth *'daß an sich der Dinge.'* Goethe's view here stands in the starkest conceivable contrast to Kant, Steiner points out.[67]

Science and creative values

As mentioned earlier, Darwin in his old age had begun to wonder whether he had lost something important by not having spent his active life on spiritual matters. In this context it might also be of interest to mention another eminent scholar, the cerebral physiologist, Ragnar Granit, who in his memoirs writes how quite early on in his scientific career, he was worried by an 'invisible destructive enemy' which he felt lay in the work of science. He cites the evidence of three witnesses. The first is Darwin fretting over the fact that during his lengthy involvement with the construction of his theory of evolution he had lost the ability to enjoy artistic expressions of culture. Something similar, Granit feels, also lies behind a comment by Tolstoy on a visit from the Nobel Laureate Metchnikoff:

> He believes in his science as in a holy image, but questions of a religious nature and a moral character are completely alien to him. He is a kind and simple man, but every person has his weakness. Some people drink, he has his science. And how many learned men have not counted the different

> species of flies? There are seven thousand! How could they ever find time for spiritual issues.[68]

Granit's third witness is Bertrand Russell, who felt that if science gave a greater number of people access to rich experiences of nature, that was excellent. But:

> when it (science) takes out of life the moments to which life owes its values, science will not deserve admiration, however cleverly and however elaborately it may lead man along the road of despair.

Granit stresses later on that:

> with a certain amount of justification [one] can say that the long, narrow, winding road to real knowledge today has become more difficult to follow. Troubled by a mounting number of disturbing factors, it has become all the more difficult for the private individual to keep his identity. An inner composure of this kind is, nevertheless, necessary for the person who intends to grow and mature within a scientific field of work. What I wish to emphasize is, that what we read, what we actively remember, what we ourselves contribute to our science, all work together to build up a living and creative structure within us. We do not know how the brain accomplishes this, as little as we know how the visible world is straightened up again after we have for a time worn inverting spectacles for experimental purposes. On that point our measure of knowledge does not suffice to explain. We must be satisfied with stating the fact that the brain has this sensible property.
>
> By keeping track of one's identity — I mean the cultivation of talents such as the gift of listening to what one's own spiritual self-activity consists of, lopping the twigs off the side-shoots and following out the main lines, gratefully receiving what the secret process generates which clothes itself in the form of automatic creativity — I can imagine that many a person would give nothing for these

> points of view and would prefer to regard them as my personal idiosyncrasies. Others, yet again, who later on in their lives make a summary of their own activities, should surely be able to distinguish a personal line of identity in their work. The majority of my older colleagues are probably willing to concede this. But I am aiming at something above and beyond this when I underline that an active brain is self-fertile. And I am deeply convinced that if one can only keep track of one's identity, it will in turn keep track of one's development.
>
> All this I bring to market with such enthusiasm since it needs saying. Life in the cities and at the universities has become more unsettled. The 'Organization Men' (Whyte's wicked book!) with their eternal paper wars, questionnaires and organizational itch, have increased their influence, while the number of teachers in relation to the number of students has decreased. This development seems to generate a clientèle of anti-scientific students who demand more and more of the universities and less and less of themselves. The scientists withdraw to their specialist institutes and this in turn leads to the standard of teaching at the ancient seats of learning, which are ultimately built upon intellectual idealism, sinking. Obviously there is a need for a number of specialist institutes, but if the university faculties are completely abandoned to professional training and neglect their scientific standard, then they no longer deserve to be called universities, but become professional schools.[69]

The modern man of science, Granit, after a lifetime's work on the physiology of the brain, wishes to call attention to the fact that human consciousness contains much that is not encompassed by logic. He can be said to have opened the door, at least a little, through his conclusions, and perhaps helps us tackle Goethe's and Steiner's critique of science more confidently.

Goethe's theory of colour — an epistemological drama

For a much of his life, and right up to his last days, Goethe worked at trying to understand the nature of colour. His writings in this field alone fill two thousand pages of papers and drafts where he describes colour as phenomena in the world of man. His method of addressing the problems is not only, nor even primarily, about physics or mathematics in our modern-day sense. Instead, according to Steiner, it is about epistemological issues, and in his theory of colour he can be said to give practical expression to the view and the method of knowledge he was aiming for. It is significant that during the same years he was working on *Faust,* the drama of knowledge.

Considering the enormous importance that Newton's observations had had for science, it is not to be wondered at that Goethe met with strong opposition and ridicule, when he wished to make critical points against Newton, and above all to point out where continuing research along Newtonian lines would lead. The prominent scientist and Rector of the Humboldt University, E. du Bois-Reymond, said in a rectorial speech in 1882 in reference to Goethe's theory of colour that it was a 'stillborn trifling by an autodidactic dilettante.'[70]

The strong and damning language which Goethe used when portraying the dangers and drawbacks he sees in Newton no doubt contributed further to the general condemnation.

Steiner carried out his research work approximately one hundred years after Goethe, at a time when mechanistic and materialistic patterns of thought were at their height in Germany. To a large extent, Steiner shared Goethe's unease at the direction science had taken and also, in many respects, his different way of thinking. As a result, he did not find Goethe's criticism of Newton as foolish as many in the scientific world did. Steiner's own particular requirements in this respect, in combination with his scientific/technological schooling, most likely contributed to his being disposed to understand what it was Goethe really wanted to attain with his research. Steiner emphasizes that Goethe was guilty of certain faults, but he wishes above all to focus attention on the fact that it is not the results that Goethe obtained that are the point of interest, but the *method* he used in his research.

Since then, it has turned out that Steiner is not alone in seeing something important in Goethe's critique of science. Some of the most prominent atomic physicists have begun to see further than the damning language of Goethe's presentation, beginning to wonder what it really was Goethe was trying to say, and they have paid serious attention to Goethe's research. I shall return to this.

One Swedish scientist — the astronomist and author Peter Nilsson — has written an essay entitled 'Goethe, Newton and the Colours.' Nilsson speaks of the subject in an exciting way here, describing how he was fascinated by many aspects of Goethe's approach, while deeming others to be sheer lunacy. He writes that Goethe's theory of colour contains:

> ... a hard and bitter criticism of science, which in the end concerned contemporary science's mechanistic and materialistic image of the world, and it is a criticism which on a number of points even today might deserve reflection.
>
> [He thinks that] ... the theory of colour is an odd mixture of misunderstanding, fine observations, bizarre deductions, brilliant ideas which stimulate the imagination, and insights which actually on occasion were a bit ahead of their time.[71]

Of particular importance for my presentation here, as previously acknowledged (see p.92), has been the Swedish edition of *Goethe's Theory of Colour* edited jointly by the physicist Pehr Sällström and the artist Arne Klingborg (1976).[72] It deals with the most important of Goethe's own texts on the subject. Reading these texts oneself is the best way of entering the issue. In this text I shall therefore occasionally relate Goethe's own words, which are often in the form of short, compact, itemized paragraphs. The book also contains pictures and background descriptions as well as commentaries by Sällström, where the problems are put into the scientific and cultural perspective of their day in a way that is invaluable for both for the scientist and layman. As already stated, Pehr Sällström stresses the tremendous value to him of Rudolf Steiner's commentaries to the Kürschner edition in working out his own commentaries on the Colour Theory.

In 1791 Goethe published a short book called *Contribution to Optics.* Here according to Sällström, he informed 'both the learned

'The human eye.' Drawing by Goethe, printed on the cover for the plates of the first edition of Contribution to Optics.

world as well as the general public enthusiastically about his findings. The book is written in a popular fashion in a charming and poetic style.[73] Along with this publication came twenty-seven small plates in playing-card size which, together with a prism, were intended to make it possible for the reader to test Goethe's observations for himself. Goethe stressed that his theory of colour could not merely be read; it had to be carried out in practice.

Twenty years later, in 1810, came the summarizing volume *On the Theory of Colours,* comprising around one thousand pages. The title suggests that Goethe did not regard this work as final. *On the Theory of Colours* consists of three parts — 'Draft for a Theory of Colours,' 'Disclosures on Newton's Theory' and 'Material on the History of the Theory of Colours.'

The first part is a collection of 914 items of the material gained from practical work that Goethe had accumulated over the years. Here he divides the colours into physiological, physical and chemical categories, and includes a section on the 'sensual-moral effect' of colours. All this material reveals what comprehensive and painstakingly systematic experiments Goethe carried out and the high degree of objectivity he strived to achieve.

The second, so-called 'polemical part,' contains Goethe's strong attacks on Newton. We can get an impression of the tone Goethe could adopt where he describes Newton's theory of colour as an old fortress ripe for demolition:

> ... to do this, and if possible, to level the ground, but also to organize the rescued materials so that they can be reused for a new building, is the laborious path we have imposed upon ourselves.[74]

I shall return later to the reactions to these polemics and their significance for the world's idea of Goethe as a scientist.

In the historical section, Goethe deals with the relationship between science and art in a way that relates closely to Steiner's interpretation. So, for example, he writes of the comparison between art and science:

> If we return, in the meantime, to the comparison between art and science, we meet with the following reflection: Since no totality can be put together either from knowledge or from reflection alone, because knowledge lacks the inner, reflection the outer, so must we, of necessity, imagine science as art, if we are to expect any comprehension of the totality at all from it. And neither can we seek the totality in the great generality, in the limitless, but instead, in the same way as art is always expressed as a whole in each single work of art, so science, too, ought as a whole to show itself in each subject treated.
>
> However, in order to be able to approach such a demand, one must not exclude any human ability from scientific activity. The chasms of presentiment, a sure eye for the given reality, mathematical profundity, physical precision, the height of reason, the focus of the intellect, animated and yearning imagination, loving joy for the sensual — nothing can be dispensed with in the living and fruitful grasping of the moment, without which no work of art, no matter what its content, can arise.
>
> If now, these elements which we demand might seem to be, if not directly contradictory, then nevertheless contrasting in such a way that not even the most eminent spirits would hope to unite them, so are they, in any case, found to

> be extant in humanity as a whole, and could on each occasion make themselves felt, were it not so that, because of preconceived ideas, through the egoism of the individual, or whatever all these unappreciative, discouraging and deadly negations might be called, they were suppressed at the very moment they were supposed to be effective, so that the phenomenon is annihilated in the same instant as it appears.[75]

According to Steiner, the differences between Goethe and Newton were not so much a contest between facts as rather about how given facts should be read and interpreted. Goethe's hypothesis did not stand contrary to Newton's. It is Goethe's method which is the important thing to try and understand — and not the individual results he arrived at, Steiner believed. What the theory of colour is about is whether one in this respect should accept today's theoretical physics or not, Steiner says.[76]

According to Steiner, it is the strong and biased direction towards mathematical calculations in Newton and the science which developed in his wake that Goethe turns against. Goethe saw risks in man — the active subject — being excluded from Newton's theories on colour. The light which could be determined in mathematical terms was dehumanized and Goethe called it *'das Totenbein des Lichts'* — the dry bones of light.

Light, according to Goethe, is not composed of different colours, and cannot be divided up in the way Newton does. Colours belong to *boundaries,* contours, crossings-over, and comprise 'pictures' rather, seen in general. Colours do not step forward out of the light; they quite simply appear, are transformed and disappear, all according to circumstances. Colours are, instead, light in transformation where the two opposite poles light-dark, and various degrees of shadow, form the colours. When light — the white — is faintly shaded, yellow colour appears, and when darkness — the black — is faintly lit up, blue colour appears, and so on and so forth. Colours hint in this way at an interplay between opposites, they are determined by the surrounding field and are subjective phenomena. Goethe understands colours as a process, something continuously happening, a kind of process of life.[77] It is necessary to know this if it is going to be possible to understand the background to the painting exercises which comprise such an important 'creative knowledge-exploration' part of the Waldorf system of education.

But Goethe does not in any way because of this view hold an uncomprehending attitude towards mathematics in general, of which he is sometimes accused. On the contrary, Goethe had a great admiration for mathematics and a profound insight into its nature.[78]

Goethe, like Steiner, realizes the decisive importance of mathematics. But he raises a warning finger to the uncritical and biased acceptance of mathematical solutions to scientific problems. He believes that Newton's optics, and the way in which colour as a phenomenon is treated there, comprises a very good example of the serious problems in the science of the time in general.

Goethe could not find that what the physicists were dealing with had any particular reference to how we human beings experience colours in practical life. This was related to Newton's and his followers' limiting themselves to a certain type of experiment where a mathematical treatment was possible. The experiments were made, therefore, more for the purpose of verifying their hypotheses, than for the purpose of really getting acquainted with the phenomena.

As regards how one should present results, Goethe says in a comment that 'it is all dependent on one's keeping everything before one's eyes as much as possible, in order to finally summarize it in a point of view, partly in accordance with its own nature, partly in accordance with the nature and convenience of people.'[79] The role of man here becomes undeniably central, on both subjective as well as objective levels.

For a theorist — whether philosopher, doctor, physicist, chemist or mathematician — knowledge is something other than what it is to the technician, practitioner or manufacturer. According to Goethe, it was the dyers, reflecting on experiential phenomena in the dye works, who first realized the inadequacies of the Newtonian theory of colour. Goethe himself approached the problems from the direction of painting, 'from the aesthetical colouring of surfaces.' And he pointed out that 'it makes a great deal of difference from which side one approaches knowledge-science, through which gate one enters.'[80]

Goethe's frequent discussions of the language of science are interesting and highly topical reading today. Here follows one

William Blake (1795): Newton.

example of many of the linguistic pitfalls about which Goethe wished to warn us:

> But how difficult is it not, to avoid putting the term in the place of the object, to always have the content alive before one, and not to kill it with the word! On this question we have in recent times become involved in an even greater danger, in that we have borrowed expressions and terminologies from all areas we know of, and know something about, to express our understandings of less complicated nature. Astronomy, cosmology, geology, natural history, indeed, religion and mysticism are made use of, and how often is the general whole not covered and clouded over by some particular thing, or the elementary by some derived thing, instead of which, it ought to be illuminated and brought closer as a result! We know quite well that need which has made it possible for such language to arise and spread, we know too that it in a certain sense makes

> itself indispensable, but only a moderate, unpretentious usage of it, with conviction and consciousness, can bring advantage.[81]

Goethe also sees a risk when the scientist transforms his observations into concepts and words, and then associates with these as though they were objects. Here, philosophy can help:

> One cannot demand of the physicist that he be a philosopher. But one can expect of him that he has so much philosophical training that he can fundamentally divorce himself from the world in order to reunite himself with it in a higher sense. He ought to develop a method which agrees with the observation. He ought to beware of transforming the observation into concepts, the concepts into words and to associate and proceed with these words as though they were objects. He ought to know about the endeavours of philosophy in order to be able to lead the phenomena onward into the philosophical region. ... The worst thing that could happen to physics, as to so many other sciences, would be to regard the derivation as being the original, and to try to explain the original using the derivation. From this would arise an unending confusion, verbose drivel and a perpetual endeavouring to seek and find excuses everywhere, when the truth steps forward wanting to take command.[82]

Goethe and the physicists

In Goethe's day there was no subject called 'physics.' Instead, scholars spoke of 'natural philosophy.' Goethe's presentation acquired a distinct mark of natural philosophy as a consequence of his contacts with Schiller and philosophers such as Fichte, Schelling and Hegel.

Sällström sketches out the main aspects of Newton's theory, and agrees that 'in itself, taken as the whole, it is valid, not to say highly attractive. But it is based on certain axiomatic premises, that are more or less implicitly taken for granted.'[83]

Trainee teacher carrying out research at the water steps, part of the biological water-purification plant at the Rudolf Steiner Teacher-Training College in Järna. (Sculptor: John Wilkes. Photo: Jan Arve Andersen.)

Sällström gives examples of such assumptions and cites Newton's atomistic way of thinking as an example. It becomes reasonable in that it reflects our way of reasoning logically in terms of structures, and that it is accepted is due to the fact that it has shown itself to be fruitful beyond all expectation. If one is educated in such a spirit, it will be obvious that light must be describable as being composed of certain simple basic elements. Sällström points out that Goethe asserts a dynamic outlook as opposed to an atomistic one, and consistently raises objections to the axioms that Newton adopted, on the following points:

- Against atomism, he wishes to place a living, dynamic outlook with phenomena that are transformed and merge with each other.
- Against the atomistic concept 'ray of light' he places the phenomenological concept 'picture.'
- Instead of the division into simple and complicated phenomena, he

speaks of a hierarchy of phenomena, with the archetypal phenomenon as the highest, encompassing all the others.

- Instead of reducing the colour scale to terms of already known and established research areas, he wishes to lay the foundation of a special kind of chromatics.

- Instead of understanding sight as a chain of cause-and-effect, he describes it as a phenomenon of resonance, a meeting and a concordance between an outer and an inner reality.

- Instead of taking colour for granted, and researching man's ability to see colour, he takes man's ability to see colour for granted, and researches, with its help, the phenomenon, colour.

- Instead of, by use of mathematical calculations, demonstrating the connection between the various related phenomena, he makes use of an inner imagination, a pictorial form of thinking, which permits development.[84]

As I understand it, it is this kind of dynamic, boundary-crossing outlook which is trained through the special method they use for painting with colours in the Waldorf system of education. If one is to understand this style of anthroposophical painting, with colours that flow into each other, one must be prepared to familiarize oneself with epistemological points of departure different from those we are used to and in which we have been schooled (see Plates 3, 4, 6, 8, 9).

In the shadow of the Second World War several prominent atomic physicists proposed a closer study of Goethe's view of science and, in particular, his theory of colour, as being one possible way of dealing with the unhealthy aspects of our high-technological civilization.

In an article on 'Goethe and the Physicists' in 1969, Stanley L. Jaki, professor in the history of physics and philosophy, wrote that anyone with any knowledge of both physics and literature might easily experience a sensation of faintness and dizziness on reading what Goethe, four years before his death, said to his friend and secretary, Eckermann:

> I imagine nothing whatever on my achievements as a poet ... But I was the only person who knew the truth in the

> difficult art of the science of colour. I would, however, have that to my credit, and this makes me feel superior to many.

It would probably be true to say that the majority of the readers of the Journal would find such a statement difficult to take seriously. But the article also describes how leading physicists such as W. Heisenberg, Max Born, Walter Heitler and Carl Friedrich von Weizsäcker have all familiarized themselves with Goethe's thinking, and have paid careful attention to it in lectures and articles.

According to Heisenberg, the foremost cultural value lay in what he understood to be Goethe's primary purpose with his study of colour, namely: to defend the sensual world of perception and the subjective values of quality against the assault from the mathematical abstraction of physical research.[85]

Jaki emphasizes that Goethe's primary aim might be said to be to defend the subjective against the so-called objective world of facts. It was also this that the Swiss physicist Walter Heitler had in mind when he said that the most profound cause of Goethe's life-long struggle against Newton's optics had to do with the poet's correct understanding that the dividing line between subjective and objective is often arbitrary and difficult to draw.

Max Born, too, writes that we ought to renew our contact with Goethe and with those who continue to cultivate and develop his ideas, and in particular to learn from them not to forget the importance of the whole, when faced with our fascination with details. He counselled his colleagues to systematically describe human colour perception from a physical as well as from a psychological point of departure, where the emotional symbolic evaluations of colours are also embraced. Born advised them to not stop at the limitations of the quantitative methods, but to go on further and develop a receptivity to those aspects of reality that science cannot reach. He warned about the wild progress of specialization and believed that the whole scientific enterprise had thereby become something unreasonable, with the consequence that the finest results of science will come to lead humanity to the brink of self-extinction.

The physicist Carl Friedrich von Weizsäcker also pointed to the cultural significance of Goethe's emphasizing the necessity of holistic thinking in his theory of colour. There are common aspects, and a dialogue between modern physics and Goethe is therefore possible, in Weizsäcker's opinion. In particular, serious reflection on the conceptual frame of modern physics could reveal an opportunity to put holistic thinking back into the foreground, and to develop a language free from the Cartesian gap between corporeal and spiritual, which has been a source of so much evil in the cultural field. When one studies phenomena by the analytical method, they are divided up, atomized, in order to gradually arrive at something general. A more immediately grasped totality is a form, a *Gestalt,* a category, which is closely related to Goethe's archetypal phenomenon and comprises the very backbone of Goethe's scientific philosophy and method. Since the threat is a result of man's impaired ability to understand totality/wholeness and connections, it is now high time to penetrate thoroughly into the deepest layers of Goethe's scientific thinking.[86]

What these physicists find to be the central issue with Goethe and worth once again bringing forth into the light, correlates strongly with the views Rudolf Steiner attached importance to in his research during the 1880's and 1890's, and which he later expanded both in practice and in theory. However, as far as I have been able to discover, Steiner's research on the subject is seldom referred to.

After summarizing the thoughts of some of the foremost atomic physicists, Jaki makes his personal observations, which rhyme ill with the opinions he quotes, but which are important as they perhaps agree better with a more general conception among scientists of Goethe's research. Jaki claims that Goethe's abhorrence — as he puts it — of exact science, and unfortunate interest in alchemy, led to increasing frustration which he was eventually able to give vent to through his fierce attacks on Newton, and which he expressed in literature in polemical form. In this polemical section, which 'typically enough,' according to Jaki, is often omitted in modern editions of the *Theory of Colour,* Goethe does not mince his words. Jaki says that one cannot gain any true feeling for 'the psychological abyss which exists in Goethe's self-deception' without reading this section. Goethe himself must have attached great importance to it since he was unwilling to agree to this part being left out when a new edition, twenty years after the first, was planned during his own lifetime.

It is often described how Goethe, as Minister, on one occasion accompanied the Duke Karl-August of Sachsen-Weimar in his resistance against the French in a battle, and how in the heat of battle he had with him an encyclopedia of physics in four volumes, and not even there could he leave off his efforts to try to get at the enigma of colour. This is usually quoted, by Jaki also, as an example of how divorced from reality he was. Was this perhaps less an expression of his being more at home in the 'sentimental aestheticism' of the Weimar milieu, which Jaki implies, than that he felt a restless, urge, in the very shadow of war, to get closer to an understanding in the way that Heisenberg, Heitler, Born and Weizsäcker were, in the shadow of a later war?

According to Jaki, what Goethe was especially proud of, was that he had succeeded in demonstrating that physics without mathematics was possible, and Goethe believed that the reason he met with such strong opposition was that no one any longer had the slightest idea that physics could exist without mathematics.

Jaki believes it was the success that Goethe experienced in other scientific fields that made him persist so stubbornly and so forcefully in his criticism of Newton, and that much of this criticism had the effect of making the scientific community lose faith in him, and also in those parts of his theory of colour which were valuable. There is probably much to be said for this point of view. But it might also be so, as Steiner claims, that Goethe understood other things, and on a deeper level, than many of his interpreters. The ultimate truth in this debate is hard to prove, and probably only the future will show.

But it turned out that the physicists, according to Jaki, did not need Goethe's faith in Nature and humanity in order to continue their own search for the laws of Nature. Evidence for this is found in Weizsäcker, Heitler, Born and Heisenberg, who all concur that Goethe's pottering about with physics is not physics. And as for their understanding of Goethe's cultural significance in the atomic age, 'one could only wish they had in mind the real Goethe, and not an abstraction of him,' Jaki writes. So the article results, as far as I understand, in expressing the disinclination to see any connection between research in a traditional, material, scientific sense, and more qualitative, spiritual aspects of Nature and culture — a connection which was the very heart of what the artist and scientist Goethe endeavoured to establish, according to Steiner's interpretation.

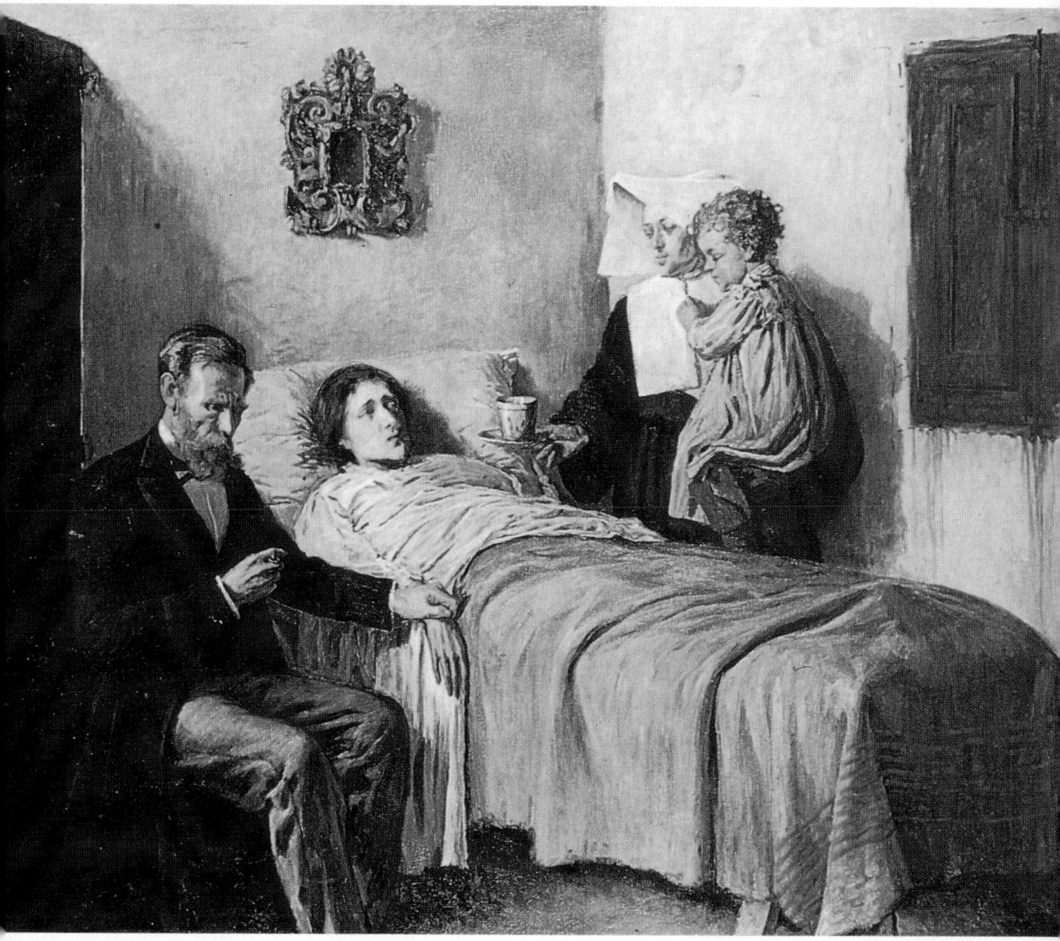

Plate 1. Science and Human Compassion, *Picasso (1897), painted by him at the age of sixteen.*

Plate 2. A Lady in Moscow, *Kandinsky (1912). The black patch stands for materialism, in theosophical terms.*

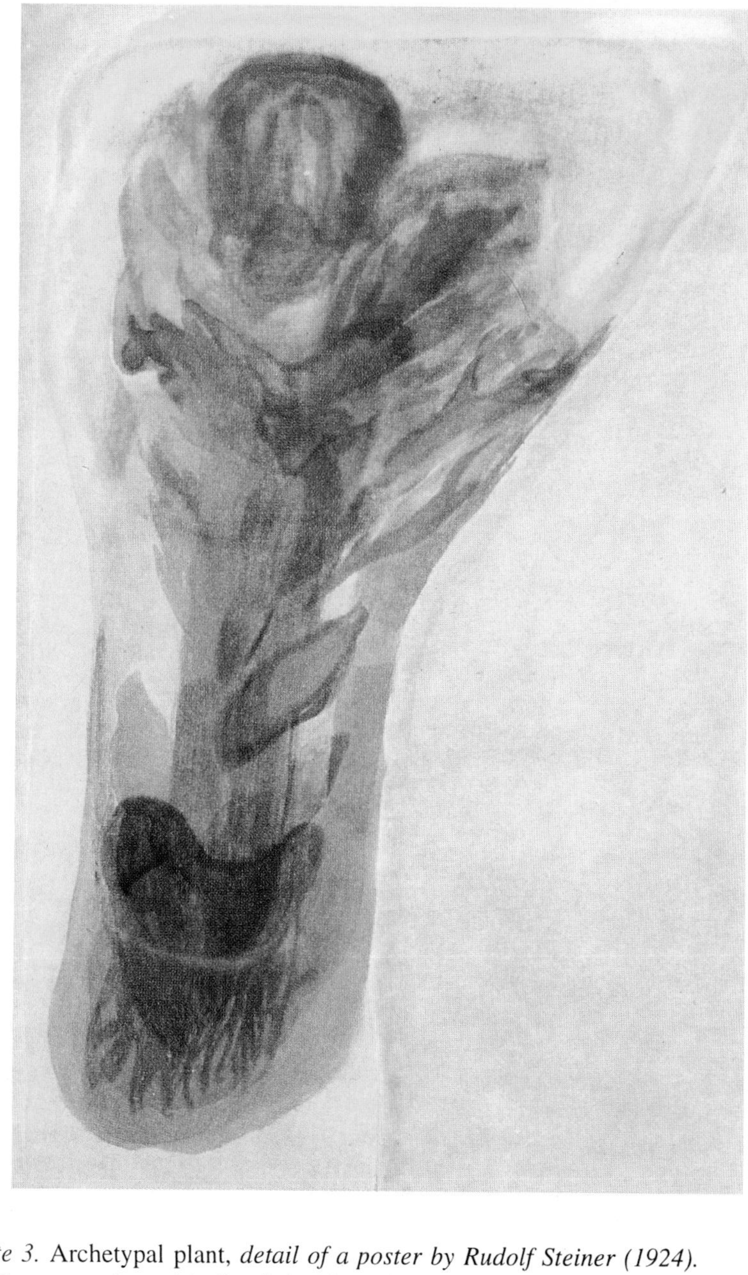

Plate 3. Archetypal plant, *detail of a poster by Rudolf Steiner (1924).*

'In connection with Goethe's idea of the metamorphosis of plants, Steiner paints this picture of the "primordial plant." From his experience of the intrinsic value of colour as a free-flowing quality, he prefers the technique of watercolours with its rich potential.' (From Goethes färglära, *1976.)*

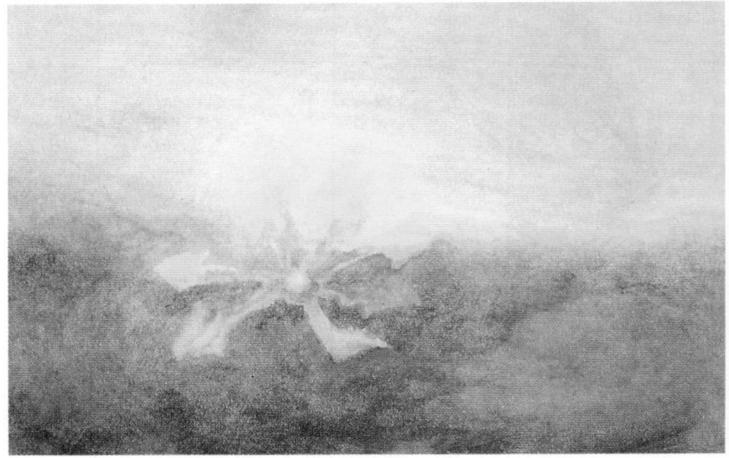

Plates 4a–d. Younger children from Class 5 'getting into' the colours — no sharp contours yet. (From Carlgren & Klingborg, 1977.)

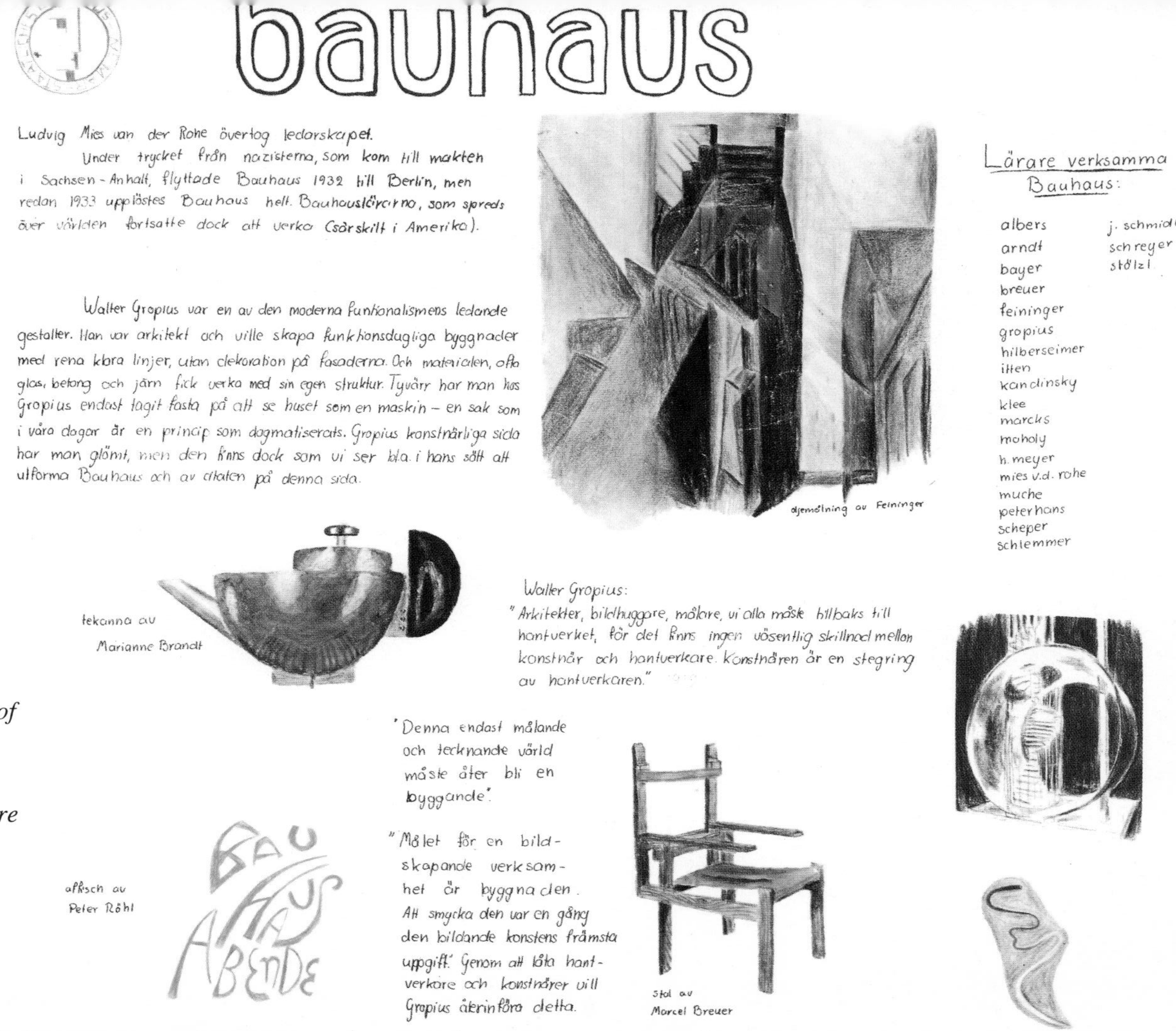

bauhaus

Ludvig Mies van der Rohe övertog ledarskapet.
Under trycket från nazisterna, som kom till makten i Sachsen-Anhalt, flyttade Bauhaus 1932 till Berlin, men redan 1933 upplöstes Bauhaus helt. Bauhauslärarna, som spreds över världen fortsatte dock att verka (särskilt i Amerika).

Walter Gropius var en av den moderna funktionalismens ledande gestalter. Han var arkitekt och ville skapa funktionsdugliga byggnader med rena klara linjer, utan dekoration på fasaderna. Och materialen, ofta glas, betong och järn fick verka med sin egen struktur. Tyvärr har man hos Gropius endast tagit fasta på att se huset som en maskin – en sak som i våra dagar är en princip som dogmatiserats. Gropius konstnärliga sida har man glömt, men den finns dock som vi ser bl.a. i hans sätt att utforma Bauhaus och av citaten på denna sida.

oljemålning av Feininger

Lärare verksamma Bauhaus:

albers
arndt
bayer
breuer
feininger
gropius
hilberseimer
itten
kandinsky
klee
marcks
moholy
h. meyer
mies v.d. rohe
muche
peterhans
scheper
schlemmer
j. schmidt
schreyer
stölzl

tekanna av Marianne Brandt

Walter Gropius:
"Arkitekter, bildhuggare, målare, vi alla måste tillbaks till hantverket, för det finns ingen väsentlig skillnad mellan konstnär och hantverkare. Konstnären är en stegring av hantverkaren."

"Denna endast målande och tecknande värld måste åter bli en byggande".

"Målet för en bildskapande verksamhet är byggnaden. Att smycka den var en gång den bildande konstens främsta uppgift." Genom att låta hantverkare och konstnärer vill Gropius återinföra detta.

affisch av Peter Röhl

stol av Marcel Breuer

Plate 5. Older pupil's workbook on the history of architecture (Class 12). Text and illustration comprise a whole, with sharp contours and a more precise presentation. (From På Väg, *No.4, 1971.)*

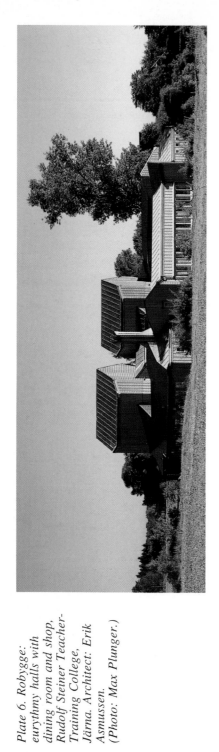

Plate 6. Robygge: eurythmy halls with dining room and shop, Rudolf Steiner Teacher-Training College, Järna. Architect: Erik Asmussen. (Photo: Max Plunger.)

Plate 7. The view from the Rudolf Steiner Teacher-Training College, Järna. (Photo: Max Plunger.)

Plate 8. Digestive mood. *(From Carlgren & Klingborg, 1977.)*

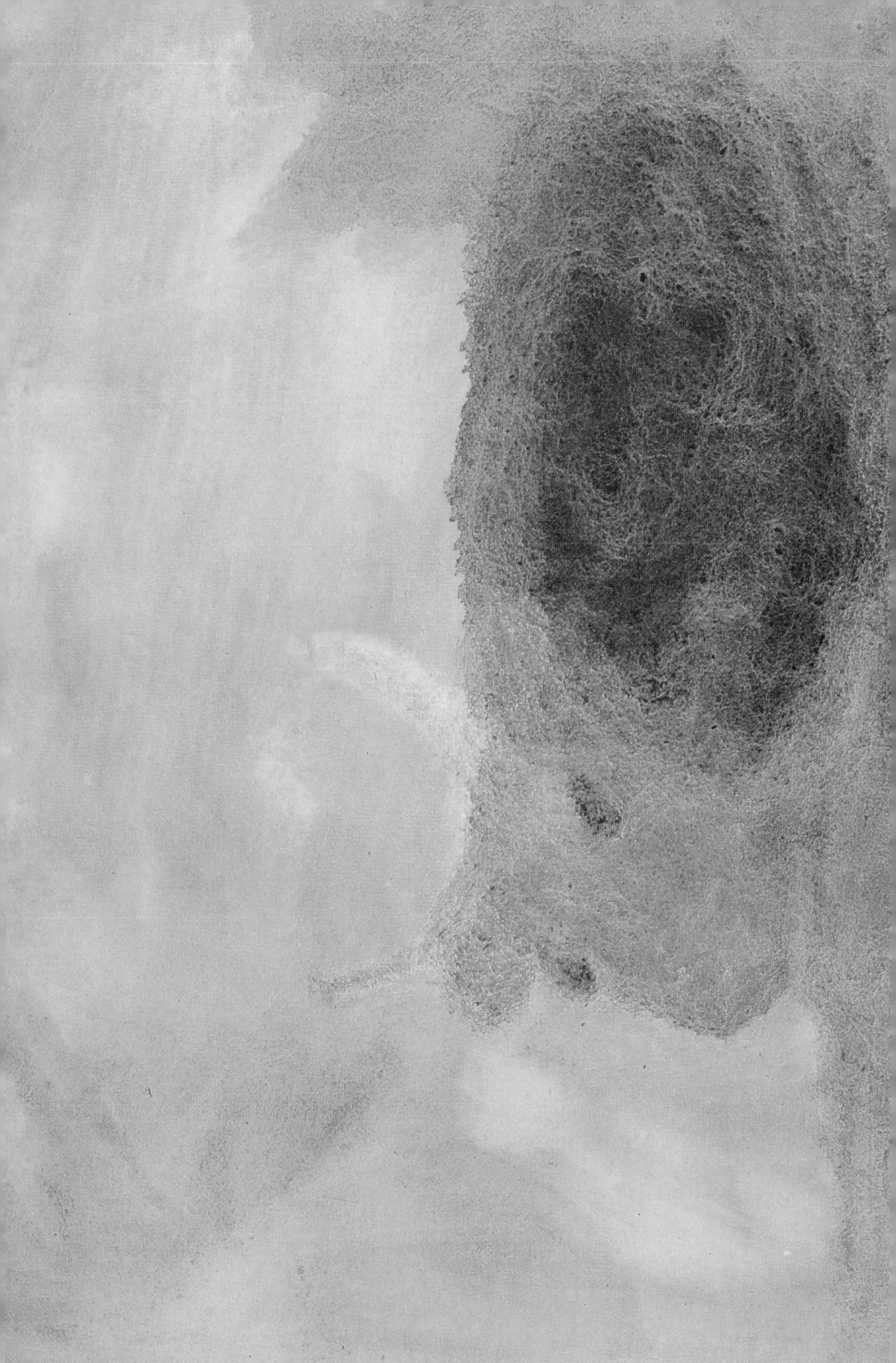

Plate 9. Eurythmy. 'Beauty is a manifestation of secret laws of nature which, without art, would have remained hidden from us.' (Goethe) (Photo: Peter de Voto, Balder, July 1980.)

Two cultures

With the atom bomb, everything was changed, except people's way of thinking, Einstein is reported to have said. It seems to have been precisely Goethe's anxiety about the way his contemporaries thought that drove him into new paths of research into Nature, at the same time as it was largely these different methods and their new perspectives that made Goethe's contemporaries incapable of understanding what he meant.

What is it in Goethe that people find so challenging? Can it have something to do with that marriage of art and science (and religion, too) which distinguishes him and makes his work so complete, according to Steiner? Here, foundations are challenged in an earthshaking way which is felt as a threat — but which could perhaps bear fruit? Maybe there are parallels here with August Strindberg's (1849-1912) comprehensive and individualistic research on Nature, which in like manner is usually by-passed with a remarkable silence, considering Strindberg's unchallenged position in other respects.[87] Goethe was of central importance to Strindberg, and it is known that he studied Goethe's scientific works.

In the preface to *Intuition* from the same period, the Lund philosopher Hans Larsson writes that his book deals with three areas — science, poetry and, indirectly, pedagogy:

> In all these three areas, I wish to make plain the need for intuitive synthesis, but this, my demand, is a demand for stricter logic, not for more lenient logic, an opposition to certain crudely formulated and basically illogical rules.

In this book, and in the following work, *The Logic of Poesy,* he turns on his contemporaries' exaggerated fear of mysticism and claims that far too little room is left for sources of inner experience and intuitive thinking in contexts of knowledge, and that they instead strive far too much to do everything as methodically as possible.[88] He believes that the highest form of theoretical thinking is really of an intuitive nature, and not at all without logical association. Science turns into art the more it perfects itself. Feeling enters into the lowest form of development, but also into the highest. When thought is fully developed and has full command of its material, the connection with feeling is rejoined. It is then not feeling in itself which guides us, but a certain kind of intelligence which distinguishes itself by being united with feeling.[89]

In our intellectually overtaxed age, it is especially important to draw attention to this, writes Hans Larsson at the turn of the century, and it becomes all the more important to make high demands

> on unity in the pursuit of science, on synthesis in poesy, science and pedagogy. Our soul is easily thrown into disorder through the multifariousness which engages it, and our intellectual life becomes peripheral, because our knowledge falls too much apart into academic scholarship to become wisdom thereof, and thus it enters into a relationship with neither our sentient life nor our volitional life; our intellectual life does not simultaneously become fully personal life.[90]

And it is the task of pedagogy to lay the foundation for such knowledge — not by means of timetables and skeletons, but by means of art, by means of the language of poetry which gives both concentration and synthesis as well as vigour and richness.

Among present-day critics of this philosophy, Elisabet Hermodsson comments how such an analytical framework — formulated with science as its model — excludes more holistic views which cut across systems. Above all she criticizes the scientific notion of 'value-free,' and turns against the 'respect for science which occasionally can take the form of blind faith ... To examine critically — instead of eternally chanting — the principles of science does not necessarily mean a vote of no confidence in science at all, but it means, rather, an attempt to attack the cold borderlines between the two cultures.'[91]

And with the language of the poet, she directs criticism at the researchers' scientific language, which:

> exchanged the holy names of Nature's events for technical terms ... And from a centre where mind and matter should

> have been one, your arsenal of concepts set about with splintering force ... You do not hear that the names you press forth out of matter are your distortions of the enigma of life. You do not hear, because the names you press forth out of matter are your distortions of the enigma of life. You do not hear because you have stopped listening ... Only those names which restore to ... matter ... the trees, the seas, the animals, their holiness, only those names give man kinship with Nature, make man aware of his responsibility for his coexistence in creation.[92]

Steiner is of the view that Goethe really begins where physics stops. The physicists have other frames of reference and *quite simply do not know the fundamental concepts* that pertain to Goethe's theory of colour, and therefore they should be incapable of judging this theory. According to Steiner, it is indicative of a superficial understanding of the matter when one continually speaks of the relationship between Goethe and Newton and modern physics, without realizing that it is a question of two different ways of looking at the world.[93] (Note that Steiner wrote this at the turn of the century, approximately forty years and two World Wars prior to the wakening interest of Heisenberg and other physicists in Goethe's ideas.)

It is in such a framework that the Waldorf system of education should be judged. Steiner's purpose is here nothing less than to make room to develop new ways of looking at and thinking of the world.

Steiner himself spoke of the modern ideal and view of Nature being to turn the world into an arithmetical example. He felt that:

> someone, whose need for causality is satisfied when he succeeds in leading natural phenomena back to the mechanism of atoms, lacks the organs necessary to understand Goethe.[94]

The special thing about Goethe was, according to Steiner, his ability to marry artistically intuitive pictorial seeing with soberly sentient observation. And it could be that no one will understand what Goethe wanted to achieve with his comprehensive studies of nature until the year 2000, as Hermann Grimm prophesied.

Sällström believes — as does Steiner — that the reason Goethe and Newton did not arrive at the same conclusions was due to the fact that they had different points of departure, different prior knowledge, different background experience and, besides this, different objectives in their studies. Goethe did not claim that Newton, based on *his* points of departure, was wrong. But, whereas Newton was a true scientist who, as a matter of course, built further on the current tradition within optics where mathematics was central, Goethe, in his natural research, also admitted his artistic nature and his profound erudition in the Humanities.

Whereas Goethe took an interest in both the phenomenon and its effect on man — the subject-object relationship — Newton took only an interest in what could be objectively measured and quantified. In the scientific method which Newton employs, object and subject are differentiated; Goethe, on the other hand, shows an interest in both the eye and the light.

Sällström points out that it is often an undeniably efficient method to do as the scientists do and study the parts, but that certain phenomena quite simply cease to exist, or slip out of our hands, as soon as we try to study them outside the context in which they appear.

> Somewhere one might imagine that this is a general problem in all research and that Goethe did the right thing — taking the theory of colour as a visible example — in reminding us that the initial stage, where one proceeds from the whole to the particular, calls for methodical awareness.

In Goethe's opinion, Newton only took an interest in the composition of the light/object and not in the importance of the human observer and the observer's power of judgment and interpretation. The phenomenon should, therefore, not be determined causally, but interpreted by man. Goethe's method was thus not an exact scientific method, nor was it philosophical. It was of a practical nature instead. Natural research and poetry-writing coincided here.[95]

It would seem that several of the disparities which have come to light here share common features with the undefined gaps to which we pay more and more attention — for example, the gap between the two so-called cultures, the Humanities on the one hand and Science and

Technology on the other; between theoreticians and practitioners; between highly educated and poorly educated; as also to the differences between male and female. Something fruitful would result from these disparities if the differences of opinion did not paralyse further action, which often appears to be the case today, but on the contrary, inspired something new. Research in this area would seem to be a pressing matter. Certain developments indicate that greater openness has arisen during the 1980's both in the scientific community and in the wider public debate. But at the same time this creates an even greater unease in certain quarters, which constitutes a serious and important part of the problem. In recent years we have been able to observe a newly-awakened interest in alternative ways of looking at science and at the relationship between art and science, which might help to cross boundaries, even if there is so far mainly a tendency to give the artistic element the character of entertainment, rather than utilizing it to get at the problems involved in research in a broader sense.

In 1987, the biggest daily newspaper in Sweden ran a long series of articles entitled 'Farewell to Newton' which the Professor of Theoretical Physics, Karl-Erik Eriksson, opened with three long articles arguing why it is high time to abandon the mechanistic patterns of thought deriving from Newton and which have had such a decisive significance, not only for science, but also for all thinking and all planning.[96] Eriksson, extrapolating from what is now happening in physics research, believes that there are now signs that the gap between C.P. Snow's two cultures — Science and the Humanities — is in the process of narrowing. Others take the view that recent developments indicate, on the contrary, a widening gap.

Steiner's dominant idea is that education and science must develop the external and narrowly limited empirical method in order to discover a way of embracing *at the same time* an internal, spiritual, artistic and moral dimension which could be the true nerve of the Humanities/spiritual science *(Geisteswissenschaft).*[97] Was it this that the scientists Darwin and Granit were searching for in their own lives?

The great emphasis placed on art and artistic exercises in the Waldorf system of education (to which we shall return in Chapter 8), is not aimed at training up artists. It is for developing the creative, artistic ability which *every* person has within — what Schiller called the uniquely human ability, and of which every machine is devoid. It is also a question of developing and training each person's intuitive ability to think as well as their sense of judgment. Placing such a weight on experiencing the interplay of colours, as also in eurythmy — where visible expression is given to the interplay between the rhythms of the body and thoughts, sensibilities and words — is related to the conviction that people, through these exercises, preserve and develop a sense of the connection between inner and outer reality, between art and knowledge. All these things are conditions which our educational institutions have systematically avoided developing, and this applies to higher education in particular.

Roger Sperry, arguing from his research on the different ways in which the two halves of the brain function, holds it likely that systems of education by mainly training primarily logical functions over a long period, have contributed to the fact that other functions which have to do with analysis of the whole, with artistry, creativity, intuition and sensitivity, have become underdeveloped.[98] Is it possible to observe the physiological consequences when a Goethean, more pictorial and synthetic form of thinking has receded into the background in favour of a Newtonian, logical-grammatical language-like form of thinking? The thought is undeniably fascinating. Would it perhaps be beneficial to train our thinking so that we could encompass a greater concurrence and integration between different ways of functioning? Is it perhaps in the border area itself between art and science that the exciting innovations which our era needs are to be found?

True reality can only be approached by allowing the outer objective aspect to flow together with the inner subjective aspect in man. But both are equally necessary to the whole. A one-sided attention to the outer, the objective, the observing of Nature, leads to materialism and the science of our day. And a one-sided attention to the inner, the subjective, leads to emotionalism, 'mysticism,' sectarianism, detachment from the world. It is first in the interplay that the totality — life — can be captured. And it is perhaps here that *'das geistige Band'* ('the spiritual band' or 'bond') can bridge the gap, as expressed by both Goethe in his poems and the artist and 'scientist' Elisabet Hermodsson who writes poetry in Sweden today:

> The idealists say: there is a spiritual reality independent of matter.
>
> The materialists say: there is only matter, and the spirit is a product of matter.
>
> The dialectician says: there is an interaction between spirit and matter.
>
> I am a dialectician and I say: 'There is an independent untouched matter and there is an independent untouched spirit, but in the touching of one another, they become Man and dependent on each other.'[99]

In the next chapter we shall follow Steiner as he leaves the academic world of research in Weimar and takes himself off to artists' and workers' circles in Berlin, and see how his ideas developed further there, gaining expression twenty years later in a well thought-out system of education.

CHAPTER 5
On the Spiritual, Art and Science

From Weimar to Berlin

After fourteen years of research on Goethe's scientific works, Steiner became more and more exercised by the problem of how to communicate his insights on Goethe's natural philosophy in such a way that the rest of the world could absorb his ideas instead of being 'struck dumb' by them. He did not wish to be struck dumb himself either, 'but [wished] to say as much as was possible to say.'[1]

Steiner found contemporary cultural development and the disinclination of science to see the intimate interplay between outer and inner phenomena — between the objective and the subjective — to be deeply harmful, and felt a 'discomfort of knowledge,' as he puts it in his autobiography.[2]

After a time he left Weimar, moving in 1897 to Berlin. Already during the last year in Weimar, he says he felt a profound change taking place within himself. This came to be even more clearly expressed in the new city. It was a stark contrast for him to leave the academic ambiance of Weimar and begin a new life moving mainly in Berlin circles of young artists and writers, at the same time as teaching workers.[3] This was to become a difficult period of his life. He himself calls it 'the Trip to Hell.' According to several biographers, he suffered periods of severe distress and is even said to have struggled against becoming alcoholic. One of his biographers — Fred Poeppig — pointed out that had he continued his path of research and become Professor of Philosophy in Jena, he would never have enjoyed the freedom for which he felt such a strong need after the Weimar period.[4]

He now embarked on an extensive literary production and became the publisher of the magazine *Magazin für Literatur.* Besides this, he took an active part in the *Dramatische Gesellschaft* (Drama Company) and *Freie literarische Gesellschaft* (Free Literary Company) and increasingly applied himself to giving lectures as well. He went outside Berlin, speaking often to artists' circles in Munich and as time went on to an increasing number of different groups in Germany as well as other European countries. From 1907 and up to the outbreak of the First World War, he conducted several extensive lecture tours in Scandinavia and in Britain.

At an early stage he stood up for workers' issues, and he did so especially at the end of the First World War when it was a matter of finding solutions to the profound problems then facing Germany. His attitude on these issues came to form the basis of later ideas in the field of education (see the following chapter on 'The Social Issue').

For five years — between 1899 and 1904 — he was employed as a teacher at the Berlin Workers' Educational Institute which had been founded by the socialist, Wilhelm Liebknecht. Here he came into close contact with workers, and now gained a type of audience different from those he had been used to in academic Weimar.

Steiner never aligned himself with any political factions. For him, the Institute consisted of working men and women and the fact that most of these were social democrats was not any of his business, he writes.[5] Certain commentators suggest that it was his independent stand and unwillingness to accept orthodoxy which resulted in his eventually being forced to resign as teacher from the Institute.

According to two students, who write vividly on Steiner as teacher at this Institute, he often spoke of Karl Marx's work with a great sense of gratitude. It concerned him, though, that an excessive focus on external economic conditions could become the breeding ground for a type of materialistic capitalism in which inner, invisible qualities of life — the spiritual — would come to be overlooked.

According to these students, his teaching was very much appreciated. He seemed to follow the inspiration of the moment and his presentation was therefore never stereotyped. He always lectured without notes and let himself be guided by the composition of the audience. In spite of the fact that his classes were held after the end of the working day, he succeeded in captivating his audience so much that lively questions and discussion arose afterwards, which often led to the classes not ending before midnight. His method of teaching was something the Institute was not used to. It was not a question of listening passively to dry facts:

Rudolf Steiner as a teacher at the Workers' Educational Institute in Berlin, 1901.

> It was as if a life-giving stream of warmth flowed through all the subjects taught, which the students previously had often experienced as dry and soporific.

He taught mainly history and literature. He also did speech training with the students, where they trained themselves in plays representing differing types of character, for example various party leaders.[6]

The workers' demand for Steiner's services as lecturer grew greater and greater. He was often requested to come and speak to associations of all sizes outside the Workers' Institute, at companies such as Bosch, Daimler and the cigarette factory Waldorf-Astoria. In 1900, on the quincentenary of Johann Gutenberg, the inventor of printing, Steiner was asked to deliver the celebration speech before seven thousand people, mostly printers and typesetters.

The things he now wrote and talked about revolved around the relationship between the science of the day and the spiritual-cultural life. He also wrote generally on issues concerning the universities and education. His writings from this period are to be found collected in *Literarisches Frühwerk* (Early Literary Works), which were published in book form.[7]

For Steiner, spiritual life at the turn of the century was characterized by a kind of dispiritedness. People were satisfied with weighing, measuring and comparing objects and phenomena, examining them with the apparatus at hand, but without asking themselves questions touching on the higher, spiritual dimension of life, and the meaning, the *raison d'être,* of things.[8] He thought it should be possible through art to recapture the link between nature and spirit which had become increasingly lost since the Renaissance, and believed it was this kind of reunion that Goethe's life and work was directed towards. For this reason Goethe came to be the point of departure for the spiritual science, *Geisteswissenschaft,* for which Steiner now began to lay the foundation.

It was now, too, that Steiner came into contact with the Theosophical movement. In 1900 he was asked for the first time to come to a meeting and talk about Nietzsche. Steiner's book *Nietzsche — ein Kämpfer gegen seine Zeit,* had come out a few years earlier, in 1895, and in 1900, on the occasion of Nietzsche's death, he gave several lectures and speeches on him in Berlin. After this first lecture he was also asked to come and speak about his research on Goethe.

In this circle he felt that he could take up esoteric questions and be understood, which was of great importance to him, since he was otherwise used to almost never meeting comprehension of such matters. In 1902 he became Secretary General of the German Section of the Theosophical Society himself — a post which he held until 1912. The leadership involved a good deal of friction, however, and parallel to his theosophical interest he now developed his own anthroposophy.

At a theosophical conference in London in 1902 he met Marie von Sivers, who later became his wife.[9] It was together with her that he entered into the leadership of the Theosophical Society. These two together came to foster the artistic interests within the Society, which were missing at that time. Art stood outside the spiritual activity which the Theosophists pursued. Steiner in some ways found this understandable, but he also found it necessary to effect change if the spiritual frame of mind fostered in the society was to develop further.

Marie Steiner had grown up in Russia and had been educated in the field of drama, her special interest being speech formation and dramatic presentation. Her activities in these fields later came to comprise the starting-point for the artistic aspects which gradually came to be developed and to occupy a central position in the anthroposophic movement, in particular within the educational activities which came into being on this basis.

Steiner held the opinion that the spoken/written word in modern time had become the slave of intellectual knowledge, and thereby also of the social life which had turned away from the spiritual. Language had stepped completely out of the sphere from which it originated, the spiritual sphere, and it had been completely ripped out of the area of art. It was therefore necessary to create increased insight into the spiritual if the enthusiasm necessary to return the spoken/written word to its proper sphere was to be resuscitated:

> A revival of the imagination through man's intellect has a deadening effect on art. The direct opposite is seen when the spiritual content, truly perceived, lights up the imagination. Then all the pictorial forces are resurrected,

> which have always produced art in earlier periods of the history of mankind.[10]

With his entrance into the Theosophical Society, several of Steiner's former research comrades broke off their friendship with him. What his relationship with the artists became after he took up this interest is apparently difficult to analyse. His statement that the Theosophists, when he entered the Society, did not show any interest in coupling art together with the spiritual activity they sought fails to harmonize with research showing to what a high degree artists and architects took an interest in theosophy, not to mention other kinds of spiritual questions. What significance did Steiner's leadership have in this case? Did he contribute to their interest being directed towards this quarter?

The Swedish art historian Åke Fant has in several books, from 1977 onwards, looked at Steiner's influence within the development of architecture. In his dissertation 'Architecture of the Future 1913-1923' he discusses the architects who took up a leading position in Germany from the time of the First World War onwards. He shows how it was not only the chaos of war that led architects to reject the old and search for innovatory models for the buildings of the future. The strong interest in spiritual issues, which at that period came to be expressed in the architectural debate also, had its roots to a great extent in the debate taking place in Europe on Nature and Spirit, a debate which was difficult to formulate. The architects were, like many artists at that time, concerned about the way science was developing. They called for a greater broadmindedness towards spiritual phenomena in life, and a similar attitude in the case of the physical formation of the environment.[11]

These were manifestly ideas which were current in the period, and many people also knew about the revolutionary findings in the then completely 'new physics.' To what degree the architects, as well as the artists, really can have been influenced by Steiner's Goethe research and his many books, articles and lectures is an area of research which attracts increasing interest. One would imagine that Steiner's two hundred or so lectures given in Berlin's Architektenhaus ought to have left some traces in the continued debate. Åke Fant mentions only a few lectures in his book.

Of particular relevance here is the artist Wassily Kandinsky and his book *The Art of Spiritual Harmony,* which he wrote first in his native Russian in 1910. It was then published in German in 1912, and translated into English in 1914. Recent research now reveals increasingly what a significant influence Steiner's lectures and writings had on Kandinsky's thought. The Finnish art historian Sixten Ringbom takes this up in his dissertation *The Sounding Cosmos* (1970) and in several later articles in the more important international exhibition catalogues.[12]

From Ringbom's research it can be surmised what a great gathering of listeners Steiner had in artists' and architects' circles of his day. It appears that Kandinsky read about both theosophy and anthroposophy and attended lectures by Steiner in the Berliner Architektenhaus at least as early as 1908. Ringbom has found notebooks showing that Kandinsky put a great deal of effort into studying Steiner's writings, just at the period when his own art suddenly changes and finds its character. As an example may be mentioned Kandinsky's ten-page summary of what he found to be the most important aspects in Steiner's book *Theosophy,* which appeared in 1904. Later the extremely influential artist, Joseph Beuys, among others, was likewise to be deeply impressed with Steiner's ideas (see Chapter 7).

Kandinsky writes about the Theosophical Movement as being one of the great spiritual movements in our time. 'This association consists of groups of people trying to approach the spiritual problems on the path of *inner* knowledge. The method is the direct opposite of positivism. Originally it was a loan from a dim past; now the theory is presented again in relatively precise form' writes Kandinsky who gives in connection with this statement the following reference in a footnote: 'See for example Dr Steiner's *Theosophie* and his article on the path to insight in *Lucifer-Gnosis.*'[13]

It is interesting to note here the ex-jurist Kandinsky's comment on Steiner's book *Theosophy* that it treats its subject 'in relatively precise form.' I have to say that I find this book extremely difficult to read, and decidedly more difficult than Kandinsky's own exposition. However, we must bear in mind that Steiner was aiming for something different from the norm in his writing, as he explains in the preface to the third edition of *Theosophy:*

> This book cannot be read in the same way one usually reads

> books in our time. In certain respects the reader must work to assimilate each page, indeed, many a clause. This is something I have deliberately striven after, as only in this way can the book become to the reader what it ought to be. The person who merely reads through it, has not read it at all. Its truths must be *experienced.* Only in this way does spiritual science have any value.[14]

It is on reading Kandinsky's text again after having spent time on texts about the role of art written by Steiner, that I discovered how closely their terminology and ways of thinking seem to agree. Kandinsky stands out for me as the more easily assimilated of the two. My impression is that Kandinsky's text, if it is 'chewed over' properly, as the Swedish art critic Ulf Linde suggests, can make it easier for a person of our time to understand Steiner's writings in the same area.

Kandinsky concentrates in particular on how artists should see their role in the development of society and how they should lead it on to new paths. His ideas connect with Steiner's and touch on central issues which were discussed amongst artists around the year 1910. At that time they reacted against positivism within natural science and many people were tired of materialism and wanted something else. Interest burgeoned for broader thinking within mystical movements and people were receptive to the direction taken by theosophy on the spiritual dimension of life. Many artists were concerned about the ability to experience the spiritual in the material and also how to express the spiritual in material form. They wanted to emphasize the content more strongly, the inner, the spiritual (the *Geist),* which they felt had come under the shadow of the outer, the material.

It is now that the former jurist, economist and scientist Kandinsky begins a whole new career as an artist. He has given up hope that materialistic and positivist science will be able to give the answers that the period patently seeks. He and several others begin instead to seek the unity between the laws of art and the laws of nature — that aspect of Goethe's aesthetics which Steiner had particularly emphasized in his many articles and lectures since the 1880's.

It is conspicuous how much the ideas in Kandinsky's book link up with Steiner's commentaries on Goethe's science. Granted, Kandinsky does not mention Goethe's name more than a couple of times in connection with the formulation of the 'general foundation' for the art of painting which Goethe prophesied. It was Goethe's opinion, according to Kandinsky, that art/painting must find its general foundation — a grammar of painting, a theory or a system of painting, which can:

> as yet only be speculated on. But when the time is ripe it will certainly be found to be established not on physical laws (such attempts have been made and are still being made — Cubism is an example), but on the *laws of inner necessity.* And these concern *the soul.*[15]

Ringbom has found that Kandinsky was specifically inspired by lectures which Steiner gave on Goethe's theory of colour. In these lectures, he stresses that the time will come when we are mature enough to understand that light does not consist only of the seven prismatic colours and purely material vibrations, but also has to do with the (scientifically hard to define) concept 'life,' which comes from the sun, and that it is to this that Goethe refers when he talks of colours as *'Taten des Lichtes'* (Deeds of the light). As long as we are only capable of seeing the physical colours it is impossible for us to understand this, and such an inner spiritual content can only be achieved and comprehended through man's artistic imagination (see Plate 2).[16]

Goethe regarded colours as being more than mere physical phenomena, intuiting that they had a 'sensually-moral effect' which Man, as the active subject, understands. The total reality in the phenomena of colours cannot be embraced by such a narrowly specific analysis as the spectrum. Kandinsky experiments with 'freely floating colours' — which Steiner too speaks of — and succeeds through a series of landscape paintings in releasing colour from its material context. And this accords, Ringbom comments, with that inner perceptive capacity, described by Steiner, which we humans characteristically have. For the observer, the colours 'float in space' without firm ground under them, as if liberated from the physical and material.[17]

According to Goethe, art can help man to understand the universal laws of nature — 'beauty is a manifestation of secret laws of nature which, without art, would have remained hidden from us,' is a quotation from Goethe that Steiner often repeats when he writes and speaks on the role of art.[18]

Is it perhaps something of this which lies behind the physicist Jacob Bronowski's statement that the layman's key to science is its association with the humanities?[19] Steiner would perhaps have thought that this is also science's key to a more genuine and life-promoting knowledge.

These laws would not remain secret from us were we brought up and trained differently, Steiner thinks. And it is against this background, as I see it, that Steiner's own art should be seen, with his ideas on the importance of training artistic aptitude and the colour exercises which are so central to anthroposophical practice, especially in education. It is a matter here of giving the pupil, the teacher, the scientist — professional people in general — a method for training awareness and experience of an active human role. The experiences of colour here take on psychological value but also have a philosophical and ethical significance and, through this, an effect on the individual will.

While Kandinsky concentrates primarily on the *artist's* central role when it comes to revealing this inner path of knowledge and its importance for the future development of society, Steiner aims at theory and in practice directly concerned with developing *the artistic side of each particular individual.* As we have seen earlier, it was this that Schiller regarded as being the very *sine qua non* for man to be man in the full sense of the word.

According to Steiner through exercises in letting colours 'float freely' on a paper, we get through in a special way to our own ability to think inwardly and to a different and more profound capacity for perception.

Kandinsky speaks of training up the artist's ability to make oneself identical with the colour. One 'turns' oneself into a weighing-machine and weighs the inner content of the material on one's own scales. In this way one's potential for insight is developed. One exposes oneself experimentally to the action of the colour, examines colours and examines contrasts and relationships of balance and equilibrium in the complementary colours. In this way one gains knowledge of the colour material, which is based more on mental experience than on any positive science. One creates at the same time as one explores or investigates by experiencing things and by identifying oneself with them.[20] Goethe says in § 763 of his *Theory of Colour* that 'one then identifies oneself with the colour, it tunes the eye and the spirit *unisono* with itself.'

In this way one comes into connection with the spiritual dimension of thinking which is necessary if we are ever going to be able to capture and better understand the ungraspable, that which has to do with life. This ability has long lain fallow with us who have only had eyes for the external, the material in life. Through the experiences that these practical colour exercises give, one can both experience the spiritual in the material — both the 'sensually-moral' (Goethe's expression) and the physical — and also express the spiritual in material form.

As I understand it, the question here is not primarily about achieving an artistically first-class result, a work of art. It is more concerned with finding a path to knowledge, a method for everyone to train their ability to get at such knowledge and understanding, which is an important part of life and reality, but which has been hidden from us for a long time above all through the methods applied within our educational institutions, and to which the science of our time cannot get through. This is why Steiner places such importance on these practical exercises in educational contexts. And this is also why Kandinsky's books and art feature so strongly in the method of teaching painting which is applied today at the Rudolf Steiner Training College in Järna.

Beyond the limits of science

The main question for the future according to Steiner — and in this he based these views also on his Goethe research — was how to resurrect the vital unity between nature and spirit. But Steiner, like Goethe, was careful to stress that science should in no way thereby lose any of its scientific nature or exactness — a way of thinking that could be extremely difficult to follow, especially for those who have received higher schooling in modern ways of western thought. Steiner was well aware of the difficulties which present themselves to many people living today, but he believed that this scientific training is a prerequisite to understand both Goethe and himself. He persists in his view that it is possible, using scientific methods, to get at much that science has not regarded as being accessible.

Mysticism [the belief in spiritual apprehension of truths beyond the understanding] is the philosophical term for spirituality. Steiner stresses that the lack of spirituality in contexts of knowledge, which we have suffered for a long time, has by no means always prevailed. Our age, according to Steiner, could have much to learn from the mystics of the Middle Ages as regards regaining contact with the inner, spiritual aspects of reality. And it is this heritage of knowledge that Goethe linked up with, and which Steiner wanted to develop further in anthroposophy.

The Greek word *muein* can mean both 'to focus the eyes' (by narrowing them), or something 'unexplained and secretive.' In contexts of knowledge it is a matter of inner, invisible knowledge, as opposed to outer, observable knowledge. But the type of knowledge which one is trying to get at here is very difficult to describe with the concepts which we employ today (compare for example the aged Wittgenstein who says that the most important parts of life cannot be described with words, similarly too the concept of so-called 'hidden knowledge').

Steiner believes that one should be able to increase understanding of these phenomena by relating how people worked in older times to arrive at knowledge outside the area that science deals with today. Much of what we today regard as faith content was knowledge content in earlier times. Some people sought this knowledge by developing 'hidden powers of the soul,' as Steiner calls them, and today we are not aware how much of what we today regard as knowledge has been discovered through older paths to knowledge.

But Steiner also emphasizes that he does not believe that these older paths to knowledge are directly transferable or suitable for those who wish to reach higher knowledge in our time. They are meant for older epochs and can even be harmful to a present-day person. It is in order that we should understand the failings in our present methods of knowledge better, and in order for us to 'go beyond the solely scientific sphere of knowledge which is valid in our days,' that he wishes to attach importance to certain aspects of these old methods for attaining knowledge.[21]

Steiner stresses in particular, the difficulties he had in trying to find forms of expression in which to explain his own relationship to mysticism. It is a complicated matter and it is quite clear from what he says that he himself, held a clearly stated scepticism towards central parts of mysticism. He warned about confusing true mysticism with the so-called 'mysticism' of the deluded. One lecture he gave for workers in Berlin had for instance the title 'Old and New Dreamers and Scatterbrains.' In the preface to his book *Mysticism at the Dawn of the Modern Age,* which he wrote in Berlin in 1901, he refers to how mysticism can go astray. He warns about a faith biased towards sensations and he writes of perception and feeling here as inseparable prerequisites for finding knowledge and a true knowing. The naïve person differentiates between the two and believes that life appears directly only in the senses, and in knowing, only indirectly. From this comes the belief that it is more important to develop the wholly and completely personal emotional life, than anything else. Such a person has taken the wrong path — a philosophy of the emotions, which is often described as mysticism, Steiner declares, going on to say:

> The delusion in a mystical outlook based solely on feeling or emotion rests in that it wants to *experience* what it ought to know, that it wants to breed something personal and individual, feeling or emotion, into something universal.
>
> Feeling is a purely individual and personal act, put more exactly, the act of setting the outer world in relation to our subject, our self, so far as this relation expresses itself in a solely subjective act of experiencing.[22]

Steiner sees man's mystical relationship with the spirit as something purely personal and therefore one cannot speak of it as trustworthy knowledge content. 'The path of mere emotion to the spiritual I rejected most emphatically,' Steiner writes. For him, as for Goethe, it was the subjective and the objective in insoluble union with one another that gave true knowledge and real learning. But neither part could be eliminated if one were to be able to claim to depict reality.[23] Goethe, according to Steiner, criticizes the mystics' method of attaining self-knowledge by sinking into themselves. Starting out from self-knowledge one should take oneself out into the world, out into the universe — that was what it was all about.[24]

What characterizes Steiner is his stubborn faith in the possibility of simultaneously being a true exponent of a scientific view and a searcher along paths leading to the soul and *truly understood* mysticism. He goes further still and believes that only the person who recognizes the spiritual in the way the *true* mystic does, can achieve full understanding of nature, and that contemporary man here can learn from the mystics' method of reaching inner experiences.

His book *Theosophy* was dedicated to Giordano Bruno — the man, Steiner says, who through a spiritual search for knowledge arrived at truths without using the empirical method but who, because of his contemporaries' and primarily the Catholic Church's unwillingness to believe in his knowledge, was burned as a heretic.

Bruno claimed that the universe is infinite. Some thirty years earlier, Galileo had been sentenced to prison for his view that the Earth moves as a planet around the Sun — a view which the scientists of his day could scarcely prove empirically. Few men stood on stronger scientific grounds, in a certain sense, than the men who combatted such ideas. 'You can see,' the Aristotelians could say with good reason, 'that the Earth does not move — a child can see that!' Nevertheless, it eventually became evident who held the truth of the matter.[25]

One Swedish scientist who, according to Rolf Lindborg, has written about the role of mysticism in the origin of modern science is Sten Lindroth. He mentions in his paper 'On the History of Learning' *(Om lärdomshistoria)* that, typical for the earliest form of science was a:

> natural philosophical mysticism often coloured by alchemical dreams of perfection. They lived in alliance with Nature, in the middle of its fields of energy. And they set up as their goals its domination by means of practical artifices. This was magic — but no demonic Black Art, instead it was what these men themselves called 'natural magic,' a secret science for initiated adepts who saw further than others behind the shroud of things and could therefore operate with a reality unknown to others. It was unknown primarily to the prevailing scholars, the Aristotelian professors at the universities.[26]

Another Swedish historian of ideas who has made a study of magic and mysticism in the seventeenth and eighteenth centuries, is Karin Johannisson. She makes the point that these phenomena have long been preponderant in the history of science yet normally have not been regarded as having any significance for the development of modern science. She refers to several recent thinkers who have shown that science and mysticism do not represent any kind of contradiction. Mysticism in the hermetic tradition — to which Giordano Bruno belongs, for instance — played a decisive part in the understanding of modern science as social activity and institution.

She also claims that the scientific ambitions of the Rosicrucian movement were progressive rather than regressive. In this movement they regarded knowledge as not being limitable to certain given methods. They had hopes that it would always be possible to go beyond the limits of the cardinal virtues of science — rationality, objectivity and critical disposition — and they dreamed of a science capable of development directly in the service of mankind. For the magician, Nature is not a mechanism which is governed only in accordance with fixed laws of Nature, but also to be found in him is the supernatural, which to him quite simply comprises the unusual, the wonderful, the artificial; the laws of Nature are not regarded as absolute and they can be overstepped by art. In its most general sense magic can be characterized as the use of art to achieve particular desired goals, not to achieve knowledge and understanding *per se.* Johanisson summarizes:

> Magic as a scientific activity starts out from a definite understanding of knowledge gathered from the hermetic tradition, it builds on experiment and rationality in a mathematical sense and is woven together with a visionary utopianism with the practical result in focus.[27]

The Rosicrucian movement was formed during a period when Europe was ravaged by war, starvation and epidemics, and by a Christianity split by the Reformation. People believed in science as a force capable of bringing about changes and there was an open outlook on the world. There was a desire to part with the authority of the Church, but a desire to believe in science as a path to development. Radical changes were called for and there was a longing for religious and scientific unity.

The appearance of the scientific association, the Royal Society, in England in the 1690s, inaugurated a neutralization of values which hit magic hard. Now science was incorporated into established society and people came to renounce ethical elements and regard them as unscientific and dangerous. But these elements did not disappear. Instead, they lived on as stimuli within the new science, but also in the form of radical activities and programmes, such as the Order of Freemasons. They regarded their experiments as being clearly scientific and distanced themselves from magic in the form of 'Black Art.' The line dividing magic from science did not exist to their way of thinking. Magic was for them the natural continuation of science, a science liberated from authoritarian faith and rigid rules, and which gained continued nourishment not only through the dream of the perfectibility of knowledge.[28]

The kind of science that was pursued in secret societies had — despite secretiveness and élitism — a progressive direction and was deeply engaged in the idea of a radical change of society. Prior to the French Revolution, in countries such as France, Sweden and Germany, the Freemasons stressed that science was, and must be, a means of struggle to be used for human development. Johannisson wishes first and foremost to show that magic is not regressive but rather progressive: not in a 'quantitative' and accumulative sense, but in a 'qualitative' sense — that is to say, when it is judged on the basis of its own premises; that it always stresses science as a power to effect change; and that science can never be divorced from certain purposes.

Steiner was well acquainted with the background of mysticism. But as with materialism, mysticism was once a positive force which went too far and therefore acquired negative consequences. Mysticism during the Middle Ages became stunted, becoming far too emotionally governed, and it lost its background of research.[29] In his opinion though, a far too emotionally governed development was now replaced by a far too one-sidedly materialistic and intellectualistic development. Steiner believed that the limits for the search for knowledge must now be extended again, there being much to learn from older seekers of knowledge as regards human knowledge and self-knowledge and the way to experience and speak of the world around us. Materialism was, to begin with, perfectly justified, but with time it has come to over-dominate, and it is from this position we must start working today.

In a series of twelve lectures on the Gospel according to St John, which Steiner first gave in Hamburg in 1908, he stresses that materialism crept into religion much earlier than into science. In the interpretations of the Bible in the fourteenth and fifteenth centuries, the ground was prepared for this. The opening words in the Gospel according to St John touch on the deepest secrets of the world, but because of materialistically-minded theologians such texts have become very difficult for people to read today. Here Steiner makes a direct comparison with our possibilities of understanding Goethe's *Faust,* and above all the second part, which has also been made difficult through the scholars' exclusively pedantic interest in motifs and their origins, thereby missing the deeper and more exalted dimensions of the work.

It is attitudes like this that have contributed to our no longer understanding the Gospel according to St John, for instance, and it is here that anthroposophy can help. By means of the form of knowledge that Steiner wants to reach, we ought yet again to be able to develop our ability to really understand texts touching on the spiritual issues of life. In his lectures he develops his idea on how the initial words on *logos* in the Gospel according to St John touch on the deepest secrets of the world and which he says the Church ought to concern itself with more.[30]

It is not, therefore, an uncritical comprehension of the mystics that Steiner wishes to present. It is important to realize this if one is to gain a correct picture of Steiner as a thinker. Much of the scepticism surrounding him as a person, which it cannot be denied exists today, can be linked to an ignorance of his way of thinking about these matters.

One feature common to all mystics is their experience of the affinity of everything, all is one — *unio mystica* — and that all division into separate independent parts is something unreal. Hegel is one of the last proponents in philosophy of this kind of thinking, according to Bertrand Russell, who himself can be looked upon as a rational positivist. However, it is increasingly clear that the developments in science, and primarily physics, at the beginning of the twentieth century have caused more and more people to think once again about these matters.

One of the forerunners of quantum mechanics, Walter Heitler, was invited by theologians at the beginning of the 1960's to lecture in Uppsala. He said at that time:

> The purposeful, holistic way of looking at things has often been reproached as being mystical or metaphysical. This is true to exactly the same high or low degree as the causal-analytical way of looking at things in physics. That the phenomena of Nature conform to laws at all is a profound question which immediately leads across into metaphysics. That a purposeful condition, however, with its accompanying conformities to law should be more mystical than the fact that the moon in its orbit follows a geodetic line, depends only on the fact that for [three hundred] years we have accustomed ourselves to causal laws and do not reflect any longer on the fact that these too are miracles.[31]

Art, science and religion

The path Steiner wished to follow — the path of anthroposophy and spiritual science *(Geisteswissenschaft)* — meant a resurrection of the old idea of a unity between art, science and religion in social life, which was a natural thing in earlier times, but which had lost its significance.

The Finnish philosopher Georg Henrik von Wright believes that our ideas of what people need have become more and more materialistic. Science in a quantitative sense has grown over the heads of philosophy and art, or has at any rate broken away as an independent component from the totality of educational life, and the understanding of the whole, threatens thereby to be lost.[32]

Steiner's desire to resurrect the unity between art, science and religion was understood by many of his own contemporaries as completely utopian and something that only a dreamer, divorced from the world, could entertain.

The many people who joined him did not see him as a dreamer, but on the contrary understood his criticism of civilization as being realistic. They saw room for hope in his attempts to analyse developments which were pursuing the wrong track and moreover, he came with practical suggestions for changes within society.

The characteristic feature of modern man, Steiner believed, is precisely that he differentiates between science, art and religion. This is a mark of our civilization. Instead of, as now, bothering to formulate a new concept of knowledge, in which art may not cross the line bordering on the area of science, we should strive to achieve the unity between these two again which existed in older times, and which in modern time is still traceable — to a higher extent in the East than in the West.

It was to a development of this nature Steiner wanted to contribute with his anthroposophy, and Goethe represented to Steiner, as we have seen, the model of a person who had truly effected this union within himself and who for precisely that reason was also capable of seeing deeper and further than most. And this was why Goethe came to form the starting-point of Steiner's continued activities, and also why his name was eventually used for the international centre for Spiritual Science *(Geisteswissenschaft)* — the 'Goetheanum' in Dornach, Switzerland.

Goethe's life and work as well as Schiller's *Letters on the Aesthetic Education of Man* thereby make up the foundation of a new and different scientific method as well as a method of teaching. Not the training of artists, but to train and develop instead *each* individual's own artistic nature, thereby became a main aim of the educational method that Steiner laid the foundation for.

Steiner's placing such weight on art in teaching is therefore directly connected with his view that the main cause of the western cultural crisis is linked to the lack of spirituality which has become more and more tangible ever since the Renaissance. Man as a living organism, and his thinking, creative capacity — that is, man as the active subject and not merely as the object — played too small a part in the cultural life and science of modern times:

> The way of thinking in the epoch in which I grew up, seemed to me to be suitable only if one wished to form ideas on inanimate Nature. In order to get to the essence of

> living Nature, I felt that this way of thinking was insufficient. I thought that in order to arrive at ideas which can give us knowledge of the organic, one must first bring to life for oneself the rational concepts which can be applied to inorganic Nature. I felt, you see, that the concepts appeared to be dead, and were therefore not designed either to encompass anything apart from that which was dead.[33]

At an International Anthroposophical Congress in Vienna, in 1922, Steiner stressed that science has led to one more admirable technical invention after the other, and the scientist has gained from this a fantastic inspirational strength. But the corresponding inspirational strength in the spiritual-soul area:

> that which concerns ethics, volition, religion — in short all that which issues from the soul of man and which ultimately leads to social reforms and social life — this inspirational strength is lacking in modern man. Here we need a force once more to influence the spiritual-soul area in the same way as the inspiring force taken only from Nature influences our external technology.
>
> ... If one, without prejudice, looks at earlier currents of world-philosophy, one will see that thinking in an obvious sort of way, appended something purely human to what emerged from experiments with, and the observation of, Nature. Examples of this are the now abandoned branches of knowledge, astrology and alchemy. In these sciences, which were adapted to ancient cultural epochs, Nature was approached in such a way that human thinking in an obvious sort of way provided something above and beyond its items of information on things in the world.[34]

Ultimately it is the question of the freedom of man that is central here. Thought as a human experience has been disengaged today and no longer appears in science other than as a means of research. But there is surely a question of a paradox here, Steiner says:

> ... [for] if thinking must be satisfied with treating the

> processes of Nature — if it only may step in formally, investigating, specifying and classifying — then it does not exist in the processes of Nature themselves, and it would therefore become paradoxical were we to put forward the question — justified from a scientific standpoint — 'How can we, out of scientific conformity to law, understand thinking as an expression of the human organism?'[35]

In Steiner's opinion, anthroposophy is about a search which does not relinquish the scientific way of thinking, but proceeds just as conscientiously as science does, but which still comprises something different and above and beyond this. Anthroposophy is a philosophy of the world and of life which really does not contain very much that is completely new. It comprises, if anything, an attempt in modern times to recreate opportunities for man to gain knowledge of the world by using various methods of knowledge which have long been abandoned.

Steiner was careful to stress that anthroposophy does not comprise a complete and ultimate philosophy, but, on the contrary, it means that one should, by trial and error, seek for paths other than those that have been followed in a more and more marked fashion over the last three hundred years. Since anthroposophy is only at the beginning of its existence, it must naturally contain many imperfections, but the attempt must be made in any case, Steiner believed.

Here, I reproduce a section from one of the ten lectures Steiner gave in 1922, towards the end of his life, to the Anthroposophical Movement's Second International Congress in Vienna. These lectures were later published under the title: *West and East: Contrasting Worlds.* In them, Steiner attempts to give an insight into how a spiritual-scientific method can complement a too narrowly one-sided scientific method, and 'thereby also reach deeper into the essence of Nature.'

> [Anthroposophy] stands in no way in opposition to contemporary science. On the contrary, it takes up the genuine temper of research characteristic in particular, of scientific investigation, and develops it by means of its exercises into a personal human skill. Present science looks

'We are all more or less involved in the issues of the art of architecture. Here, social, private, economic, rational, aesthetic, ethical, biological, ecological issues touch on one another. No form of art is so tied up with the burning issues of society, as is the art of architecture.' ('Introduction' in Klingborg & Fant, 1985.)

Above: *The second Goetheanum building — organic forms in concrete.*
Below: *Adolf Loos' house in Wittgenstein's Vienna.*

It should be possible to see from the outside of a building what its purpose is.

The central boiler plant at the Goetheanum — organically alive.

The transformer building at the Goetheanum — geometrical, straight.

Model for a new hall at the Teacher-training College in Witten-Annen, West Germany, 1989. Architect Imre Makovecz, Hungary.

Projekt för salsbyggnad till lärarseminariet
i Witten-Annen. Västtvskland. modellfota 1989

for exactness and experiences particular satisfaction when it can look for this exactness through the use of mathematics applied to the processes of Nature. Why is this so? Quite simply because the perceptions of external Nature, which our sense of observation and experiment gives us, are outside of us. We investigate it with something which we train up in our innermost human nature completely on our own, that is, with our mathematical skills. The words of Kant are often uttered, and are practised even more often by those who think in a scientific manner: Every item of knowledge contains only as much science as there is mathematics therein. — This is one-sided, if ordinary mathematics is intended. But by applying it to the inanimate phenomena of Nature, and, in our day, by even seeing a certain ideal in it, for example, the possibility of being able to count the chromosomes in the cells, one shows a sense of satisfaction in being able to explore the external phenomena round about us by means of mathematics. Why? Because one experiences mathematics as something absolutely secure — something which we, to be sure, often must visualize by means of drawings, but these are not what is important for the truth. The proof is mathematics are inwardly perceived and what we find within us we connect with what we see externally. Consequently we feel satisfied.

If one sees into this process of cognition in its totality, one must say to oneself that only that which man really can see and experience by means of the forces within himself can satisfy him in terms of knowledge, only that can lead to a science within him. By means of mathematics one penetrates into the facts of the inanimate world and also somewhat into the animate world, even if it happens in a primitive way. But one needs an inner idea as equally exact as the mathematical idea, if one would penetrate into the higher modes of operation in the physical world. Even Haeckel's school, through one of its most prominent representatives, has expressly admitted that one must arrive at a completely different way of carrying out research and looking at things, if one would reach through to the organic from the inorganic. For the inorganic one has mathematics and geometry, for the organic, the living, one has as yet nothing which in its inner nature is so formed as, for instance, a triangle, a circle or an ellipse. It is through living thinking that one arrives at this. One does it, not by using ordinary mathematics, but by using a higher mathematics, with a thinking which is qualitative, which acts in a formative way and — even if I thereby must utter something abominable to many people, so it must be said in any case — which takes into account the artistic elements.

Through our penetration, by means of such mathematics, into the worlds to which we otherwise do not have access, we expand scientific thinking into the biological area. And one may be certain that epochs will come when it shall be said: Older times have justifiably emphasized the fact that one can obtain the same amount of science from inorganic Nature as one, in the broadest sense, can reach inorganic Nature by means of mathematics, to the extent that the mathematics are quantitative; from the life processes, one can obtain the same amount of science as one is in a position to penetrate the processes of life with a living train of thought and an exact clairvoyance.

One would not imagine that this modern clairvoyance stands so close to mathematical thinking particularly, as it in point of fact does. And when we one day realize that we should appropriate knowledge of the spirit by using the working methods of modern knowledge of Nature, we will come to find the spiritual science referred to here, with its starting point from this area of the modern knowledge of Nature, justified. For this will not set itself up in any opposition at all to the significant, magnificent results of science. It wishes to try something else. When we, with our physical senses, look at a person's physical form, his gestures, his play of features, the special look in his eyes, then it is only that person's exterior we get to know. But if we, right through the exterior form, can see something spiritual within him, only then do we have the whole person in front of us. In the same way it is, so to say, only the outer physiognomy

> of the world, its gestures and mimicry that we see when we use the scientific way of regarding things. We first learn to know something of what we ourselves are akin to, and which is eternal in this world, if we go beyond the external physiognomy which the phenomena of Nature provide us with, beyond this mimicry and its gestures, and penetrate into the spiritual elements of the world.
>
> This is what the spiritual-scientific view should do, whose methods to begin with, I have wanted to portray today. It should not be an opponent to the triumphant modern science, but should completely accept it in its importance and its individuality, just as one completely accepts the external human being. But just as one penetrates through the external human being and can see his spiritual aspect, so would anthroposophy — not in an amateurish and layman-like manner, but by serious research — penetrate through the laws of Nature and their physiognomy to the spiritual and non-material which lies as the basis of the world. Thus would this spiritual-scientific philosophy not create any opposition at all to science, but would instead be the soul and spirit of science.[36]

That we so readily resort to mathematics in various connections should therefore, according to Steiner, be linked to the fact that it gives us the opportunity to exploit and come into contact with what we find in our inner self, and this is exactly what gives a sense of desire and satisfaction. However, this applies almost exclusively to the inorganic. If we wish to gain knowledge also of the organic, then it is not enough to use ordinary mathematics; instead, a higher mathematics is called for and this is where art enters in.

Many years earlier, in 1897, Steiner had written the following in a paper, which he also reproduced in his autobiography towards the end of his life:

> Our understanding of Nature sees plainly and clearly as its goal the explanation of the life of organisms according to the same laws by which the phenomena in inanimate Nature must be explained. Mechanical, physical and chemical

> conformity to law is sought for in animal and plant forms. The same kind of laws that govern a machine should be active in an organism, although in a form which is infinitely more complicated and difficult to explore. Nothing should be added to these laws in order to make the phenomenon we call life possible ... The mechanical understanding of the various phenomena of life is gaining more and more ground. But it will never come to satisfy him, who can see deeper into the events of Nature ... The natural researchers of today are too timid in their thinking. Where knowledge runs out in their mechanical explanations, they say that it is not possible for us to explain the matter ... A bold kind of thinking elevates itself to a higher outlook. What is not of a mechanical nature, they try to explain with higher laws. All our scientific thinking comes to a standstill before our scientific experience. Today, one praises the scientific way of thinking. One speaks of us as living in the scientific age. But in reality this scientific age is the most pitiful age that history has ever beheld. Getting stuck on mere facts and mechanical explanations is its distinguishing feature. Life can never be understood through that way of thinking, since a higher world of ideas is called for in order to grasp something like this, than is necessary to explain a machine.[37]

This extra something, which has to do with life itself, cannot be got at by us only using our scientific methods. Here we must employ creative art to help us. This is what Goethe realized, and it is this insight which Steiner wanted to perpetuate into our time. The same year in which Steiner wrote the above, the sixteen-year-old Picasso painted a large picture which he called *Science and Human Compassion* (see Plate 1).[38]

At the beginning of Steiner's research career, 'spirit,' according to his way of explaining the matter at that time, was everything that produces 'culture' through human thinking, feeling and volition. Only later on did he venture on an explanation which also meant that, as a base for what was spirit in man and in nature, there lay something which was neither spirit nor nature, but a perfect unity composed of both, and this only the creative spirit inside man could get at. To understand something such as 'life' was an impossibility without this unity.[39]

> If one pushes on through to this kind of an inner experience, one no longer senses any relationship of opposites between natural knowledge and spiritual knowledge. It becomes clear to one that the latter is only a metamorphosis and a continuation of the former.[40]

It was this understanding that made it possible for Steiner to give the sub-title 'Results of Spiritual Observation following the Scientific Method' to his book *The Philosophy of Freedom.* And he says that 'if one keeps oneself strictly to the scientific method in spiritual research, it will lead specifically to insight into this area too.'

According to Steiner's interpretation of Schiller, man can teach himself through aesthetic education to create those things which have not been provided for him by Nature:

> He can bring reason into the activity of the senses and elevate the sensory dimension to a higher plane of consciousness, so that it acts as though in a spiritual way. In this way he achieves a state of the spirit between the compulsions of logic and Nature *(Stofftrieb* and *Formtrieb).* Schiller regards man as being in such a state of the spirit when he lives in art. The aesthetic understanding of the world looks at the sensory dimension, but in such a way as to find the spirit therein.[41]

It is in art and in play that man can gain an outlet for his creative ability — that which makes him man. And it is also first in this act of creating that he can gain a holistic experience of existence — both of external, material objects as of inner subjective experiences. And it is first here that he can be made to go beyond knowledge which only underlines facts, and beyond items of information on existence, to encompass the spiritual phenomena, which an understanding of the concept 'life' presupposes.

Perhaps it is something of this that Saul Bellow (himself inspired by Rudolf Steiner's writings) means when he says that we in our time 'are informed about everything, but know nothing.'[42] And perhaps we would be better equipped to deal with the ethical problems that science today has presented us with in most areas, concerning our ability to manage life, if our aesthetic education had been of a different kind. That is at any rate what Goethe, Schiller, Steiner, Read and the Waldorf educationalists of today believe.

In Steiner's view we must open ourselves to a total rethinking if modern developments are not to lead to the total destruction of life. And to this end the educational system in the schools as well as the universities is called upon to renew the unity between science, art and religion which existed in older times.

From Theosophy to everyday life

In 1912 Steiner came to relinquish the leadership of the Theosophical Movement, expressing his criticism of the far too profuse theorizing that went on there. He wanted to work in a different way by trying to get in more of spiritual dimensions in *practice* — in the real life and thinking of all people.

Steiner felt that a movement that spends its time merely theorizing on subjects such as cosmology, philosophy and religion, '... degenerates into an ultimately insufferable dogmatic bickering.' Since Steiner believed that anthroposophy wished to be something that not only theoretically devoted itself to cosmology, philosophy and religion, but which instead, in accordance with the present requirements of the spirit of the age, should intervene in the truly practical life, it gradually became impossible for the anthroposophical movement to collaborate with the theosophical movement. After a longer period of friction and conflicts, they severed their connections. Steiner wanted to achieve something other than what the theosophical movement primarily stood for. His anthroposophical movement had to fight to gain an independent standing for itself in the world as a movement of practical importance for life.[43]

The very name 'anthroposophy,' as he termed his own philosophy, says something about how he wished to distance himself from theosophy. It is here not in the first place a matter of God — (Theo-sophy) — but a matter of people and their practical reality. The term anthroposophy should not be translated into 'wisdom of man' but is rather about *becoming aware of one's humanity.*

This more practically-oriented direction of interest was not something new for Steiner; it was what all along he had endeavoured to express in his writings. After leaving Weimar and moving to Berlin, his authorship, which apart from literary and theatrical reviews also dealt with education-political issues, etc., witnesses even more plainly to his efforts in this respect. In the same way his interest in questions of general education in the teaching of workers, from 1899, and also his writing on the upbringing and teaching of the child, from 1907, show how, at an early stage, he actively strove to try to bind together theory and practice in the context of education (see Chapter 8).

CHAPTER 6
The Social Issue

Social questions in post-war Germany

'The Social Issue' was a living question in Germany at the turn of the last century, as it was in Sweden. The issue concerned the future social prospects for improved living conditions in the organized modern community. The most debated area was the so-called workers' question, which at that time particularly concerned the effects of industrialization on the life and work of factory labour. The issue of women's rights was also seen as part of the social issue.

As a result of the chaos in which Germany found itself after the end of the First World War, Steiner came to apply himself intensively to those theoretical and practical problems which he saw as related to the social issue. In April 1919 he published *The Threefold Social Order* (available in English as *Towards Social Renewal).* In his opinion the catastrophe of the War was largely the result of not having sufficiently taken notice of 'that which lived in the will of the proletariat.' The book should be seen as a first step towards the restructuring of society that Steiner, like many others, regarded as necessary for the preservation of peace. One basic criterion for such a restructuring is a radical change in the educational system, and his ideas in the book also came to form the basis of the school which only a few months later he started for workers' children at the Waldorf-Astoria Factory in Stuttgart. Afterwards, he was to come to spend the greater part of his time on questions of education.

An appeal to the German people accompanied the book, signed by several hundred prominent persons from various walks of cultural life — mainly professors and doctors. The appeal was also published in many German and Swiss newspapers.

The immediate reaction to the book did not lead to the revolutionary changes which Steiner thought necessary and had hoped for.

Its influence, however, was significant, not only in Germany. Basic ideas in it still apply to the anthroposophical activities within various sectors of society today and are the object of a steadily growing interest in different parts of the world. In Scandinavia it created so much attention that it was translated into Swedish and published here the same year as in the German-speaking countries. Here, too, it was accompanied by an appeal to the Scandinavian peoples, signed by 'The Scandinavian Threefold Society Association' with headquarters in Stockholm, Copenhagen and Christiania (Oslo).

The book was reviewed prominently in Scandinavian newspapers — for instance, in the *Göteborgs handels-och Sjöfartstidning* (Gothenburg Mercantile and Marine Newspaper) and by Ivan Oljelund in *Socialdemokraten* (The Social Democrat) of 3 and 5 January 1920 under the heading 'A Modern Reformer.' Oljelund seized on the idea of how the World War and the false ideals exposed by it had led to an intensified attention to spiritual issues where much was of a 'fleeting and confusing nature, much of a good and lasting kind.' In this latter group he felt one should count Steiner's book. He fastened onto the idea that Steiner's thoughts were 'independent in that [they] cannot be captured by any of the prevalent party programmes but also original in that he applies an inner, spiritual view to the social issues and is drawn to the essence and heart of the phenomena.' Oljelund accords the book great significance in its analysis of the psychology of the workers' movement and the social situation. He observes that Steiner tries to look at the social question from within and he ends the second of the two articles by stressing that the book 'reveals that the problem of society is a many-sided complex tissue of many-sided complex issues. With reference to both these circumstances, the book is recommended first and foremost to our Conservatives and Bolsheviks.'

Similarly, the leader of the Swedish People's Liberal Party in Finland, Axel Lille, wrote two lengthy articles on the book in the *Dagens Press* (The Daily Press) of 17 and 28 August 1920 with the heading 'Towards new social conditions.' Axel Lille found the book an epoch-making work and believed that Steiner here more clearly than anyone else underlined the basic impulses of the modern workers' movement.

In Germany itself the book was subjected to a great deal of criticism, not least from academic quarters. Steiner was well prepared for this and emphasizes in his short preface that he is aware that various categories of people for various reasons will object to his presentation. 'Many a person will find this presentation "abstract," since for him only that is "concrete" which he is used to thinking of, and the truly concrete becomes "abstract" when he is not used to thinking of it.' He adds in a footnote that the author has deliberately avoided using the phrases commonly used in socio-economic literature and that he is aware of the fact that he will therefore be called a dilettante by the 'experts.' His desire however is to be understood outside the specialist circles, but above all he believes that the ideas which are based on real experience of life, and not merely on bookish studies by specialists, call for another form of expression.

The experts within different sectors in society must now relearn their subjects, since their 'expertise' has demonstrably proved itself to be completely wrong. They must learn to see many phenomena as practical, which *they* have hitherto regarded as eccentric and distorted idealism. Using his personal knowledge of life as his point of departure, Steiner says he was forced into realizing that the faults of the past will only multiply unless attention is paid to the spiritual life of modern people and to their knowledge, instead of concentrating on the material and economic aspects of life. On the other hand, it is not a matter of any spirituality whatsoever, but of that spirituality which is directly involved with the practical reality of living.

One of the most important, but far too neglected aspects is then according to Steiner, the workers' *own* inner understanding of what gives work and life vitality and purpose. The workers abhorred the idea that their work should become a piece of goods, a commodity, and not even the socialist theories emphasized this fact radically enough, in Steiner's opinion. They did of course point to the problem, but only as an economic factor. What they had not understood was that this is built into the economic system and that everything which is incorporated into it *must* take on the nature of commodities. It will never be possible to release human manpower from its characteristic of being a commodity without radical rethinking. Steiner believes that the tragic attempts to solve the social problems were due to a misinterpretation of the proletarian struggle and a misjudgment of what the workers *were really striving for.* The development of events has not kept an even pace here with the development of thinking. Through capitalism and the advancement of technology the worker has lost the prospect of experiencing human dignity in the actual execution of his work. His own thinking and creativity no longer have any importance, or else they are a direct obstacle to rapid product development. (Schiller's idea that it is when man is creative that he is man had not had any penetrative force in social planning.)

Since the workers felt that this deep human element in social life, as regards both their working and living conditions, had been lost for their part, they turned with faith and confidence to science to seek an understanding of their situation plus a new awareness and new values. But Steiner felt that the science of the time was not designed to help them in their situation. However, they were not capable of realizing this themselves, Steiner says, because their awareness had lost its deeper human connection with their immediate life, and consequently they were far too uncritically open to scientifically moulded ideas.

The science of the time was the pursuit of the leading classes. It was materialistic and disregarded the spiritual dimension of the social problems. This had not been the case in the old days, and the question now at bottom was to understand how the spiritual aspect has significance for practical reality, as it appears today, not only for the privileged classes, but also in the first place for the proletariat.

Modern science, along with capitalism and the technologizing of society, had developed in such a way that they together constituted an obstacle to a more human existence in practical terms for the worker.

The class consciousness of the proletariat had been filled with concepts which were derived from modern science. It was economic science and not an economic life based on human impulses of will which governed the development. 'Notwithstanding that the worker at his machine stands far enough away from science; he hears his situation explained by those people who have gathered the means of the explanation from this "science".'

According to Steiner the workers' movement is in a certain sense the first movement to have taken its stand on purely scientific foundations, and through the direction and deficiencies of modern science it has come to fail to observe very essential connections. The reality of spiritual life, which many of the leading scientific personalities simply ridiculed as being no more than ideology, is concerned with the workers' own inner thoughts and feelings — their own innermost experience of their existence as it appears to them in practice out on the factory floor and at home in the worker's housing of the industrial towns, where the prospects of feeling oneself to be a freely creative human being anchored in a liberal cultural life were extremely restricted. It is necessary for science to see the whole context in this way if it is to have a favourable effect on practical living. Here, Rudolf Steiner criticizes science as being just as unpractical as philosophy.

The threefold social order

The social issue which Steiner presented in *The Threefold Social Order,* concerns three dimensions of social life which must be made to function partially independent of each other if they are to contribute to an entirely balanced organization of society. These three parts are:

- *economic life,* which has been developed through modern technology and capitalism in such a way in society that it has come to dominate over the other parts of social life;
- *public legislative life,* political life, the State. This only concerns matters referring on purely human grounds to the relationships between people, while the economic system is only concerned with the production, circulation and consumption of merchandise;
- *'spiritual culture,'* that is, all education and research and culture — everything concerned with spiritual life, which is composed of both the spiritual as well as the physical gifts of the private human individuals — which must be allowed to develop independently in the social organism.

Just as the economic system concerns everything which must be provided so that man can organize his material relationship with the outside world, and just as the legislative system concerns everything that must exist in order to make it possible to regulate the relationships between people, so does the spiritual, cultural system concern everything developing from the human individualities themselves, and which must be incorporated into the social organism.

Unity and balance in the social organism depends entirely on the economic and the spiritually cultural parts being allowed to develop free from one another. Should this not be the case, human work input will become a piece of merchandise in the material economic sense. Between these two, the third part — the legal system — should then have a regulatory function, so that results from the economic and the spiritually cultural life can be integrated in a human and egalitarian way in society. This has not worked in more recent times. Therefore there now exists a state of imbalance, which is related to the economic life 'quite simply taking on quite definite forms by itself. It has become especially powerful in human life through unilateral activity and has come to control the other two parts as well, which have not been given the opportunity to establish themselves properly in the social organism.'

To give a thorough account here of how Steiner envisioned the role of the economic and legislative political parts in the whole would be beyond my present aims. I shall mainly concern myself with the third part of the system — the spiritually cultural life — as it encompasses the educational system in society.[1]

The psychological analysis he makes is that when a person is deprived of the possibility of a free spiritual life and becomes instead like a cog in a machine performing a routine job, then he loses his identity as a human being. His vitality wanes, and he feels a sense of apathy and unhappiness, which adds to putting his conscious social volition out of action. This produces directly negative effects both in economic as well as governmental life. When the labour input itself becomes merchandise or when the State regulates everything in detail for the people so that no room is left for personal impulse and initiative, then people become 'for the greatest part deprived of the true foundations of their own lives, since these can only consist of that vitality which they must develop within themselves.' People can then not develop their talents. They feel no sense of responsibility, are unhappy and cannot perform their work efficiently. When people's vitality disappears in this way, they can neither drum up any energy to fertilize economic life nor any other part of the system of society with their ideas, and the whole social organism suffers as a consequence.

This applies to people in working life on the whole, and not least to teachers and students in the institutions of education. It is a view of man which embraces the potential each person should have freely to develop his or her talents. Through the provisions of the legislative system, each person should be credited equally with worth in the entire social system and should be able to count on an understanding for what he, in accordance with his talents, is capable of accomplishing. If not given room, freely, to develop talents, people become paralysed and passive, which leads to inefficiency and poor health. So that people may develop their talents freely in order to become whole people, they must be given the opportunity of development in a spiritual sense as well. One prerequisite for this event is that art, education and world-philosophy issues and everything concerning the spiritually cultural life, should have an independent status in the body of society. Otherwise, they will never be capable of furnishing the entire organism of society with anything of value beyond the material.

Steiner takes up an example here in connection with science education, which is a topical subject for today's education debate in Sweden, too. He writes:

> Even if mathematics and physics cannot immediately be influenced in their content by the needs of the State, the things developed from them, people's ideas of their value, the effects studying them have on the rest of spiritual life, and much else, become, however, determined by these needs, when the State manages branches of the spiritual life.

Quite different conditions exist in this case if a teacher, responsible for the most elementary schoolteaching, follows the stimuli of national government in this respect, or if he receives these stimuli from a spiritually cultural life Steiner goes on to say.[2]

Many people today believe that a shortsighted and utilitarian thinking, above all from business life, controls the direction of schools and also of the universities. To what extent does this inhibit the system of education and total role in the social body, by not giving teachers the freedom to promote the development of their students into individuals and in so doing encompass cultural-spiritual dimensions of life? The maths teaching of today, often less than inspiring, not least from the point of view of creativity, would probably then also become more effective by approaching something of the play and art which higher mathematicians usually say that mathematics should really be all about. Do the school mathematicians not have time, and are they not allowed, to develop these aesthetic dimensions of mathematics because of other demands placed on them by business life and by politicians with little understanding of what growing children and, in a deeper sense, an effective educational system demand?[3]

According to the idea of the threefold society, it is an ultimate requirement that people develop a better social understanding than is the case today. Such an understanding can only be developed out of a sound spiritual life which presumes a life of culture and a system of education developed independently of economic demands, and independently of governmental systems of regulations, which can never consider individual talents and needs at certain precise stages of that person's development. The clearest expression of how such external influences can stunt and sometimes paralyse the healthy growth of children is found in regular testing and grading which do not take into account the child's own growth. For this reason traditional kinds of grades were abolished in the Waldorf Schools.

Women's rights

Here I only mention briefly how central Steiner felt women's rights were to a solution of the social issue. He does not take up this question in *The Threefold Social Order,* published in 1919, but we find these issues discussed both earlier and later in articles as well as in lectures. He also mentions in his autobiography how important were his friendship and long discussions with Rosa Mayreder while he was writing *The Philosophy of Freedom.* Likewise, he underlines the decisive contribution of Marie Steiner in evolving the art exercises of his practical pedagogy.

In his opinion, the women's issue was one of the great cultural questions of the time, with significance for the workers' issue as well as for the scientific discussion. He claimed not to have any solutions to present, but only wanted to point to perspectives.[4]

According to the view of man that Steiner embraces, and which comprises the very basis of anthroposophical activities, each person can be said to be composed of two parts — a more open, material and masculine part, which has become extremely dominant in our modern civilization, and a more concealed, artistic, spiritual and feminine part.

The masculine part of man looks more to external palpable facts, and less to the invisible heart and soul and to things concerning the interrelationships of people in practical life.

It is the feminine part in man that has receded into the background in our time, with an accompanying imbalance in thinking as well as in our actions. Man must therefore in the future learn to know himself better, starting out from this totality, and it is here that the educational system has such a central function to fill, so that gaps can be bridged over and the balance restored (see further, Chapter 8).

One dominating idea with Steiner here is as we have seen, is that science should develop away from the outer, far too one-sidedly empirical method and find a way to include *also* an inner, spiritual dimension of life, which more concerns art and the intuitive in man. One must be aware of Steiner's way of thinking, in order to be able to understand why he regards it important, for instance, that boys in the first class should learn how to crochet and knit, together with the girls. It is not here primarily a question of sexual equality. According to Steiner, certain talents and a certain type of thought activity and a particular kind of logic are trained by crocheting and knitting, which it would be good for both sexes to practise and develop so as to approach one another's minds and to lessen the effect of specialization and differences in ways of thinking. Ultimately it was about training the individual to be able to imagine himself as, and understand, others, those who did not share the same views and interests as himself — to increase mutual understanding. For the same reason the girls should spend time at school doing woodwork and metalwork, techniques that more often lie within the boys' areas of aptitude and interest.

Steiner himself mentions in *The Threefold Social Order* that the ideas on social understanding which he puts forward here are difficult for a modern person to take seriously. He is aware that his viewpoint can be taken as fanaticism. Consequently he dwells on this and points out that such a view need not be fanatical:

> Of course, fanaticism has caused an enormous amount of harm in the area of social volition, as in other places. But the view presented here is not dependent, as one can see from the foregoing, on the illusion that 'the spirit' will perform miracles, if they, who claim to have it, speak as

> much as possible about it. Instead, it becomes clear from the observation of the free collaboration of people in the spiritual area. This collaboration would obtain a social form from its own essence, were it only allowed to develop itself *truly freely*. It is the fact that the life of the spirit is unfree that has prevented this social form from making its appearance up to now. In the leading classes, spiritual vitality has developed itself in such a way that its procreation has been reserved for certain circles of mankind, in an anti-social fashion. What was created in these circles could only be conveyed to the proletariat in artificial ways. And the proletariat could not ladle up any soul-supporting vitality out of this spiritual life, because they had no *true* part in it. Institutions as 'information for the people,' 'educating the people' to make them enjoy art and such like are, in truth, no means to the end of socializing the spiritual. Because 'the people' stand with their innermost human essence outside this spiritual life.[5]

And again:

> In the sound social organism, the worker should not stand by his machine and have his thoughts directed only on running it, while the capitalist alone knows the course of the goods produced in the circulations of economic life. The worker should, as having a just interest in the matter, be able to form an idea for himself on how he participates in social life by producing the goods. Lectures and discussions, which should be counted as part of the running of the machinery as much as the work itself, should be regularly arranged by the company owner with the purpose of developing a common circle of conception including both the employer and the employee. A healthy activity in this direction should arouse in the worker an understanding for how correct cooperation on the part of the capitalists benefits the social organism, and thereby also the worker as a part of it. The company owner should, by making his business leadership in these ways an object of

public scrutiny, be obliged to act in an irreproachable manner.

Only the person who has no sense of the social actions of an inner common experience in the process of a job of work performed by united efforts, can regard this as unimportant. It will become transparent to the person who does have a sense of this, how economic productivity is promoted when the capital-based leadership of the economic life is subjected to the administration of the free spiritual life. The interest in capital and in the creation of capital which at present is a result of profit interest, can only on this prior condition give place to an objective interest in the production of goods and services.

Those who think in socialist terms in our time strive after the take-over of the means of production by society. The justification of this endeavour can only be achieved by their administration being taken over by the free spiritual organization. Through this the economic coercion practised by the capitalist, if he develops his enterprise starting out from the forces of economic life, would be made impossible. In this way one would also avoid bringing people's personal capabilities to a standstill, which must be the result were the political state to force personal initiative under its administration.

The result of the collaboration between capital and personal capability must in the sound social organism, as is true for every spiritual accomplishment, partly be evident from the company owner's free initiative, and, partly, from other people's free understanding of his actions serving to benefit them. The company owner may in this area also possess the freedom, after the expenses for starting his company and after the costs for running it, etc., to claim compensation for his work. He would, however, find his claims complied with only if he is met with understanding in his work.

Through social institutions constructed along the lines specified here, a basis is created for a truly free agreement between the employer and the employee. This agreement should no longer be based on an exchange of commodities (or money, respectively) for labour, but on a settlement of the shares to each of the parties involved in collectively producing the commodities.

That which is produced by means of capital on behalf of the social organism, is as a *consequence of its nature* dependent on the way in which the individual talents intervene in this organism. These talents could nevertheless only acquire the social impulse required for their development from the spiritual life. The real productivity in all that which requires capital should depend on such free individual forces battling on despite paralyzing institutions, also in a social organism which turns over this development to the political state or to the own forces of the economic life. However, development under such prior conditions are unsound. It is not the free development of personal capability by means of capital which is to blame in the conditions in which the human labour force appears to be a commodity, instead it is the pressure of the State on the personality or its being tied down to the cycle of economic life. An unprejudiced comprehension of this is presently the prerequisite for what should now be happening in the social area. For more recent times have given rise to a superstitious belief that the cure for the social organism should appear all by itself out of the political State or the economic life. Were one to go further along this path of superstition one would create institutions which would not lead to the desired goal, but on the contrary, they would lead to an unlimited increase in the oppression which it seeks to avert.

Steiner continues by stating how little one is prepared in our time to bring the social idea, which is supposed to square things with capitalism, into immediate connection with the spiritual life. Instead, the social issues are far too unilaterally linked to the economic life and, most recently, to the idea of cooperation, which leads to the formation of associations into one big State-owned company. No one then reflects on the fact that it becomes more difficult to let people have the kind of position in these firms as is hinted at here, the bigger the firms are.

That we are so badly equipped today for recognizing the significance of the spiritual life for the social organism is due to the fact that we have accustomed ourselves to regarding the spiritual as something extraneous to the material and practical. But Steiner is well aware that the kind of viewpoint which he expresses is regarded as absurd by many people today, and this is due to certain currents of thought having been allowed to prevail, which have prevented the appearance of a true social thinking.[6]

> These currents of thought flow — more or less unconsciously — away from that which gives inner experience its proper impulse. They strive after a philosophy, an intellectual, scientific knowledge which isolates them and which can therefore be likened to an island in the whole of the great life of man. They find then no way to throw a bridge from this life across to the everyday life of people. One can observe how in our time many a person finds it 'fashionable' to reflect in a certain, scholarly abstract way in their ivory towers about all sorts of ethical-religious problems. People muse over how they should acquire virtues, how they should behave in love towards their fellow men, how they should become endowed with an 'inner meaning of life.' But they hereby also betray their incapability of finding a transition from that which they call good and loving and benevolent and just and moral to that which in the outer reality, in everyday life, surrounds people in the form of capital, wages, consumption, production, the circulation of commodities, the credit system, the banking and stock exchange systems.
>
> One perceives how two world currents flow side by side in the habitual thinking of people: the *one* world current, which to a certain extent strives to keep itself on a divine-spiritual height, does not wish to throw a bridge between that which is spiritual stimulation and the common realities of life; the *other* current lives without thinking in everyday life. Life, however, is a unity. It can only develop soundly

when all the forces of the ethical-religious life are active in the simple everyday life, in the particular kind of life that appears less fashionable to many a person. For, in neglecting to construct a bridge between these two areas of life, one lapses in religious, moral life *and in social thinking* into pure fanaticism, which stands far from the everyday, true reality; and then this everyday, true reality avenges itself. Man then strives, impelled by a certain 'spiritual' impulse, after all sorts of ideals, after all sorts of things he calls 'good,' but devotes himself thereby without 'spirit' to instincts, which stand in opposition to these 'ideals,' but which form the basis for the ordinary, daily needs of life, which must be satisfied through the national economy. He knows of no viable path from the concepts of the spiritual to the everyday life. Through this, this everyday life takes on forms, having nothing to do with ethical impulses, which remain at fashionable, spiritual heights. But then everyday life takes its vengeance, so that the ethical-religious life, which keeps itself distant from everyday life, from the immediate praxis of life, is transformed into an inner lie, without this fact ever being perceived.

How many are they in our day who, driven by a certain noble ethical religiosity, *covet* a proper or just life together with their fellow men, who only desire the very best for their fellow men, but who because they were not able to acquire for themselves a social means of comprehension, leading to *practical* conduct in life, remain unreceptive to the sensibilities that would make this possible.

It is such people, at this moment in world history when the social issues have become so urgent, as fanatical spirits taking themselves to be genuinely practical, who place themselves as an obstacle in the path of a true conduct of life. One can hear them make comments such as: People must raise themselves out of materialism, out of the external material life, which has driven us into the disaster and misfortune of the World War, and they must acquire for themselves a spiritual comprehension of life. — In order to show mankind the path to spirituality, they do not tire of

> quoting personalities who, in by-gone ages, were honoured for their spiritual ways of thinking. If, however, one tries to indicate what the spirit must necessarily accomplish today in practical life, how daily bread must be produced, it is immediately contended that first of all people must be brought once again to acknowledge the spirit. But the heart of the matter today is that the guidelines for the recovery of the social organism are to be found in the strength of spiritual life. It is in this respect not sufficient that people should occupy themselves with spiritual matters as a sideline. On the contrary, everyday life must be formed in accordance with the demands of spiritual life. The tendency to treat 'spiritual life' as a sideline has led the hitherto ruling classes to acquire a taste for social conditions, which have resulted in the current state of affairs.

Societies, like the individual person, may be seen as living organisms which grow and exist in a state of continual transformation. Neither can be governed and regulated like a machine by a system of generally accepted regulations controlled from above or outside. In order to keep one's mind open to the continual changes which life implies for the social body as well as for each person, one must preserve and look after the free creative force in each individual person. Each person's creativity is anchored in that person's own personal conditions of life, in that exact cultural phase in which he exists. This is why Steiner, in educational contexts, emphasizes very strongly how important it is that teaching should not start out from defined pedagogical formulae but must be directly connected with the prevailing culture in any given period, and that it must take into account the differing talents and life courses of the teachers and, above all, the students.

The people must also themselves, from their inner life and outwards *(aus sich heraus)* create this development, according to Steiner's way of seeing it — just as Goethe's plant, which *aus sich heraus* goes through a metamorphosis from seed to fully developed plant, and which the whole time bears within itself the embryos for developing each stage and each portion of the whole, but which is dependent on the surrounding environment for its complete development. It is therefore disastrous for sound social thinking to start out demanding 'evidence' for what is socially necessary, before going into action, in the same way as one demands 'evidence' in science:

> Evidence for a social philosophy of life can only be put forward by one, who is capable of grasping not only that which lies in the established order of things, but also that which, like a seed, lies in the impulses of men — often unnoticed by them themselves, and which strives to be realized.[7]

This is the reason, as I see it, why the teachers, parents and pupils at any Waldorf School must themselves plan, create and transform the school, all the time and freely, to suit each individual child's needs at any particular moment so that it may grow, and to suit the general cultural environment of the same moment.

Steiner, in *The Threefold Social Order,* draws up guidelines towards a new way of thinking, but he stresses that it is up to each individual person to make up his own mind himself on the ideas presented in the book. Perhaps people's ideas will lead to something quite different from what has been put forward here, he writes in the final paragraph. Ideas must always be adjusted to the current cultural environment, and his ideas are intended as *impulses,* not programmes which it might be imagined one could carry out to the letter.[8]

Anthroposophy and Marxism

In recent years, Steiner's ideas on the social issue and the cultural questions woven into it have become the object of growing attention. The interest does not seem to have any distinctive pattern, nor to follow any party-political lines.

In Sweden, as the world over, there are people in completely diverse fields of work who are trying to find alternatives to modern capitalism and who have been inspired to reflect on Steiner's principles as a means of finding new paths. It has been difficult to establish a constructive debate on the epistemological foundation on which anthroposophical activities rest. And yet it is precisely

Rudolf Steiner in 1923.

there, as far as I can understand, that much of the interest is to be found.

In the early days of the Labour Movement in Sweden, there was, as we have seen, an openmindness towards Steiner's work which has long since been forgotten and besides which probably never filtered through to the general public.

Steiner lived in the midst of the cultural debate of his time, where he continually forged his own way. He was well acquainted with the ideas of Marx (1818–83) and pondered over the consequences these might have. He was himself, as we have seen, a teacher for four years at the Workers' Educational Institute in Berlin (see Chapter 5), and agreed with many of the intentions of Marxism for social change. Steiner's ideas, especially on the social issue, are on many points a further development of Marxist points of view. But the fundamental failing of Marxism in his opinion was that it did not see social change in the light of the private individual and his inner development.[9]

In an article entitled *'Astral-Marx,'* the author Joseph Huber expressed surprise at the resemblances which can be found between anthroposophy and Marxism, but he points above all to important differences. Huber stresses that both Marx and Steiner claim to lay out a perspective of the whole. Marx exaggerates the importance of the material in this respect, and Steiner the importance of the ideal. Marx adhered too closely to a mechanistic picture of the world, while Steiner sought to put more accent on organic ways of thinking. Marx placed his emphasis on the economy while Steiner wanted to attach primary importance to what we today call ecological considerations. Marx dwelled primarily on society, while Steiner wished to establish a kind of thinking where one looks more to man as living on the earth and in the universe. Both sought the dignity of man, but Marx looked principally to changing the system and centralization, while Steiner underlined more the need to change people within themselves, stressing autonomy for the parts in the whole. Capital for Marx was only an expression of the material, while Steiner, in the cultural situation which then existed, stressed the significance of the spiritual to the social organism.[10]

Steiner was critical of Marxism which he felt led to a narrow class consciousness instead of to a human self-awareness which must be achieved if changes were to be possible. Huber underlines that what was implied in the word 'anthroposophy' — being conscious of one's humanity — was an unattainable reality for the proletariat after the growth of industrialism and wage employment. For Steiner there was something positive in that context about a so-called *Unternehmungsgeist* (spirit of enterprise) — that is, to be allowed to live out such a spirit in fellowship and in a responsible way — while for Marx that was a more negative aspect, in Huber's opinion.

Marxism is often criticized for its bureaucracy. In a similar way, anthroposophy is often criticized as being sectarian. Huber himself would not call anthroposophy a sect, but speaks rather of a subculture. 'Spirited ideas can be spiritualistic mischief, but can also mean inspiration.' Huber ends his article by stating that there is more to be learned about this.

A full comparative analysis of Marxism and anthroposophy was carried out in Germany in 1986 by Christoph Strawe. There is no room here for a full account of this study, but I would like to take up some of his findings.

In Strawe's opinion, both Marxism and anthroposophy have much to gain from a fruitful dialogue. The Movement of '68 in Germany strove towards a humanization of society and towards increased opportunities for self-realization for the citizens. Many people saw Marx as a leading figure at that time. Today, many are finding their way to Steiner and Strawe therefore finds it imperative to make a comparison between these two currents of the time.

Strawe presents an in-depth analysis of the concept of materialism in Marxism and anthroposophy. This concept is regarded as comprising the crucial point for an understanding of the relationship between the two different directions of ideas. He stresses the decisive importance Steiner attached to material needs, but estimates that these had come to be far too overemphasized in the existing cultural situation of the day. Strawe claims however that in the Soviet Union there had later been a development away from a mechanistic-materialistic psychology of development, towards Vygotski and Leonchev, underlining more the inner activity of man and the reciprocal action between subject and object.[11]

Strawe's account ends with a short chapter suggesting that a dialogue between the two schools of thought could be particularly profitable in the field of education. It is emphasized that in the Soviet Union, in the official principles of pedagogy, there exists a latent interest in the Waldorf system of education. At least, it is claimed, such an interest awoke before it did in the academic pedagogy of Anglo-Saxon countries.[12]

Strawe emphasizes that if one looks at Steiner's so-called 'art of teaching,' one will understand from the phrase itself that it cannot be a question of some elevated pedagogical theory, but an understanding of the growing human being which can only do justice to itself in an immediate pedagogical praxis. Everything here depends on the teacher's ability to apply a pedagogical creativity based on human knowledge. This is not achieved through pedagogical knowledge gained from books. Teaching is rather about making science, art and religion come alive.

It is also made clear here how Steiner endeavoured after the First World War to create a school and a science suited not merely to one class of society, but to *all* people. The new and revolutionary aspect of his school model is its social formulation. Parents, teachers and other friends of the school have here a common legal and management responsibility. The educational work is taken care of by the teaching staff, who are at the same time responsible for administration. Everybody participates in the common management — freely, under personal responsibility and without a headmaster, for instance by holding conferences once a week.

Strawe points out that in the first Waldorf School the idea of the comprehensive school was already being applied. Both sexes were taught together throughout their whole school life. The religious instruction was non-confessional. The state schools' complicated and differentiated course systems were not applied; on the contrary, great importance was placed instead on the social relations themselves in the class. Those students who wished to advance further and take their General Certificate of Education were obliged, in Germany, to supplement their education with an extra year after completing their Waldorf schooling. The strong emphasis on practical elements in the teaching is also reminiscent of socialist pedagogy.

But at the same time Strawe emphasizes that one should not underestimate the differences. His book aims at being one step towards a profitable discussion. To that end it would be particularly important, he says, to provide more opportunities for getting acquainted with practical illustrative examples, which he sees as a necessary prerequisite for serious exchanges of opinion in the future.

The book ends by giving an example of the importance a 'visit to the site' can have. He relates the Bulgarian Minister of Culture, Ludmilla Shivkova's impression of anthroposophical institutions in Järna, Sweden, which she visited during an official visit to Sweden in 1980. On that occasion, she made the following statement:

> If one's goal is that the people of the future shall be more and more creatively active in the development of society, then it is education which must pave the way for and support that development. Such a form of education must be artistic the whole way through. Steiner's pedagogy is pervaded with this in particular. That is why it is the pedagogy of the future. It is not merely something for Sweden or Bulgaria, it is the pedagogy for the human race.[13]

As a thank-you for the visit, the Minister of Culture sent one thousand

Bulgarian rose bushes to the Rudolf Steiner Teacher-Training College outside Stockholm, and they now make up a rose garden there.

It might also be added that several other Eastern politicians have shown interest in anthroposophy, among other alternative movements, as a consequence of the revolutionary development which has taken place in the wake of *perestroika.* This makes further research into this area a matter of importance.[14]

The Russian soul

More and more research points to Steiner's influence among artists and intellectuals, especially in Russia, during the years just prior to the outbreak of the First World War. Primarily due to Sixten Ringbom's research and his book *The Sounding Cosmos* (1970), we can clearly see what significance Steiner had for the Russian artist and former jurist Wassily Kandinsky and thus also for the growth and development of Modernism (see for example Plate 2 and Chapter 5).

But other investigations point to Steiner's influence elsewhere in Russia.[15] An insight into this influence can be gained from the dissertation by the Slavonic student Magnus Ljunggren on one of the greatest modern Russian writers, Andrei Belyi, and his limited but strong bond with Steiner.[16] According to Ljunggren, one can discern a dualistic attitude and a fundamental ambivalence in all Russian Symbolists in their attitude to Steiner and 'spiritual science.'[17] The eminent philosopher, Nikolai Berdyaev, says he for his part could not be a 'Steinerian,' but he recognizes Steiner's 'colossal' historical significance — a symptom of an imminent universal revolution which both the Church and science have lacked the ability to foresee. According to Berdyaev, it is also the eternal 'femininity' of the Russian soul which can be discerned behind the great popularity of anthroposophy in Russia.[18]

Steiner came to break away from theosophy and its Indian-Buddhist focus, wishing instead to give esotericism a Western anchorage. In this connection he then took a close interest in Russia, lying as it does on the borderline between Eastern and Western cultures and ways of thinking.

One apparently overlooked reason for Steiner coming to take such a degree of interest in Russian aspects might also have been his close friendship and marriage with the Russian artist, Marie von Sivers. It was of course she who, according to Steiner himself, brought him to place increasing stress on art in contexts of knowledge. It is also possible that she came to comprise a link between Steiner and the many Russian artists and intellectuals who were interested in theosophy and later also in anthroposophy, if more often than not with ambivalent feelings.[19]

Several people warned about Steiner's 'Germanness' and about his rationalization of spiritual experience. Belyi felt that his own collaboration with Steiner was an extremely harrowing experience but maintains at the same time that it was as if Steiner had moulded together the contrasts within him — as if Germanic rationality and Russian pathos of the soul had contracted a union, as if he thereby had become the first 'cosmic human being.'[20]

After the outbreak of the First World War, repudiation of the 'German' Steiner became all the more distinct amongst the Russian writers. Belyi, however, retained his interest. His elated relationship to Steiner is reminiscent, according to Ljunggren, of that of Edith Södergran, and his state of tension was intensified by the increasingly sceptical attitude of his friends towards anthroposophy.

Steiner did not receive permission to travel to St Petersburg. But Russian revolutionaries and Theosophists found a place of refuge in Helsinki, and when Steiner gave a series of lectures there in 1913 between thirty and forty Russians turned up. Apart from Belyi and Berdyaev, there were many other members of the Symbolist movement in the audience.

Berdyaev held the opinion that Belyi was the greatest creative talent among those who followed Steiner. Anthroposophy is, according to Berdyaev, hardly designed to favour artistic activity, but Belyi had in this respect shown himself to be an exception, and 'spiritual science' had provided him with important artistic impulses. Berdyaev himself was attracted by anthroposophy, but he also had serious objections, not only to Steiner's 'rationalism' but also to the relatively little attention that he, according to Berdyaev, paid to the Dionysian 'creative elements' of the personality.[21]

Berdyaev's judgments about Steiner's 'rationalism' and poor capacity for promoting artistic activity are remarkable, not least considering what an inspiration Steiner then, as today, represented for many people in various artistic *avant garde* movements.

It was during the first decades of the twentieth century that 'the new physics' came to have crucial significance for the whole picture of the world, and for those physicists who were familiar with the problems, this meant revolutionary experiences.[22] There were probably only a very few who in the beginning could possibly understand what it was all about and who were capable of setting the findings into a broader epistemological and philosophical picture. There are reasons for presuming that Steiner could at an early stage have had unusually good grounding for seeing beyond conventional limits or boundaries. He was a graduate from an institute of technology and held a high academic degree in philosophy and was, besides this, active in many different fields of art. This was an unusual mixture which had fundamental significance for his picture of the world. Could it perhaps have been a different kind of rationalism in him that many people — especially searching and free-thinking artists — were enthralled by in his lectures?

Was it perhaps this that captivated the former jurist Kandinsky and contributed to his interest in the role of art and the artist in relation to science and the new picture of the world — ideas that flow through his book *The Art of Spiritual Harmony* — ? Many other artists and writers came during this time to take an interest in the border area between art and science.[23] As with Kandinsky, they gained inspiration for a new creativity and the way was now paved for abstract art and for the so-called 'Modernism.' There is good reason to take issue with Berdyaev, by drawing attention to Steiner's special ability to inspire artists and to the keynote importance he places on creative elements for all — in theoretical as well as in practical contexts, whether in science, the social issue, or elsewhere.

Regarding the significance of the Dionysian creative elements of the personality in scientific connections, it appears that an in-depth study of what Steiner really intended should be able to produce profitable new angles. Is there perhaps really a sort of spiritual fellowship, as Steiner himself claims, that makes it easier for Russians to understand Steiner, than for many others? Steiner maintained what a great task the Russian soul would have for the future of mankind (which, Dostoevsky also believed).[24] In his lectures in Helsinki, Steiner claimed that anthroposophy should be able to 'heal' the young Russian national soul and help it to fulfil its mission between East and West. The vigorous interest in anthroposophical activities which has surged up again in the countries of the Eastern bloc, should be seen in this longer perspective.[25]

With Steiner it is a matter of bridging over divisions, and of searching for methods, also within the framework of science, of training man's ability to experience intermediate positions and his potential to work across disciplinary boundaries rather than in isolated fields. How Steiner in this respect inspired one of the most influential artists in the west today — Joseph Beuys — is examined in the next chapter.

CHAPTER 7
From Goethe to Beuys

A wider concept of art

Joseph Beuys, the artist and pedagogue, was born in 1921 and died in 1986. In the great number of books, exhibition catalogues and films about him which have appeared over the years, some touch on the fact that he was inspired by Rudolf Steiner. This is apparent above all in how their views on art connect with their ideas on changing society, as well as in how they both see the systems of teaching and education should be constructed with the aim of developing people who can contribute positively to society and nature. Increasingly I realize that an understanding of Steiner can lead to a deeper understanding of the sometimes problematic art of Beuys, and vice versa.

Beuys, who lived in Germany, had intense personal experience of the War both as fighter-pilot and prisoner of war. His chief idea is that it is through art, through our own acts of creation, and through our own inherent creativeness that we can achieve an intensified understanding of what life is — of the processes of life and of the structures of society. He seeks democratic creativity and assumes, just like Steiner, that every person is born with an aptitude for art. He sees it as imperative, in a period of estrangement, that man should have the opportunity of training his creative ability, and that he should be able to express it in everything he does. At the present time the opposite is the case. The system of education merely reproduces knowledge, and man's own creative gifts are suppressed both in his work and in his free time.

Beuys has become an unofficial institution and a legend, especially among young people in many parts of the world, for instance in Japan. At the same time, paradoxically, he has remained virtually unknown to many, or else is looked upon as unintelligible, contrived, not to say quite mad. I have the impression that this is so even among art experts

Andy Warhol: Joseph Beuys. *(Photo: Tom Bonnalt.)*

in Sweden in spite of the two great exhibitions of his work in Stockholm, at the Museum of Modern Art in 1971 and at the Liljevalch Gallery of Art in 1987 — not forgetting several minor exhibitions. And his pedagogical ideas and activities appear to be even less known.

It is interesting to compare Beuys with Steiner in terms of the way the surrounding world understands them. Both are contradictory and controversial personalities and phenomena, difficult for our time to grasp. When I saw the 1987 exhibition in Stockholm I really did not understand much of what it had to say and felt the deepest sympathy with all those who had left the exhibition in a state of irritation. I vaguely recollected, however, that Steiner was said to have influenced the work of Beuys, a fact also briefly mentioned in the exhibition catalogue.[1] I therefore became interested in trying to understand in what respect Beuys had been impressed by the ideas of Steiner. I shall give an account here of my conclusions so far, as it is my opinion that this can throw light on Waldorf principles of art and knowledge.

Of permanent importance for Beuys is the aim of making the world more humane — that is, getting the main teaching of Christianity to be applied in our time. To achieve this, society has to be transformed.

A method has to be found to overcome capitalism as well as communism, and to continually develop new alternatives. It is a question of giving people back their capacity to understand the inner, spiritual qualities of things. As a child, man has this ability. A child is able to imagine what a brick in a wall feels and experiences — but once in school all this knowledge is systematically squeezed out of us and is then gone. And with it the basis for our thinking of life as a whole as well as for our consciousness of ecology.[2] Discussions on such issues must take place continuously with everyone taking part, not only artists as at present. Every person is a permanent part of material processes and is a participant in the production of entire and complete contexts of life. Each person has a more or less conscious need to think in terms of the whole. The important thing now, says Beuys, is to find a pedagogic method which will make it possible for people to feel more sure of what they already possess in their heads, because in the future each individual's own thinking must have much greater importance. Art and the artists are necessary in this respect as models for people, to help them dare to trust in their own spiritual experiences.

It is through art that society is shaped and change is brought about. For this we need a wider concept of art — an anthropological concept of art which contains something more than the currently predominating concept. With his own art, and in workshops, seminars and

Joseph Beuys: Brick wall.

interviews, Beuys wants to give expression to and explain how he sees art as a science of freedom. To achieve this aim another kind of knowledge of man and nature is required, as a complement to what science has produced to date. Here, too, he underlines the capacity of art to capture dimensions of human life and the whole 'principle of life' which we suppress in our present way of looking at knowledge.[3]

As a young student Beuys began by studying science. The 1939–45 War interrupted these studies and in that global disaster his experiences led him to feel that everything must be changed radically — more radically than ever before. This cannot be done through physics, he said, nor through the sort of studies or lectures encompassed by the universities. So he left his studies of the natural sciences and went over to art which he considered to be another, more universal, kind of science. Eventually he became professor at the Düsseldorf Academy of Art, initially in Sculpture and later on in a subject called the Principle of Social Formation.

Very soon after starting at the Academy of Art, he discovered that ever since the Renaissance art and science had developed side by side towards a rigid academism. This continued well into the period of modern art. Granted, art strongly expresses man's individual freedom, but it does not accept any consequences, Beuys says. He asked himself what the next step of modern art should be and believed that we must extend the concept of freedom to embrace every kind of work done by man. And he embarked on his search for what he calls a wider, anthropological concept of art.

He now became politically active, working closely with students and youth movements. In 1967 he started the 'New German Student Party' and called it his greatest work of art — not as a provocation, but in accordance with his idea that it is through people that ideas can be developed and produce a true change in practical reality. In art, when this becomes a question of art products and different -isms, the ideas wither away and are consequently abandoned. In 1972 the Party was renamed, becoming an 'Organization for Direct Democracy' and it eventually came to play an important part in the founding of 'Die Grünen' in Germany.

Beuys was inspired by Rudolf Steiner in his political and artistic purpose of getting cultural movements to go beyond theories and art products, and above all activate people into dealing with problems of real life. The point at the heart of the social question is for Beuys, too, man's capabilities in his work and new economic values. Like Steiner, he stressed the importance of the formation of education for producing a basis for change.

In 1973 together with the author and Nobel Laureate Heinrich Böll, he started an association with the aim of working for 'A free international university of creativity and inter-disciplinary science' in Düsseldorf. Similar initiatives were later taken elsewhere in Germany.[4] The principles of this 'Free International University,' FIU, were presented in a manifesto written by Böll and Beuys together, which I reproduce here:

> *Manifesto at the founding of a 'Free International University of Creativity and Interdisciplinary Research'*
>
> Creativity is not limited to people practising one of the traditional forms of art and, even in the case of artists, creativity is not confined to the exercise of their art. Each one of us has a creative potential which is hidden by competitiveness and success-aggression. To recognize, explore and develop this potential is the task of the school.
>
> Creation — whether it be a painting, sculpture, symphony or novel — involves not merely talent, intuition, powers of imagination and application, but also the ability to shape material that could be expanded to other socially relevant spheres.
>
> Conversely, when we consider the ability to organize material that is expected of a worker, a housewife, a farmer, doctor, philosopher, judge or works manager, we find that their work by no means exhausts the full range of their creative abilities.
>
> Whereas the specialist's insulated point of view places the arts and other kinds of work in sharp opposition, it is in fact crucial that the structural, formal and thematic problems of the various work processes should be constantly compared with one another.
>
> The school does not discount the specialist, nor does it adopt an anti-technological stance. It does however reject

the idea of experts and technicians being the sole arbiters in their respective fields. In a spirit of democratic creativity, without regressing to merely mechanical defensive or aggressive clichés, we shall discover the inherent reason in things.

In a new definition of creativity the terms professional and amateur are transcended, and the fallacy of the unworldly artist and the art-alienated non-artist is abandoned.

The founders of the school look for creative stimulation from foreigners working here. This is not to say that it is a prerequisite that we learn from them or that they learn from us. Their cultural traditions and way of life call forth an exchange of creativity that must go beyond preoccupation with varying art forms to a comparison of the structures, formulations and verbal expressions of the material pillars of social life, law, economics, science, religion, and then move on to the investigation or exploration of the 'creativity of the democratic.'

The creativity of the democratic is increasingly discouraged by the progress of bureaucracy, coupled with the aggressive proliferation of an international mass culture. Political creativity is being reduced to the mere delegation of decision and power. The imposition of an international cultural and economic dictatorship by the constantly expanding combines leads to a loss of articulation, learning and the quality of verbal expression.

In the consumer society, where creativity, imagination and intelligence are not articulated, and their expression is prevented, they become defective, harmful and damaging — in contrast to a democratic society — and find outlets in corrupted criminal creativity. Criminality can arise from boredom, from unarticulated creativity. To be reduced to consumer values, to see democratic potential reduced to the occasional election, this can also be regarded as a rejection or a dismissal of democratic creativity.

Environmental pollution advances parallel with a pollution of the world within us. Hope is denounced as Utopian or as illusory, and discarded hope breeds violence. In the school we shall research into the numerous forms of violence, which are by no means confined to weapons or physical force.

As a forum for the confrontation of political or social opponents the school can set up a permanent seminar on social behaviour and its articulate expression.

The founders of the school proceed from the knowledge that since 1945, along with the brutality of the reconstruction period, the gross privileges afforded by monetary reforms, and crude accumulation of possessions and an upbringing resulting in an expense account mentality, many insights and initiatives have been prematurely shattered. The realistic attitude of those who do survive, the idea that living might be the purpose of existence, has been denounced as a romantic fallacy. The Nazis' 'Blood and Soil' doctrine, which ravaged land and spilled blood, has disturbed our relation to tradition and environment. Now, however, it is no longer regarded as romantic but exceedingly realistic to fight for every tree, every plot of undeveloped land, every stream as yet unpoisoned, every old town centre, and against every thoughtless reconstruction scheme. And it is no longer considered romantic to speak of nature. In the permanent trade competition and performance rivalry of the two German political systems which have successfully exerted themselves for recognition, the values of life have been lost. Since the School's concern is with the values of life we shall stress the consciousness of sublimity. The School is based on the principle of interaction whereby no institutional distinction is drawn between the teachers and the taught. The School's activity will be accessible to the public, and it will conduct its work in the public eye. Its open and international character will be constantly reinforced by exhibitions and events in keeping with the concept of creativity.

'Non-artists' could initially be encouraged to discover or explore their creativity by artists attempting to communicate and to explain — in an undidactic manner — the elements and the coordination of their creativity. At the same time we would seek to find out why laws and disciplines in the arts invariably stand in creative opposition to established law and order.

It is not the aim of the School to develop political and cultural directions, or to form styles, or to provide industrial and commercial prototypes. Its chief goal is the encouragement, discovery and furtherance of democratic potential, and the expression of this. In a world increasingly manipulated by publicity, political propaganda, the culture business and the press, it is not to the named, but to the nameless that it will offer a forum. (FIU, 1972)

Social sculpture

Beuys talks about his contact with Steiner's works mainly in a number of interviews.[5] For his part, he does not find that it conflicts with any claim to originality to declare openly that he starts out from Steiner's ideas. As he sees it, there has never been any originality — Steiner proceeds from Goethe and also from the French Revolution, which in reality was an unsuccessful threefold social movement. Such insistence on originality rather shows a lack of interest in other people, Beuys says.

When Beuys read Steiner the first time he put the book aside, just as many people do. This was during the War. Later, during his student days, he again came across a book by Steiner on a bookshelf in the house belonging to the family where he rented a room at that time. This was the *Threefold Social Order.* He says he now experienced an immediate spontaneous relationship to the book and in particular to the ideas expounded in it on a three-way division of the organism of society. Social, political work through artistic formation — so-called social plasticity or social sculpture — which Beuys increasingly came to study together with his students, is based on these ideas put forward by Steiner.

Beuys was deeply impressed by the lectures Steiner had given — especially by a series entitled 'About Bees' which he had given to the workers who built the first Goetheanum. Beuys became interested in the bees' plastic processes, their honey secretion and their wax. He was strongly inspired by Steiner's description of structures in nature which found expression in the hexagonal wax cells, as also in the mystery of liquid honey, in pollination, and so on, where he found analogies to living forms and processes of change connected with human organization.[6]

These are ideas that Beuys later gave form to in such things as his great installation 'The Honey Pump at the Place of Work' which took place over a period of one hundred days at the Dokumenta Exhibition in Kassel in 1977. The idea here, from the starting-point of sculpturally articulated activities, was to start discussions and ideas on the subject of living forms and processes of change in man, in the system of education and in society.

The installation had enormous proportions. It filled the central stairway of the building where the exhibition was held. Two tons of honey and one hundred kilogrammes of liquid margarine were pumped through plastic tubes around the interior of the building with the aid of two aeroplane motors. The installation was accompanied during the whole period of the exhibition by discussions, seminars, lectures, demonstrations and films, all organized by the Free International University. When the hundred days that the exhibition lasted had passed, the whole thing was dismantled and can now be seen in its static form at the Louisiana Museum of Art in Denmark. When I saw all the pieces there in the spring of 1990 they filled an entire room. I can imagine that many unprepared visitors might react with anger — or does curiosity perhaps overcome the incomprehensibility, spurring them to make up their own minds on what it is all about? A few photos and short descriptions of the apparatus at work at the Dokumenta Exhibition were also to be found on the walls of the room, but they were of no great help to the visitor.

The greatest action that Beuys inspired was a monumental time-sculpture called '7000 Oaks' which went on for a period of five years. This action too was part of the annual Dokumenta Exhibitions in Kassel. It was an attempt this time, too, to visualize a totalized and expanded concept of art. A tremendous pile of basalt pillars was heaped up in front of the building where the exhibition was held. These were gradually taken away one by one and erected in different places in the town; at the same time a tree was planted next to each pillar. In this way the historical point at which man had begun to reshape the social organization was indicated. The first oak was planted in Kassel in 1982 and the seven thousandth oak five years later, thereby completing this lengthy action. The message was: 'React against all forces destructive to Nature and life!' After these five years the project had attracted attention far outside the limits of the town of Kassel.

When Beuys talks about a totalized, expanded concept of art he means the formation of connections or relationships in the world. Formation merely in the form of art products to be hung on the walls at home or in a museum is not enough for him. He is trying to bypass everything motionless, static, objective and external. His social sculptures comprise all social formation — such as the formation of legislative conditions, conditions within economy, farming, environmental care and in particular within the educational system. He regards his actions as a kind of philosophical theatre with the help of which he tries to get at indifference and stereotypical thinking. By his frequently provocative actions he wants to activate people into thinking for themselves. The communication of knowledge should not primarily be a matter of a verbal one-way communication between teacher-pupil but should also comprise practical elements. His goal is the achievement of vitality, movement, fellowship and action in man. As Professor of an Academy of Art he does not want to spend time on lectures and orations. He can be said to be seeking a unity between form and content by permitting ideas and arguments to grow and take artistic form. His actions are neither products nor states but instead they have a kind of an inquisitive nature in which the absurd helps to intensify the question. This is accomplished by addressing not only the intellect but also all kinds of sensitivity and intuition. All impressions of the senses are activated — 'use the senses to come to one's senses,' as one might say in English. His type of art is not easy to digest nor should it be. It is all aimed at liberating processes of thought. He deliberately aims to upset people — to create movement and provocation in order to get a discussion going which could lead to action and in the long run have an effect on the constellations of power.

Yet another example: in 1964 Beuys declared that the Berlin Wall should be raised five centimetres — for aesthetic reasons. With this declaration he achieved great political excitement and debate. His reason was yet again to provoke people and make them reflect — to put not so much stress on the physical, visible wall but above all on the invisible, inner reasons which were its cause. Humour is also an important ingredient in his pedagogical methods.

Beuys says Rudolf Steiner's artistic works in the Goetheanum had made intense and stimulative impressions on him too. But the impressions he came away with had faded for his part, on account of the kind of 'business with devotional objects' which he felt had grown up there. He stresses in an interview in an anthroposophical journal that:

> at times there is something unbearable about the anthroposophical art of the 'anthroposophical' artists: they have no real theme. It is often a continual repetition, really an imitation of Steiner's sketches; nothing moves in it.[7]

In the same interview Beuys asks why one so rarely finds Waldorf school pupils who, after leaving school, carry the ideas onwards. One reason, he believes, is that these schools have not succeeded in becoming as free as they should, but have instead become private schools which only a small minority of people in Germany can enjoy. For instance, his own children were not admitted to a Waldorf School. The schools were afraid of what other fee-paying parents might think of such a notorious person being a parent of the same school. Beuys also discusses the significance of anthroposophical developments taking place in step with the enormously powerful forces at work in the modern world.

The situation in which society currently finds itself works in a repressive manner and many people are now demanding a radical change, according to Beuys. If we are to change the structures of power so that democracy can survive, a new process of education is called for, as well as a reformation of the system of education. Beuys maintains that nothing can be achieved except through art. His educational theories are based on the assumption that humans are creative and that it is important we should realize this. Only then can we look upon ourselves as free beings, and this is a necessary prerequisite for our being able to remain anti-authoritarian. Freedom and creativity place us in the position of being able to make decisions, bring about changes and shape things. It is the business of the artistic sector, as well as of the rest of society, to help us become conscious of our own potential.[8] This revolutionary force is to be found in human creativity.

Art equals capital

Separating 'the artistic' and 'the pedagogic' from 'the political' was not adequate for Beuys. From his point of view these have each developed logically apart from one another. From this it follows that a wider concept of art means a wider stimulation of freedom with wide-ranging significance.

This in turn means that all governing and planning on Earth lies in human hands. As a result Beuys rejects all centralized governing and regards instead creative humankind as the only capital for the future.[9] Beuys, like Steiner and Schiller, believes art to be a concept whose reference is the human being. It is identical with what is generally thought of as our creative power. If we are not allowed to use our creative artistic gifts, we lose our volition and life energy and become unable to deal with our studies or work in an energetic, enthusiastic or effective way. Besides which, according to Beuys, if we were given freedom and this potential, we would produce other things — things which humanity and Nature really need. Without freedom humans are not productive in any significant sense.

This is in short what Beuys means when he says that the concept of art is applicable to the concept of capital. It has to do with people's competence in their work. And Beuys thinks that the threefold representation of the organization of society that Steiner describes bares the heart of the social issue and that one can thereby — at any rate in principle — counteract the impotence people experience when their own thoughts and ideas are regarded as insignificant.

Today we humans act fragmentarily. The complete person does not as yet exist. We are either protesters in the form of punks, rockers or hippies, or else we approach the issues on a more theoretical level as intellectuals.

Beuys also worked on examining the trustworthiness of Marxism. He wanted to search out a more honest concept of capital. He felt, as Steiner did, that the spiritual — as this is expressed in art and in the formative creativity of man — has been overlooked and that it, rather than the economy, should be considered the base. Capital is not money but human ability, in his opinion. This is why it is necessary to widen the concept of art into a concept that makes it clear that

Art = Capital. He is well aware that this formula is provocative but he does not regard it as final; instead, he sees it rather as a stimulus.

In his later years Beuys worked more and more with what he called 'social plasticity' — that is, living works of art out in workshop halls together with peripheral activities around the theme of the work of art, and where the social issue was taken up in discussions. As well as this he worked on expanding 'The Free International University' in connection with the ecology movement. Beuys' proposition is wholly and completely practical. But this main direction did not prevent him however, from throughout his whole life simultaneously attaching great importance to painting, drawing and sculpture. In his opinion everything will be altered the very instant the spiritual and industrial production areas of man meet. Then, for instance, an iron rolling mill would at the same time be a university.[10]

Training creative talent

Beuys says it is necessary to point out the great and positive importance materialism has had for the development of mankind. Without materialism no freedom would be possible. But having said that, one must also recognize its many detrimental effects. Man has reduced everything to fit in with the same type of laws as govern matter, where materialism is the norm. Materialism is an ingenious method for analysing matter in order, for example, to develop high technology. But if such a narrow concept of science is allowed to penetrate the whole of our culture then that culture will founder. A one-sided materialism develops the principle of death.[11]

What matters now is to get a hold on the whole picture. Using art it is possible to get through to the spiritual. Art is not something merely retinal, something apprehended by the eye. The retinal aspect is something cold and what must be added is warmth. Here it is basically a matter of substance, the essence, and that is something spiritual.[12] Appreciation of such things has to be trained — for example, by using colours. Or through the use of other materials which Beuys works with in particular, such as grease or wax which change their forms when heated, or felt which has an insulating effect.

Artists should assist in getting people to develop true pictures and to revitalize their talents for experiencing life with all their senses. Beuys does not shun the concept of materialistic science, but he believes that it must be widened through art. Only then will the whole man be developed and only then will he be able to see whole contexts.[13]

Both Beuys and Steiner have a way of approaching questions of knowledge which is both strange and unfamiliar to us. They are both themselves of the opinion that this unfamiliarity applies in particular to highly educated Westerners. Both wish to provide impulses for new ways of behaviour, new thoughts and new ideas. They wish to pose the questions in different ways, but do not claim to have the answers.[14]

I find that Beuys' ideas concerning art and knowledge, in central elements comprise a transformation into modern time of Schiller's ideas on the aesthetic education of man, and also of the work of Goethe, in the way Steiner has interpreted it as the basis for his alternative educational principles.

A principal theme for Beuys is the attempt to make the quest for knowledge an active occupation. The great challenge as he sees it is to get people to be more than mere recipients of ready-made knowledge, which is what education today consists of to such a high degree. It is a question of giving people the opportunity of experiencing phenomena closely and of being able to work on those experiences, to reflect on them and to actively relate with what comes from one's own inner self. This is achieved by using various artistic forms of expression. Ultimately, it is also a question of acting as a human being, as the subject, facing the surrounding world and the stuff of knowledge — using one's 'power of judgment through observation' *(anschauende Urteilskraft)* in order to unite disparate parts, cross over boundaries, grasp the whole, take a stand and obtain the energy to act. It is now a question, Beuys says, like Goethe in his day, of seeing art and science in one context and in addition to this of making thoughts and ideas of this nature become a reality right down to the political attitudes.[15] Only then can art and science be said to be part of 'the green tree of life.'

CHAPTER 8

From Theory of Knowledge to Waldorf Education

Colour is the soul in nature and the whole cosmos, and we are participants of this soul the instant we experience the colours.
Rudolf Steiner

Knowledge of the growing child

At the heart of Waldorf education lies the desire to establish a harmony between the spiritual and the worldly — between the intellectually-spiritual and the physically-corporeal — in the teaching of children and young people. Instead of separating these two aspects of life from each other, points of unity are sought in their teaching. For Rudolf Steiner, this was primarily a question of expanding the limits of both science, art and religion, and of composing a form of education which could more completely develop the talents and aptitudes of human beings. In this chapter I shall try to show something of what Steiner regarded as necessary for his theories to become practical reality in a school.

Long before Steiner came to start a school in 1919 he had thought about what consequences his view of art and science would have for the education of children. He gave lectures on the subject which he was requested to publish in printed form. He revised them himself and in 1907 published a small book entitled *Die Erziehung des Kindes vom Gesichtspunkte der Geisteswissenschaft (The Education of the Child in the Light of Anthroposophy).* This is the only book Steiner published on child upbringing and teaching, apart from what he wrote in his autobiography. However, he gave over three hundred lectures on education which have been published, dating mostly from the start of the first Waldorf School until his death in 1925.

The ideas on education and the development of knowledge which

Steiner formulated prior to 1907 came to practical realization at the end of the First World War. In the chaos which then prevailed, people craved something new and there was a spirit of openness towards experiments in education.

Steiner regarded the causes of war, and conditions in the world in general, as being related to our understanding too little of others. This was true of the different ways of thinking between East and West, between women and men, and especially — in regard to the causes of the First World War — the incapability of those in power to truly understand 'that which lived in the will of the proletariat.'

The workers at the Waldorf-Astoria factory in Stuttgart now wanted Steiner, whom they had heard give lectures at the factory, to start a school for their children. During the previous months Steiner had written his short book *The Threefold Social Order* accompanied by an appeal throughout many German-speaking countries, and also in Scandinavia (see Chapter 6). The factory director also knew Steiner well, and he helped to establish the school without delay. Steiner then gathered a dozen or so highly qualified teachers about him. Some came from far away, and all were well acquainted with Anthroposophy. In other respects they had widely differing backgrounds — some held high academic degrees, and some were practising craftsmen.

Here there is not sufficient room for an in-depth description of the work, or the content of the syllabus. There is already a comprehensive literature on this subject.[1] What I wish to concentrate on here instead, starting out from the epistemological background which I have treated in previous chapters, is to take up what Steiner himself has said and written on how this can and should be realized in practical teaching.

In this respect, I wish to provide insights into and examples from Steiner's lectures on education, from the work at the Waldorf School in Stuttgart, and also, to a certain extent, from the Waldorf system of education which is being developed today, primarily in relation to the training of teachers at the Rudolf Steiner Teacher-Training College in Järna. There has been a lack of studies encompassing both Steiner's theories on art and knowledge, and his views on how this can be incorporated into teaching methodology. A link of this kind between the epistemological and practical points of departure is necessary if we are to understand the approach employed in Waldorf Schools the world over today.

The entire planning for the first Waldorf School in Stuttgart was done within the course of a few summer months. During an intense fortnight the future teachers were given further training by Steiner. Each day began with lectures on the general knowledge of man. Thereafter followed a methodology course and at the end of each day there followed common seminar exercises and discussions, often where tasks given out the day before were gone through and discussed.[2]

In the following, I shall try to show what was regarded as important in this course, and give some examples from some other courses for teachers that Steiner held. He makes a point of saying that in these lectures he only wishes to give stimuli. It is then up to each teacher to formulate his teaching himself. Here it is thus not a matter of concrete tips and formulas, but more about making the teachers reflect on what attitude they themselves should adopt towards the children and towards the subject-matters they are conveying. One problem in the context, as previously mentioned, is that most of what is to be found in written form on education comes from the three hundred or so lectures taken down in shorthand, the accuracy of which may be in doubt. He returns with a certain amount of variation to the same themes, and in my presentation I shall concentrate on these.

Steiner believes that all improvements in teaching must rest on an enhanced general knowledge of man. Since the things he says in his lectures on this subject have also been formulated in writing by him in *Education of the Child.* I shall mainly refer in the following passages to this publication.

Steiner begins by pointing to how many unsolved issues there are 'buzzing around in the world' and invading people's lives. The multitude of formulas, programmes and manifestations for the solution of the problems which are presented deal far too often only with 'the surface of life,' showing little knowledge of the fundamentals of life, and they rarely explore its 'innermost depth.' 'The whole of life is like a plant, which not only contains what one can see with the naked eye, but which also conceals a future state in its inner self,' says Steiner, and gives his example of the transformation of a plant in the same way Goethe does when he speaks of the metamorphosis of plants which one can never fully understand without also acquiring knowledge of the nature of the plant.[3]

Science now draws conclusions only from sentient impressions and believes that it is impossible to gain knowledge of anything lying above and beyond this:

> For spiritual science, this is the same thing as if a blind man were to only accept all the things he can touch and everything that can be inferred from the things he touches, and who therefore rejects the statements of people who can see, as lying outside the possibility of human knowledge.[4]

In the same way as there are colours and light around the blind man which he cannot perceive because he lacks the organs to do so, so spiritual science explains that there are a lot of things around man which he would be able to perceive if he would only train the organs necessary to do so. And it is here that the system of education and pedagogy shows such a tangible failing, resulting in the system of education itself helping to breed spiritual cripples.

Above all, our age needs more knowledge of man in order to be able to give real meaning to practical solutions in the area of education. Steiner's way of talking about and of describing man's inner, concealed nature, is however sometimes difficult to follow. Is it perhaps, in spite of everything, his academic and rational side which comes into play here? I find it strange to create, as he does, systems and classifications of phenomena in life which science tries to steer clear of. But interest in the human subconscious was a response to the needs of his time.

It was at approximately the same time that Freud made his division of the personality into the 'superego,' the 'ego' and the 'id.' In the same way, the psychologist Jean Piaget's attempt to divide human mental development into different stages — which in many ways shows great similarities with Steiner's idea — was something science has found easier to accept. But Steiner tried to also embrace something other and more than this — something which has to do with human beings in the cosmos — and this undeniably presents particular difficulties. Every Waldorf teacher must have a feeling for, and knowledge of this as a basis for teaching.

Steiner speaks of the four essential parts of man — the physical body, the etheric body or life body, the astral body, and the 'I.'[5]

The *physical organization* is something we can observe with our senses. It is really the only element in man's being that current materialistically-focused science accepts. But, according to Steiner, this only comprises one part, one element of the nature of man. This physical organization is subject to the same laws, and is composed of the same substances and forces of physical life, as the whole of the rest of the so-called 'inanimate' world.

Above and beyond this physical organization, Steiner, within the framework of his science, wishes to also differentiate a second element of man's being — *the etheric or vital organization.* He points out that it was regarded for a long time as extremely unscientific to speak of something like the etheric life. But during the first half of the nineteenth century, certain circles began to discuss again the idea that there must be something more and different in a living organism which is not present in dead matter — the something that makes it impossible to dissect a beetle into its various parts and then put it all together again and expect it to live. But in the face of a more materialistically-minded climate, they again abandoned this idea of a special 'life force,' believing that an animate being is built up in the same way as an inanimate one, and that it is only a matter of increased complexity. Steiner says, however, that it is only the most obstinate materialists who continue to deny 'the life force' wholly and completely, and he points out that many scientists have stated that one must assume that it is something resembling this life force or principle of life which man has in common with plants and animals.

As regards the third element of man's being, this is something he has in common only with the animals. Steiner calls this element the *astral* organization. It is the mediator of pain and desire, of instinct and covetousness and so on.

Finally, man also has a fourth element of his being, which he does not share with any other creature on earth, and that is the 'ego' or 'I.' For the person who correctly contemplates the nature of this little word, the gateway to the knowledge of human nature is opened.

> All other names can be applied by all men equally, to the things they designate. Each and every one can call the table 'table' and the chair 'chair.' On the question of the name 'I,' this is not the case. No one can use it to mean someone

> else. Each and every one can only call himself I. The name 'I' can never come to me from outside as a term for me myself. In the act of designating ourselves as 'I,' we must name ourselves, in ourselves. A being who can say 'I' to itself, is a world in itself. The religions which are founded on spiritual knowledge have always realized this. It is for this reason that it has been said: With 'I/ego' the 'divinity' begins to speak from within; for lower creatures the divinity shows itself only in the phenomena of the outer surroundings. The carrier of the ability described here is the 'organization of the ego/I,' the fourth element of man's being.

It is the ego which then works with the subordinate elements of the being. Thus, the ego can even influence the physical organization — one's appearance, gestures and movements. It is in this work of the ego that the cultural development, as far as man is concerned, is expressed.

The various means of culture and education have different effects on different individual elements. Insight into the spirit of art operates particularly on the etheric the vital/life organization:

> When man, through the work of art, gains a sense of something higher and more noble than what the sentient surroundings have to offer, he reshapes his life organization.

In the same way, the life organization is disciplined and ennobled through religious stimulation, and what we call 'conscience' is nothing more than the result of the work of the ego on the life organization. The gathering of knowledge itself concerns the astral organization, but true insight presumes a reshaping of the material, which amongst other things is dependent on higher ideas and concepts — for example, art experiences, religious stimuli — touching on the life organization.

As a tutor one should work on influencing all these four elements of man's being. To do this correctly and at the right time, one must also be aware of certain laws of development. Steiner expresses these in the form of different sheaths which are shed during the process of growing up in the following way: Up to the point when a human being is born, he is surrounded by a physical *maternal sheath.* Thereafter, he is enveloped by two further sheaths — an *etheric sheath* and an *astral sheath.* The etheric sheath disappears at about the age of seven, at the time when the second set of teeth are cut, and the astral sheath remains up until the time of puberty.

This means that as long as the growing human being has not matured sufficiently, there is no point in trying to furnish him with impressions which he is completely incapable of absorbing. So, for example, before the age of seven, certain impressions which ought to get through to the astral organization cannot reach it, just as light and air in the physical world can scarcely reach the physical organization as long as it resides in the maternal womb.

The teacher must be aware of this fact. Otherwise, he will not formulate his teaching in such a way that it can have a formative effect on people in the various stages of development in which they find themselves.

In particular, up to the age of seven, it is important for the tutor to arrange such a physical environment for the child that its physical organs can be moulded in the forms appropriate to this stage. During this period the child's relationship to its environment is developed through *mimicry* and *models.* Everything which is enacted in its surroundings, and which the child can perceive with its senses, now operates on the spiritual forces of the child. 'To this also belong all moral and immoral, wise or foolish acts, to which it may be witness.' It is not modes of expression and wise explanations, not verbalizations or admonitions, which have an effect on the child now, but only everything the adults do, purely visibly, in the child's surroundings. Learning, admonition and various kinds of regulations do not operate to form the physical organization at this stage of development. Such things cannot have any influence on the child until the life-organization stage is reached, and this becomes 'accessible' first at the age of seven and the second dentition, when its protective sheath disappears.

Joy and delight are also part of the forces which have a formative effect on the physical organs. It is therefore important for the tutor/teacher to observe carefully what the developing child demands, covets and takes pleasure in. An art of teaching based on spiritual science must start out from a living realism and not from some 'grey' theory. In this respect a great deal of harm is accomplished beyond doubt 'because of the mistakes committed by many of our friends,' Steiner states.

Apart from joy in the surroundings, an honest, but not forced love is necessary above all things. 'Such a kind of love, which streams warmly through the physical surroundings, hatches in the real meaning of the word the forms of the physical organs.'

In the same way, during the early childhood years, children's songs and beautiful rhythmic impressions have an organ-shaping power. At this age it is also a good thing for the children to imitate letters of which they will learn to understand the meaning first much later on. It is especially important for the children to learn to speak by imitation during this time, since rules and artificial teaching will not accomplish any good, according to Steiner.

If imitation belongs to the phase of development of the physical organization, then the perception of an inner meaning of things speaks to the etheric or life organization. When the outer etheric sheath disappears, roughly at the same time as the second dentition, then the time has come when one, from outside, can begin to have an educational effect on the etheric life. Now it is no longer primarily through physical models that one can influence the developing human being. But it is still a matter of pictures. Now the pictures are filled with imagination, and allegories are filled with inner sense and value which can develop the life organization and become a guiding principle. It is still not abstract concepts which can influence the child, instead it is a matter of visual pictures, not physically visual, but spiritually visual pictures, that is, living inventive or skilful pictures which can be conveyed through oral narration, reading out loud, through painting, dance or through other forms of expression.

It is in this period between 7-14 years of age that the artistic ways of expression have an altogether special significance for the development of the human being. Between the age of seven and puberty it is crucial that the young person:

> does not assimilate the secrets of Nature and the laws of life in terms of rational, sober concepts, but in terms of parables.
>
> Parables for spiritual relationships must present themselves to the soul in such a way that one senses and

discerns life's conformity to law lying behind the parables, rather than grasping it in rational concepts. 'All transient things are parable,' this must be a maxim for education during this period. It is enormously important for man that he receives the secrets of life in parables, before they step forward to meet him in the form of laws of Nature etc. An example may illustrate this. Suppose that one wished to speak with a young person about the immortality of the soul, about its exit from the body. One should do so by taking as example a comparison with the butterfly, how it emerges from the chrysalis. Just as the butterfly raises itself out of the chrysalis, so does the soul too leave the dwelling of the body after death. No human being is going to understand the actual situation in rational terms, if he has not first received it in the form of such an image. Through this kind of allegory one speaks, you see, not merely to reason, but to feeling, to perception, to the whole soul. A young person who has gone through all this, addresses himself to the matter then in a completely different atmosphere when it is *later on* conveyed to him in terms of intellectual concepts. It is even really harmful if man cannot first approach the puzzles of life through his feelings. It is actually imperative that parables should be at the disposal of the teacher in explaining all the laws of Nature and the secrets of the world.

This can illustrate exceedingly well how inspiringly spiritual science can affect practical life. When someone formulates parables in a materialistically rational method of presentation and lets young people partake of them, he will as a rule make little or no impression on them. For then, you see, he must first work out the parables in his mind for himself with all his powers of rationality. Such parables, which one has oneself forced out first, do not have any convincing effect on those who listen to them. When speaking to someone pictorially, you see, then it is not simply so that that person is influenced by what one says or shows, instead, a fine spiritual current flows from the narrator over to the person receiving the message. If the narrator himself does not have a warm feeling for his parable, and does not

> believe in it, then he will not make any impression on the person he is addressing. In order to be able to have an effect in a correct way one must oneself absolutely believe in the parables as in reality. One can only do this when one's thoughts are alive with spiritual knowledge and if the parables themselves have their origins in spiritual science.[6]

One cannot prove the correctness or incorrectness of such questions as deliberated here. It is the task of the reader/listener to judge for himself what he wants to assimilate, and out of which to create his own understanding on which he then can act. Have we perhaps left too little room for reflection and expression of this kind in pedagogical contexts? For my own part, after having associated with texts of this nature over a long period of time, I have come to believe that there might be something important highlighted here, which is missing in the objective, compressed and 'complete' presentation of facts, such as, for example, in the books on general subjects for children at the junior and middle school ages.

An inner, living methodology

Steiner often stressed that the decisive factor for all pedagogy is the nature of the teacher, and that the teacher's first task is to become aware of the fact that she must make something of herself if a beneficial relationship between teacher and pupil is to arise. A teacher can only manage her task if she understands it to be *both* intellectual-sensual and moral-spiritual. Up to now people have worked far too much as if humans only functioned on the physical plane.

All teaching must take into account the general cultural situation of the day. Steiner told the future teachers at the first Waldorf School that the special and chaotic conditions of the time demanded a special kind of pedagogy, saying that we must not forget that the whole of the culture of our time, right up to the spiritual, is focused on human egoism. This must be fought against in all areas.[7]

The teacher must endeavour constantly in her thinking to achieve increasing breadth and flexibility. She must accustom herself to conceiving the syllabus as a whole and approaching the pupil as a whole person, as well as considering how she can collaborate with other teachers on the staff.

A Waldorf teacher normally teaches her class in all subjects, except for a few practical subjects, over a period of eight years. The so-called 'main period teaching' gives the teacher the opportunity to work in a more comprehensive way. Here, teaching is focused on one subject during the morning hours, for a period of four to six weeks. Thus it is really and truly demanded of the teacher that she penetrate into the subject-matter in a diversified way if her teaching is to get through to the pupils. In this way one can also more easily find time for the more artistic aspects of the subject-matter, as also for the pupils' own personal expressions when they are asked to make an account of what they have learned. It then becomes a matter of working with a section without ever forgetting the whole. And being able to at grasp what the whole entails, according to Steiner, is an artistic issue no matter what the subject might be.

By and large, Waldorf teachers try to proceed from the whole to the part in teaching. In the first reading and writing lessons, for instance, they advance from picture to letter, to the annoyance of many people who would like to progress faster. And in mathematics, they do not begin with the complete formula but try first, on the contrary, to find the basic phenomena in observation and in one's own thinking. That is, they do not take the formula first and thereafter the confirmation.[8]

The teacher transforms the subject-matter by starting out from her own thinking — *aus sich heraus.* This makes the subject-matter come alive, and through this it can become sustenance for the child. The teacher herself serves as the instrument, just as in Goethe's method. It rests in the hands of the teacher to awaken creative powers in the pupils, by means of a living, free, artistic teaching. Only then can a relationship, a dialogue arise between the teacher and the pupil. Turning all education into an art has to do with life. One cannot experience the organic unless one is oneself inspired, as well as the subject-matter one is teaching. It is here that our method becomes effective — not as a postulation but because I myself become the instrument. It has to do with one's personal ability to judge (compare Goethe's *Urteilskraft,* or power of judgment).

Returning to Goethe, he approaches the theory of colour as an artist and not as a professional dyer. He sees the whole rather than the part, and he is *at the same time* attentive to the phenomenon and its influence on man, and vice versa (the eye and the light), in a perpetual interplay between part and whole, between subject and object *(aus sich heraus).*

Steiner himself points to our not really being able to explain and comment on Goethe's conceptions, for instance, when it comes to man and colour, within the structure of our given frames of reference. The same is probably true of Steiner's way of expressing himself, as well as that of Waldorf teachers and also of the anthroposophists in general. Is something different demanded of us if we are to understand? In a lecture from 1967, Werner Heisenberg says, in reference to Goethe's scientific publications:

> Maybe they contain a seed, which through careful tending can be brought to development, particularly when the somewhat naïve belief of the nineteenth century in progress has been obliged to step aside in favour of a more sober outlook. One must then once again pose the question what really is the characteristic of this Goethean view of Nature; in what way does its method of looking at Nature differ from that of Newton and his followers? In that connection it is emphasized above all that Goethe's view of nature starts out from man himself, that man and his immediate experience of Nature in Goethe's view of Nature form the central point of departure from which the phenomena submit themselves to a purposeful order.
>
> ... We still have much to learn from Goethe today, that one must not allow all other organs of knowledge to wither away in favour of *one* such organ, the capacity for rational analysis; that it depends instead rather on our trying to grasp reality with all the organs of knowledge given us and that we can rely on the image of reality we then gain also reflecting the important aspects of reality. Let us hope that this will succeed better in the future than it has in our own time, in my generation.[9]

If we are to understand the artistic approach in Waldorf Schools perhaps we must activate several of our organs of knowledge. It is a

Light and shade studies (Class 7). Teenage pupils find themselves in a period of contrasts. Long periods of working only in colour are interspersed with long periods when they only work with black-and-white techniques. (From Carlgren & Klingborg, 1977)

question here of a path to knowledge, starting out from a different subject-object relationship in the process. It is a question of being able to feel the shades of emotion in colour. Perhaps it can be compared to making oneself identical with colour — turning oneself into a wave, as Kandinsky says.[10] Goethe speaks of tuning the soul in unison — *unisono* — with colour, and Steiner says *'Farbe ist Seele der Natur und des ganzen Kosmos, und wir nehmen Anteil an dieser Seele, indem wir das Farbige miterleben'* (Colour is the soul of nature and of the whole cosmos, and we partake of this soul when we experience the colours). At the Rudolf Steiner Teacher-Training College they talk about practising 'breaking the object situation' into which we so easily fall, and about trying to unite oneself with the object. The subject 'creeps into' the object. This is why knowledge of oneself as human being becomes so important.

The approach is also about training oneself in going beyond limits, and in seeing the interplay between complementary colours, and what role man himself as a human being plays in the context as a consciously active creative subject. To be able to live in, and also with, opposites or contrasts means to have an understanding of life. Life itself is a continuum of conquests, but at the same time this implies a regeneration of opposites or contrasts. By being allowed frequent working with colours, the organs of knowledge are trained up, for which we otherwise have no method of development. Such practice offers the opportunity of observing the play between opposites and contrasts in a more reflective and meditative way not only in regard to colours, but also in regard, for instance, to the antithesis spirit-matter.

Steiner gives a more concrete example of how the child can be trained to rely on its own inner thinking, and thereby eventually develop organs of knowledge which we often extinguish rather than stimulate. He writes:

> As the muscles of the hand grow firm and strong in performing the work for which they are fitted, so the brain and other organs of the physical body of man are guided into the right lines of development if they receive the right impression from their environment. An example will best illustrate this point. You can make a doll for a child by folding up an old napkin, making two corners into legs, the other two corners into arms, a knot for the head, and painting eyes, nose and mouth with blots of ink. Or else you can buy the child what they call a 'pretty' doll, with real hair and painted cheeks. We need not dwell on the fact that the 'pretty' doll is of course hideous, and apt to spoil the healthy aesthetic sense for a lifetime. The main educational question is a different one. If the child has before him the folded napkin, he has to fill in from his own imagination all that is needed to make it real and human. This work of the imagination moulds and builds the forms of the brain. The brain unfolds as the muscles of the hand unfold when they do work for which they are fitted. Give the child the so-called 'pretty' doll, and the brain has nothing more to do. Instead of unfolding it becomes stunted and dried up. If

> people could look into the brain as the spiritual researcher can, and see how it builds its forms, they would assuredly give their children only such toys as are fitted to stimulate and vivify its formative activity. Toys with dead mathematical forms alone, have a desolating and killing effect upon the formative forces of the child. On the other hand everything that kindles the imagination of living things works in the right way. Our materialistic age produces few good toys. What a healthy toy it is, for example, which represents by movable wooden figures two smiths facing each other and hammering an anvil. The like can still be bought in country districts. Excellent also are the picture-books where the figures can be set in motion by pulling threads from below, so that the child itself can transform the dead picture into a representation of living action. All this brings about a living mobility of the organs, and by such mobility the right forms of the organs are built up.
>
> These things can of course only be touched on here, but in future Anthroposophy will be called upon to give the necessary indications in detail, and this it is in a position to do. For it is no empty abstraction, but a body of living facts which can give guiding lines for the conduct of life's realities.[11]

In the introductory courses for the first Waldorf teachers, as also in many later courses for teachers around Europe, Steiner also criticizes the predominant psychology and pedagogy of our time which, according to him, had forgotten, or was incapable of understanding, how the spiritual in man stands in relation to the world and the universe. In these disciplines, man is not described at all in his spirituality, but only in his corporeality. Steiner wanted the teachers in the new school to be pioneers in uniting the abstract sciences — history, geography and physics — and knowledge of man — anatomy and physiology.

But one can only teach like this by linking different subjects together — by letting one subject be woven into another, as he often puts it. One can teach history by pouring life into anatomy using history, and one can teach anatomy by giving life to history. The physical and the abstractly spiritual should be fitted into one another, and then you will notice that you have the class with you — that your words actually gain weight at the same time as they gain wings, Steiner says.[12]

The tutor must have a certain feeling towards the developing person — an inner, living methodology, as he puts it, which again leads our thoughts to Goethe *(aus sich heraus,* and so on). Without such a disposition it is impossible to carry on any education at all. We began to lose the capacity for this already in the fourteenth century when an increasingly stronger intellectual and rational development was initiated. Interest then turned outwards instead of inwards and they regarded the matter as one-sidedly as we do today.[13]

There is a great risk as a teacher that one slackens off and becomes lazy. It is therefore necessary to appeal to the imagination everywhere and especially in teacher-training. Steiner develops this theme in various ways in his lectures on education. The categorical imperative for teachers ought to be — 'Keep your imaginations alive!' It is a matter then as a mature person, of making a continuous effort to try to let the liveliness and mobility of the child live within oneself — of not always being staidly adult but of also being able to take pleasure in things as a child does; of being a little childish in one's inner being; of being curious and full of wonder in the face of life.

In order to formulate a subject-matter in a dynamic and flexible fashion, it is not sufficient merely to repeat what it says in a book. In order to counteract the trivial, the emphasis on routine and things that destroy joy, one must make the effort to keep the subject-matter alive within oneself. That ability can be trained up by recounting the subject-matter orally from memory, or by presenting something on the blackboard in the form of a drawing or a painting. One must oneself be captivated by the subject-matter if the children are to be captivated. By creating the story oneself, one becomes flexible in the soul or mind. One becomes stimulated and liberated oneself by this, and can then also convey that enthusiasm to the children. In this way each teacher constantly develops his own ability through constant practice. This is overlooked in teacher-training, according to Steiner. And one can only speculate on what he would think of so-called 'teacher-proof' systems, which recent teaching has so largely come to depend upon, and where the personal creativity and planning of the teacher can be almost entirely avoided.

As far as I understand, it is about *training up a flexible, creative method of conduct towards knowledge, as a counterweight to the risk that the teaching might become routine and locked tight in rules, concepts and formalized classifications.*

The seminar exercises Steiner held every afternoon during the fortnightly course for the first Waldorf teachers give an insight into how he went about his task. Over a period of five days when he covered scientific and mathematical sections of the teaching, he would begin each seminar with speech exercises. The fifth seminar, up to and including the thirteenth, would begin with such exercises — often with the aid of some nonsense, almost idiotic rhyme or a poem which was to be read aloud and preferably learnt by heart.[14] For example, one seminar discussion was begun with this rhyme:

Pfiffig pfeifen aus Näpfen,
Pfäffische Pferde schlüpfend
Pflegend Pflüge hüpfend
Pferchend Pfirsiche Knüpfend

Kopfpfiggig pfeifen aus Näpfen
Napfpfäffische Pferde schlüpfend
Wipfend pflegend Pflüge hüpfend
Tipfend pferchend Pfirsiche Knüpfend.

Steiner emphasized that the *pf-* sound should be pronounced in a lively and athletic way *(turnerisch).* After that, everyone was required to read the poem *'Das Gebet'* from Christian Morgenstern's *Galgenlieder.* Steiner stressed that this was a piece where one should take note of the form as well as of the content:

Die Rehlein beten zur Nacht,
Hab acht!
Halb neun!
Halb zehn!
Halb elf!
Halb zwölf!
Zwölf! ...

Directly after this they went on to lessons on the plant world. The participants of the course contributed various points, and among his comments on these, Steiner pointed out why it is wrong to let children make the acquaintance of scientific concepts too early on. Scientific systematization comes later, he said. First the children must make the acquaintance of the spiritual in the forms of the plants.

When the group met the next day after the morning lectures, they again began with a speech exercise of the tongue-twisting kind, designed to train up the elasticity of the speech organ, suppleness, and also rhythm and breathing when speaking.

Ketzer petzten jetzt kläglich
Letztlich leicht skeptisch.

One should get used to the tongue saying it, as it were, by itself, Steiner commented:

Zuwider zwingen zwar
Zweizweckige Zwacker zu wenig
Zwanzig Zwerge,
Die sehnige Krebse
Sicher suchend schmausen,
Das schmatzende Schmachter
Schmiegsam schnellstens
Schnurrig schnalzen.

After this the first stanza of another poem by Morgenstern '*Wir fanden ein Pfad*' was read:

Wer vom Ziel nichts weiss,
Kann den Weg nicht haben,
Wird im selben Kreis
All sein Leben traben;
Kommt am Ende hin
Wo er hergerückt,
Hat der Menge Sinn
Nur noch mehr zerstückt.

After this, the lessons on the plants were continued. The following afternoon began with the following speech exercise:

Ketzerkrächser petzten jetzt kläglich
Letzlich plötzlich leicht skeptisch.

Steiner observed that it was correct only when one could reel it off by heart *(sie auswendig herschnurren kann).* 'Consciously pronounce every syllable!' he added. Then the first and second stanzas of Morgenstern's poem were read aloud, before going on to the science lesson. Then they went on to map-drawing, area calculation, etc.

The next day began with this rhyme, accompanied by a recommendation to memorize and practise it:

Klipp plack plick glick
Klingt Klapperrichtig
Knatternd trappend
Rossegetrippel.

After this followed the Morgenstern poem *'Wir fanden ein Pfad.'* And after this, discussions on the calculation of area, arithmetic, moving on to algebra and the calculation of interest, which children can easily understand, according to Steiner.

Can we perhaps develop a more flexible intellect in such a way? Can we — by means of a new and different kind of purposefulness — train children into ways of thinking of the whole *at the same time as* thinking analytically in terms of parts?

The words a teacher uses must be warm and emotionally tinged, and this can be attained if she is imbued with a genuinely spiritual-scientific frame of mind. All pedagogy and all education is dry and dead if it does not constantly have a fresh input from a source of this nature, Steiner believes.

The artistic aspect has a significance here on many different levels. So, for example, it is up to the teacher to be able to keep a source alive within himself which can enable him to devise visual images for the children. But equally important are the art exercises, so that the children's ability to learn for themselves and to develop by creating their own inner images can be constantly trained. By virtue of this, they develop and lay the foundation of a life-long capacity to attach importance not only to outer visible things, but also to the inner, invisible, spiritual qualities of life.

Reason is really first born at puberty and prior to this 'one must not shrivel up the spirit by overloading it with rational concepts.' Between the years of 7 and 14 one need not place such great weight, as is generally the case, on the children having to comprehend everything taught. Concepts are only *one* of the means of gaining an understanding of the things of this world.

Here Steiner cites Jean Paul, whose book on education he regards as excellent. There it is underlined that one should not be afraid of appearing to be incomprehensible:

> If the eight-year-old child, with his developed speech, is understood by the child of three, why do you want to narrow down your language to the little one's childish prattle? Always speak to the child some years ahead — do not the men of genius speak to us centuries ahead in books?

Regarding the importance of a joyful time together with the children in the context of teaching, Steiner quotes Jean Paul here as well:

> The very brightness and decision of children should give us brightness and decision when we speak to them. We can learn from their speech as well as teach them from our own. Their word-building is bold, yet remarkably accurate! For instance, I have heard the following expressions used by three- and four-year-old children: — 'the barreler' (for the maker of barrels) — 'the sky-mouse' (for the bat) — 'I am the seeing-through man (standing behind a telescope) — 'I'd like to be a ginger-bread-eater' — 'he joked me down from the chair' — 'See how one o'clock it is!' ...[15]

Training the memory through retaining information — such as a multiplication table, which one does not necessarily have to comprehend — is another example of what should be done during the years before puberty.

Comprehending nature with the heart

A teaching which depends too much on sense-observation is not appropriate for children before puberty. Such teaching, according to Steiner, has its origins in a materialistic philosophy, and the spiritual and emotional dimension which must be made visible for the children at this stage of their development, is then missed. Steiner stresses that as a teacher one must make everything visual in a spiritual and artistic way for young pupils:

> One should not, for example, be satisfied with only objectively demonstrating a plant, a grain of corn or a flower. Everything should be an image of the spiritual. A grain of corn does not consist only of that which reveals itself to the naked eye. Inside it, the whole new plant conceals itself, invisible to the eye. That something like that is more than what the senses can apprehend, must be apprehended in a living way through feeling and the imagination. A divining of the secrets of life must arise in the soul. One cannot object that the purely sensory observations would become blurred through such a procedure. On the contrary, when we halt at the mere objective demonstration, the truth falls short of the mark. For the whole reality of a thing consists of *spirit and matter,* and a correct observation need not be less accurate if one activates all the powers of the soul, and not only those of the physical senses. If only all people, in the same way as the spiritual researcher, could see how much of *soul* and *body* is devastated by a solely sentient method of teaching by object lessons, they would not adhere so closely to it. What use is it, in a higher sense, to show all sorts of minerals, plants, animals and physical experiments to young people if this is not associated with one's using the sentient images to allow the young people to divine the spiritual secrets? In all probability, a materialistically-minded person will not know what to make of what has been said here. This is something the spiritual researcher understands only

> too well. But for him it is also clear that a really practical art of education can never grow out of a materialistic way of thinking. Practical as this attitude thinks itself to be, materialistic thought is impractical when it comes to understanding life in a living way. In the face of true reality materialistic thought is often sheer fantasy, though indeed to the materialist the practical presentations of spiritual science appear as sheer fantasy. There are, beyond doubt, many obstacles to be overcome before the principles of spiritual science, which have been engendered entirely by life itself, penetrate into the art of education. But this is of course completely natural. For the present the truths of spiritual science *must* still appear strange to many people. But they will be incorporated into culture, if they really are the truth.[16]

In nature study one must also teach in such a way that the pupils can get a sense of the connection between Nature and spirit — between outer and inner Nature. This is of fundamental significance for the feeling for Nature the pupils will gain, and for their awareness of Nature. In the 7-14 age-group it is important, as in all teaching, that the teaching does not become too intellectual with a multitude of lifeless concepts and definitions of the kind which science employs. This intellectual subject-matter can be brought to life by the teacher. The spiritual dimension existing in everything can be brought forward for instance, by a more artistic formulation of the teacher's presentation and by the pupils expressing themselves creatively in their workbooks and other schoolwork, as well as in dramatizations and such like. In such ways they will acquire a more all-embracing and more intimate understanding of life, which will have both a social and an hygienic effect.

In the teaching methods at the Rudolf Steiner Teacher-Training College in Järna, I have seen how they endeavour, not least in the science subjects, to give the future teachers an idea of what it means to teach not merely in an objectively correct way, but also in a way that takes Nature more 'to heart.'

Steiner also maintains in the methodology course that one should never teach facts, nor analyse these, during trips together with the pupils out into the countryside. On these nature-trips, one should only take in the beauty and joy of the experience of Nature. One may point to various remarkable and droll things — such as how a small beetle crawls through the undergrowth, and so on. One should listen to the music of Nature — and to the peace and quiet, and allow the pupils to experience how humanity is part of Nature. Before leaving for home, one may collect various products of Nature to take home to the classroom, but it is important to save the business of analysis until afterwards, so that their experience of Nature itself is not disturbed. One should also underline this difference to the pupils — the difference between analysing lifeless natural matter indoors and of experiencing the life out there. Both are necessary, but we must not lose our sense of the difference, Steiner says.

He also warns, as we have seen earlier, about using teaching purely by object lessons too soon. It must not be allowed to become banal, one should instead try to lift it up onto a higher level. This is possible with geometry and when teaching Pythagoras' theorem, for instance. But this endeavour should exist everywhere in dealing with the younger age-groups. If, for example, the pupils are being taught about some animal, they should be allowed to experience the animal and its life in a pictorial way that emphasizes the whole aspect of the animal — where the animal appears in its total context, preferably also in its cosmic context. On one occasion, during my observation work on Waldorf teaching, I met an older, experienced Waldorf teacher, who told me with horror in her voice that she had heard that the children in an ordinary junior school, were dissecting a fish and also cows' eyes. She regarded this as completely wrong for children at that age, who were not yet mature enough for that type of learning. One should avoid the fragmented and the particular as well as far too objective facts and should instead try to give a more artistic presentation, via fairy tales, painting, songs and other forms of expression. If this is done in a proper way in the younger age-groups, the pupils can then assimilate a more objective and factual type of learning further along the system of education, and still not lose their grasp of the whole.

Steiner would probably have serious objections to many of the textbooks used today in which compressed presentations in factual prose describe things such as the development of the embryo. This is what he had to say on textbooks in a lecture in 1924:

> In modern manuals one can read accounts of the most wonderful courses of Nature, such as the presentations of the embryonic life, and this is then taken up in our schools. But one can also become completely desperate over the intellectual chill which meets one and how everything artistic — and there is nothing purely intellectual in living nature — how this artistic aspect has been deliberately and methodically obliterated here. If one exaggerates this intellectual aspect and is not able to transform the subject-matter into images, then there arises a fine, subtle disarray in the child's creative exploration of knowledge.[17]

One prerequisite for effective teaching then is that the teacher should be aware of the four essential parts in the development of children. As well as this, they must know how *thought, emotion* and *will* should be dealt with during the various stages of growing up, in order for the *whole* person to be able to be developed to the maximum.

During the first seven school years when the etheric or life body is developing, the will power and the character are influenced by the correct development of the feelings. The child then needs such things as religious stimulation so that the individual can feel incorporated into the cosmos. If he does not feel himself to be securely bonded with something divinely-spiritual, then his will and character are bound to become uncertain, disunited and unsound, in Steiner's view. I imagine that it is probably when these stimuli are missing that the teaching adopts a lecturing tone instead of an enthusiastic one.

The world of feeling is developed in the correct manner through artistic allegories and symbols. It is particularly important here to venture to enter deeply into the beauty and secrets of nature. There one will find the best opportunities for nurturing the aesthetic mind and of arousing one's sense of wonder in life. Through music the etheric body is furnished with the rhythm which then makes it possible for man to experience the hidden rhythms existing in everything. In the same way, all the other forms of art should be practised, especially during this period. Provided the teacher has the right feeling for what should be done in these respects, the whole thing is very simple and calls only for the simplest of means.

The joy of life, the love of existence, the strength to work, all this develops for one's whole life if one nurtures a sense of beauty and art. And relationships between people — how noble and beautiful they become under this influence. The moral sense is of course also developed during these years through images from life as well as through the model authorities the child looks up to, and it becomes assured if one feels through one's sense of beauty that what is good is beautiful at the same time, and what is bad, is ugly.

Thinking, as a form of its own, as an inner life lived in abstract terms, must, during the period of life in question, as yet remain in the background. Without outside influence, it must as it were develop itself by itself, while the soul partakes of the parables and images of life and the secrets of nature. Together with the other soul experiences between the age of seven and puberty, thinking must thus develop, and the power of judgment mature. And it must take place in such a way that the person then, after puberty, becomes capable of forming his own opinion on life and knowledge, with complete independence. The less one has previously directly influenced the development of the power of judgment, and the better one has indirectly done so by developing the other faculties of the soul, the better it is for the young person's entire later life.

Spiritual science provides the right bases not only for the spiritual side of education but also for the physical side. To give a typical example here, I shall touch on gymnastics and sports for young people. Just as love and joy must permeate the milieu during the first years of childhood, so too must the developing etheric body really and truly feel itself growing, feel its powers perpetually increasing by means of physical exercises.

Gymnastics exercises must for example be composed so that the following feeling in the young person appears at each movement and at each step: 'I can feel strength growing within me.' And this feeling must fill his whole inner being as a wholesome joy, as pleasure. In order to be

> able to think up what gymnastics exercises might fill these requirements, one must definitely possess more than a rational, anatomical and physiological knowledge of the human body. In addition, an intimate, intuitive knowledge of the connection between happiness and pleasure on the one side, and the positions and movements of the human body on the other, is a necessary requirement. The person arranging such exercises must be able to experience how a movement or a position of the limbs produces a pleasurable, pleasant sensation of strength, while another produces a sort of loss of strength, etc. ... If it is going to be possible to perform gymnastics and physical exercises following these guidelines, then something is demanded of the teacher which only spiritual science and, above all, an anthroposophical habit of mind can provide. It is therefore not necessary for a person to be directly able to see into the spiritual worlds. He need only have a sense for using in practice what emerges from spiritual science. If the insights of spiritual-science were to be applied in particular to practical areas such as education, then the completely unnecessary discussion which says that these insights must first be proved, would soon cease. For the person who uses them correctly, they will be proved by life itself, by virtue of their using them in a wholesome and strong manner. Precisely because these insights are confirmed by practice, he will find that they are true, and he must thereby find them better proved than through all the 'logical' and so-called 'scientific arguments.' Spiritual truths are best discerned by their fruits, not by alleged, however scientific, evidence, which can be scarcely more than a logical skirmishing.[18]

This leaves room, of course, for many objections. One might be irritated by, and critical of, the self-assured and unreserved way Steiner presents his case. But I leave it up to my reader to decide whether or not they can find something in this which could stimulate new ideas. More than that was not actually Steiner's intention:

> However interesting it may be to follow a great spirit on his way, I will only follow someone as long as he develops me personally.

We might of course consider whether we could possibly develop a better feeling for Nature and thereby treat Nature and people and life differently if we were really allowed to develop more artistic means of expression, in contexts of knowledge as well. Would we then perhaps have a greater sensitivity towards the role of man in the general scheme of things and towards his inner spiritual needs, as well as towards the connection with the spiritual aspect of nature? We are hardly going to find methods of examining and answering such questions within the framework of the limits of our present science, with its demands for proof or concrete examples, as starting-points. But still I imagine that most people today believe that many of the problems of the earth must *also* be analysed from the perspective of aspects of life which are more difficult to define and gauge. This discussion is necessary, and here Steiner's ideas and practical advice on the role of art in the context of education can inspire to new and different ideas, not only for the Waldorf Schools themselves, but also far beyond these, in ordinary schools and universities.

From soul to soul

The teacher's task of bringing physical life into harmony with mental-spiritual life — and allowing these to harmonize with each other — should naturally not be formulated expressly in the teaching. But as teachers, we must be pervaded with the idea — then a relationship between teacher and pupil will arise through inner powers which can provide a profitable basis for learning. The stuff of knowledge should be passed on, not from mouth to mouth, nor from eye to eye, but from soul to soul.

To achieve this, all of teaching and methodology must be infused with the artistic aspect. It is only then that we can grasp the whole human being and *also reach through to his will.* Life and living must be approached with an artistic frame of mind — something which has today vanished from our way of thinking about teaching.

Above: *Eurythmy class at the Kristoffer School.*

Below: *Dramatization of 'The Fisherman and his Wife,' Järna Waldorf School.*

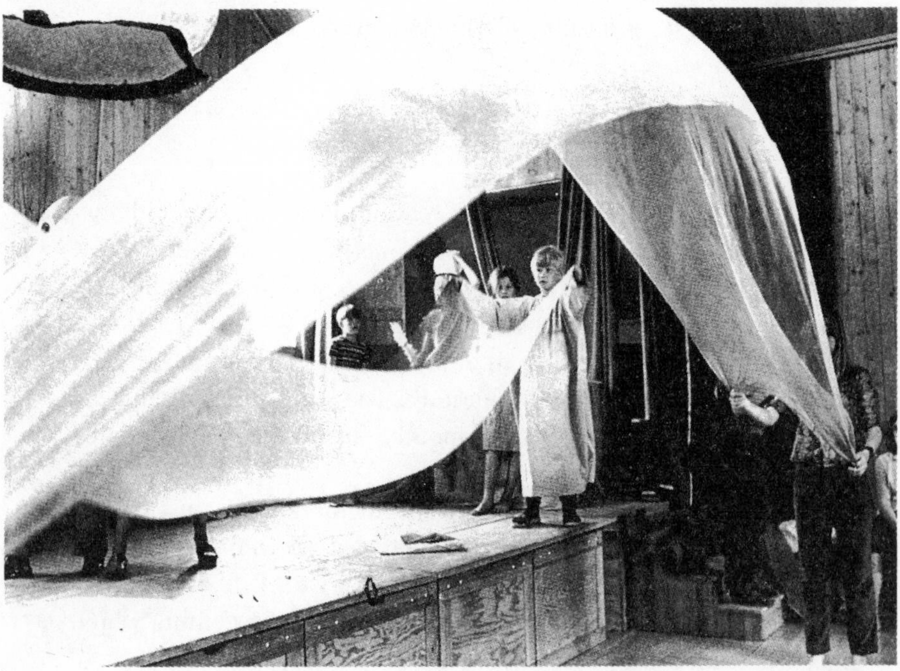

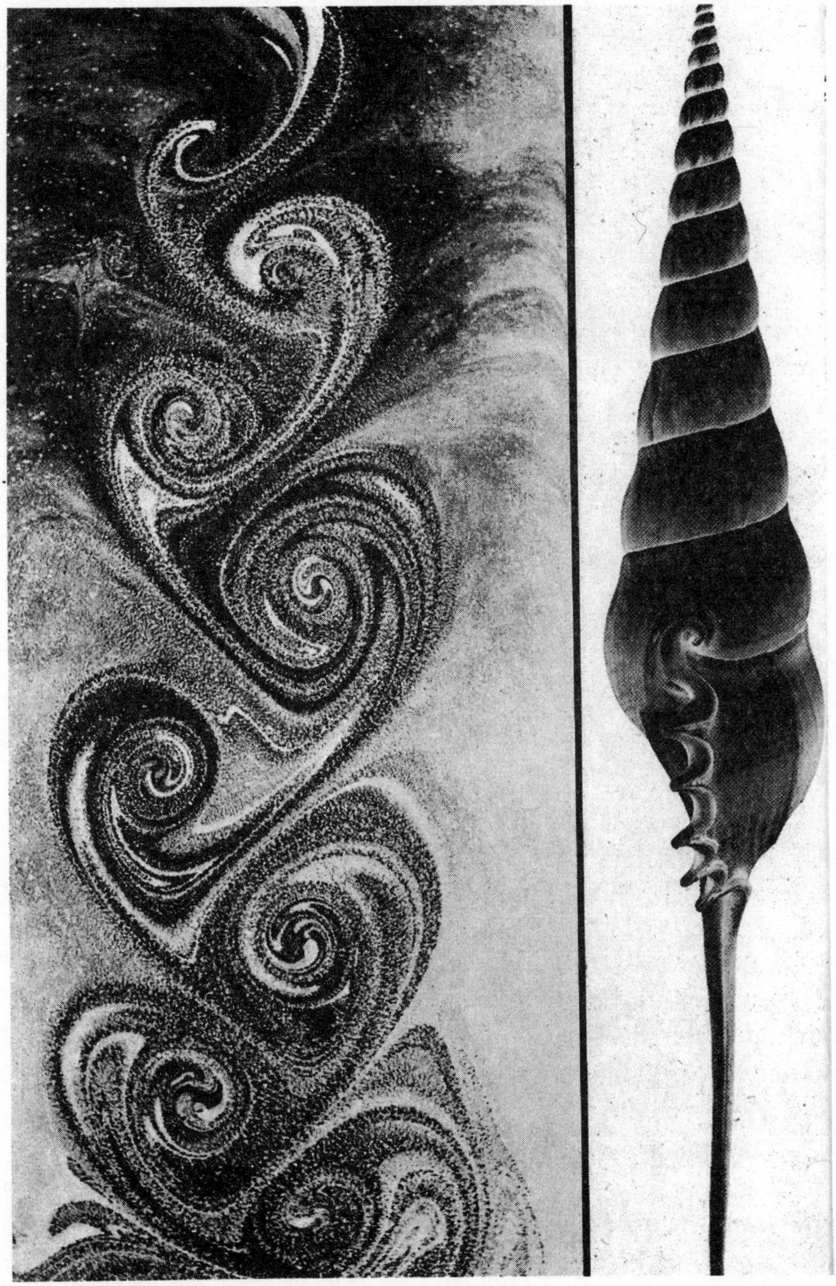

Water whirling in eddies. (From Sensitive Chaos *by Theodor Schwenk.)*

The teacher's own knowledge has no meaning for the very young child. It is not good enough to pass on knowledge to a child in the same form one has assimilated it. Learning loses its meaning for the child if it is merely passed on. One must transform learning with the aid of art — transform everything into pictures, pictures which can become seeds for the children: 'the whole human being resounds when you work in images.' The teacher must awaken imponderable powers between herself and the child. Up to the age of puberty, it is of far less significance how much teaching matter the teacher carries in her head, than that she can convert everything she does in the presence of the child into visual images in living form. In the pupil, independent learning really gains significance only after puberty.[19]

Establishing a harmony between the physically-corporeal and the mental-spiritual is a matter of being able to deal with the substance of knowledge, the teaching matter. Steiner differentiates between three levels of knowledge material. The first level is exemplified by learning to read, which is built on human writing which has arisen through human activity — through conventions on the physical plane. This, according to Steiner, is somewhat different from teaching number. In that subject, one must be aware as a teacher that the main thing is not what shapes the figures have, but that what is actually signified by these shapes, the ideas inherent in them, have a more spiritual character than the letters on which reading and writing are constructed. And when we finally come into the artistic area we come to the spiritual/mental area.

Thus we work most physically when reading and writing, somewhat less physically in number; and when we teach music, drawing and other areas of art, we teach spiritually/mentally. In a rational kind of teaching we can bind these three stimuli together, and in precisely that way we can produce a harmonization of the human being.

In teaching these age-groups it does not help to instruct and explain or to arouse interest by means of sensations; instead, the most efficacious method is to tell fairy tales and myths and let the children paint and draw, so as to try and develop an interest out of the child's own being. This presupposes partly that one likes the children and does it out of love, but partly also that one is oneself enthusiastic about what one is relating. We cannot present something theoretically to children for them to learn from it, if we ourselves do not have real insight into the material and are not captivated by it.

One area that Steiner attaches particular importance to here is the area of linguistics. He gives incentives in a number of different ways to what attitude one should adopt to problems in language teaching in the Waldorf educational system.

He speaks against the rigorous spelling rules employed in the German school system. He warns that the intimacies of the language will disappear and, along with them, important qualities in life, if the school and the teachers do not feel themselves free in linguistic respects. He takes Goethe, here too, as an example and tells of the many spelling mistakes he made, especially in his youth, and which would not have been passed in the language exams the schools employ. In the methodology course for the Waldorf teachers of 1919, Steiner says:

> We can thus always link up with man and his relationship with the world around him when we teach the children to write, and when we teach them to read by making them read what they have written.
>
> Something which we should not forget to pay attention to is that a certain longing to be completely free is part of teaching. Note how a certain freedom flows into this method of telling you how to organize the teaching, because it has something to do with a freedom coming from inside. I beg you to pay attention so that you do not make yourselves unfree by directly sitting down and swotting up how the art of writing arose during the change-over from Egyptian to Phoenician culture; instead, you should develop your own abilities. There is nothing to stop one teacher from doing things in one way and another in a different way. Everyone cannot use a dancing bear; someone will perhaps use something much better for the same purpose. The final result, though, can be achieved just as well by one teacher as the other, but each and every person gives part of himself when he teaches. His freedom remains quite inviolate. The more a body of teachers wishes to retain its freedom in this respect, the more it can enter into teaching, the more it will be enabled to devote itself to teaching.

This is something that has been almost completely lost in recent times. I shall give you an example. Some time ago — the younger members of the audience have perhaps not experienced this, but for the older ones who understood what it was all about, it was a great nuisance — some time ago something was to be introduced into the cultural sphere which resembled the famous 'Imperial German National Sauce' of the material sphere. You know, how it has been stressed that all inns that did not reckon on having foreign visitors, only on German ones, were required to prepare a standardized sauce. It was called the 'Imperial German National Sauce,' they wanted it to be standardized. Now they also wanted to formulate spelling, orthography, in a standardized fashion.

In questions of this nature, people have a remarkable attitude. One can study this disposition in concrete cases. There happens to be a very beautiful and tender relationship described in German cultural life, namely, the relationship between Novalis and a young woman. This relationship is so beautiful because Novalis, after the death of the young woman, consciously continued to live together with her when she was already in the spiritual world. He also speaks of this coexistence. He follows her through death in an inner, meditative activity of the soul. It is one of the most exquisite and intimate things one can read about in German literary history, this relationship between Novalis and his beloved.

Now there is a very shrewd, strictly philosophical dissertation, which is also very interesting, on the relationship between Novalis and his beloved. It is written by a German scholar. In it, the tender, beautiful relationship is 'cleared up,' as it is proved that the female party died before she had learnt to spell correctly! She made spelling mistakes in her letters! In short, we are given a thoroughly banal picture of this person who had such a special relationship to Novalis — all according to the strictest scientific accuracy. This scientific method is so good that each and every person writing a dissertation in which he employs this method deserves to get top marks in his diploma.

I should only like to remind you that Goethe could never really spell correctly, that he actually made spelling mistakes all his life, especially in his youth. In spite of this, he was able to rise to his Goethean greatness! Not to mention people he was in contact with and whom he estimated very highly — indeed, their letters, which now often come out in facsimile, would be riddled with red ink if they fell into the hands of a schoolmaster. They would get very bad marks in an examination.

This is linked together with a fairly unfree aspect in our lives which should not be allowed to gain a foothold in teaching and education. A few decades ago it was, however, allowed to prevail in a way that the more enlightened teachers found rather irritating. A standard German orthography was to be introduced, the famous 'Puttkammer Orthography.' Thus, the State not only ran the country, it also regulated orthography by means of legislation. And the result is also only as can be expected! For we have essentially lost a great deal through this Puttkammer orthography which would still have been able to make us attentive today to certain intimacies in the German language. Through reading so much abstract scribbling today, people have lost a lot of things which could previously live in the German language. These get lost in the so-called 'written language.'

In a question of this nature it is important above all to have the right attitude. One cannot permit any old kind of spelling to flourish, naturally, but one should at least be aware of how the one and the other extreme stands on the question of this subject.[20]

Life must surge through all intellectual work in school. And this takes place through a spiritualization of the teaching, which in turn can be achieved through art and artistic formulation. This is when teaching becomes an art. If the teacher succeeds in this, it leads to effects on many different levels. It can imbue the teacher with a feeling of freedom and security which may be necessary if one is to be able to handle the many difficult situations one can be faced with. Here the role of humour is also emphasized. If one were to enter a classroom, for example, and be met by a collection of rowdy children laughing at one, Steiner says, one should be so strengthened by such thoughts within one, that one would take no notice of the laughing — that one could take it as an external fact only, like the fact that one went out without an umbrella and it suddenly began to rain. Of course it is unpleasant, and of course there is a difference between being subjected to an outburst of laughter and to a shower of rain but, as a teacher, one must learn to take such a outburst of laughter in the same way as a shower of rain.[21]

With the passing of time, Steiner became increasingly convinced of the importance of the artistic aspect in educational contexts, and is said at the end of his life to have emphasized that this aspect in particular should be given even greater weight in the future, not only in the education of children but also in the education of adults. It seems that Waldorf education in Sweden has certainly followed this counsel, with children and adults.[22]

Reverence for the work of the hand

The first lesson at all Waldorf Schools is devoted to the importance of the hand.[23] The small beginners class pupils arrive, accompanied by their parents, all prepared for this new period of their child's life. They know that now, above all, intellectual training is about to begin. To counteract this at the outset, the teacher should devote this lesson to highlighting what a remarkable tool we have in the human hand, and how fundamental the work of the hand is for our lives. Everyone should, from the very beginning, have the sense that at this school, in the development of knowledge, the hand is accorded equal importance with the head and purely intellectual work.

Here the aim is to get us, as adults, not to make such a sharp division between body and mind or spirit. Steiner wants to make the future Waldorf teachers, as well as the children's parents, see the physically practical aspect and its connection with the spiritual. This reminds us of the philosopher who, in Steiner's view, can never be really prominent in his profession if he cannot also sew a button on to his trousers. It is once again a matter of being able to work with the whole man. And Steiner persists in his view that the person who would assert some theory or other really must stand much closer to life than a person who is a cobbler or a tailor. Otherwise all the ideas expressed turn into something which have very little to do with life and praxis. But to make theory and practice interplay with each other, and thereby, to couple thinking to the hand as well as to the whole body, is one of the most difficult tasks a teacher has. The basis for this must be laid from the first year of school, but the task is just as important throughout the whole of school life and in the final year, when the pupils are preparing to go out into the community where the connection between theory and practice rarely works, they need to have this made lucidly clear.

In the Waldorf School the emphasis throughout the whole of school life is placed on tangibility in teaching contexts. They endeavour to make the various craft subjects, with the professionals who teach these subjects, an integrated and equally qualified and important part of the life of the school as the theoretical subjects and their teachers. Today, at least in the Swedish Waldorf Schools, craft teaching is regarded as more important than ever, as the opportunities afforded for developing knowledge in an intimate, physical, practical way are so extremely curtailed. They therefore still invest, despite the tight financial conditions in which they work, in building craft centres of high quality and thereby tangibly accentuate the importance they place on this aspect.

This highlighting of the importance of handiwork and handicraft is built largely on traditions from the first Waldorf School. Here, among others the artist and geometry teacher Hedwig Hauck was responsible for the teaching. In 1937 she published a book entitled *'Handarbeit und Kunstgewerbe — Angaben von Rudolf Steiner'* (Handiwork and Applied Arts — Statements made by Rudolf Steiner), a comprehensive work gathering all of Steiner's references on this subject. The greater part of the first edition was destroyed during the War, but interest in later reprints has been great, and in 1981 the book came out in a fifth edition. It includes every reference to the significance of handicrafts made by Steiner in his books, lectures and articles, and, because he frequently refers to a wider context, an enormous number of of the texts deal with art and handicrafts in a broader sense. Steiner believes for example that we must ask ourselves what it means for us when an artistic handicraft vanishes. Throughout the modern world technology is taking over — both at home and at work — and the inner connection between humans and their work is at risk of disappearing. The nature of our surroundings becomes increasingly divested of human characteristics. The teacher must feel within herself, and understand in depth, the significance of handicraft.

Hauck states in her preface that the book is important not only for teachers and those who work particularly with handicrafts and applied arts. Technicians, doctors, educational therapists and theologians should also be able to find inspiration in this material.

In the Waldorf School all the children are taught co-educationally for the whole of their school life. But in the 10th class (age 16) a certain amount of division according to sex can occur in the practical teaching. The boys are taught from the first class to both knit and crochet together with the girls, without their male dignity coming to harm. This is not done primarily to teach them the skills as such. The main reason instead is for every individual to be given the opportunity to develop an understanding of various phenomena and of various directions of interest. One of the main problems of our times is that the one person understands too little of what the other is doing today, and we must therefore establish a better understanding of one another's interests and fields of work. But in addition, in Steiner's view, by knitting and crocheting one develops a clear way of thinking and a sound logic, something which many men know nothing of today. One's thinking becomes sound and solid because it is always corrected by reality in such a palpable way — if you do not follow the rules, you drop stitches, and that has a serious effect on the whole end-product.[24]

In the usual over-intellectualized kind of school, handiwork can also be important for creating harmony and well-being. Pupils with learning difficulties or merely tired of too much intellectual work, can join special handicraft groups in the afternoons for a period of several weeks. At the Kristoffer School (the oldest and biggest Waldorf School in Sweden), for example, they work in areas resembling workshops rather than classrooms. There they help to manufacture things used in the school, for instance, things which the younger children need but cannot make themselves; or bind exercise and other books, or make theatrical props for the school plays, and so on. Here school-work and voluntary work are combined, and it inspires a sense of security and pride to feel that one can make something beautiful oneself. The craft teacher at the school emphasizes that this sort of activity adds to the pupils' general sense of well-being.

One important part of the teaching is to give the pupils a *feel for various materials.* Wood plays an important part in handicraft teaching, but is also important for an appreciation of Nature. A skilfully carved surface makes a special impression on a person who has developed a sensitivity to this. A teacher who enjoys the qualities of the wood sufficiently can convey reverence for the forces of life and for the whole order of the world. In the structure of the wood can be seen more clearly than in many other materials how and in which direction the tree has grown. One can also draw the pupil's attention to the rhythm of the annual rings. Such aspects are important both from a technical and an artistic perspective, for the wood will split and will function poorly unless we are aware of them. When we work with wood we also work with ourselves — rhythm and direction are important aspects in education, and influence both our volition and our thinking.

In our technological age it is important that children and young people train their feeling not only for materials but also for the connection between the aesthetic and the mechanical. In this context Steiner regarded it as particularly suitable to let the pupils themselves design and make mobile wooden figures performing some kind of task. This type of figure is still being manufactured today in Waldorf schools.[25]

As regards music, too, which is something profoundly fundamental to man and which pervades most things in life, it is not the external musical influence that is the primarily important aspect. Here Waldorf teachers are trying more to appeal to the child's inner self — to that which exists in one's own body, that which pertains to dance, the rhythmic. So here too it is the link between the spiritual and the physical they want to try and establish.

The same thing applies to gymnastics classes and physical exercises for children. Here, a truly deep human knowledge and a feeling for each child is demanded of the teacher. Something much more than an

'Uniting the mechanical with the aesthetic.' Wooden figures made by pupils during craft lessons. (From Carlgren & Klingborg, 1977.)

intellectual knowledge of anatomy and so on is called for. Steiner turned against the gymnastics of the times, with its physical military style. He wanted instead to develop a kind of spiritualized physical culture, where the external, visible performance and measurable records would not be the important thing. One should instead strive to get the children to feel within themselves a growing strength — a sense of liberation and inner happiness and well-being. One would then have established a connection between the physical and the spiritual which could lead to something constructive.[26]

It is the same in teaching small children mathematics. Here the methodology starts out from the child's own body through a wide variety of games, dance, rhythmic exercises and so on. And ways are sought, too, of linking the physical games to the mathematical way of thinking.

Teacher trainees at the Rudolf Steiner College in Järna are given training in mathematics for the junior classes by the Danish teacher Henning Andersen. He has reluctantly — because Waldorf teachers are really against textbooks — let himself be persuaded to write down his ideas and methods in three books intended as teacher guides.[27]

This illustration (below), like many others in the books, was drawn by the teacher/author/illustrator himself. In the Waldorf system of education it is generally regarded as important that the teacher should draw and paint as much as possible for the children. Proficiency is not what matters, but rather that the pupils should become freer and more sure of themselves in their own drawing and painting if they see the teacher doing the same thing. Along with other physical exercises — in particular they start out from the child's own hand in arithmetic exercises — these books also contain drawing exercises which are intended to link up with arithmetic.

In the first teacher guide there is also a whole-page illustration of hands drawn by Dürer. It is a picture one would hardly expect to see in a guide for maths teachers. But once again, it is the importance of

'Count and hop!' Illustration by Henning Andersen, a Waldorf teacher.

Hands, by Albrecht Dürer. (From the mathematics book, 'Count and hop!')

the hand which is highlighted here and, in this instance, in an artistically inspired fashion.

Much of the content of these books is connected with the teaching in mathematics developed by teachers in the first Waldorf School in Stuttgart, in particular the works of Hermann von Baravalle, who wrote textbooks on mathematics, geometry and physics which are still used by teachers today, and not only in the Waldorf Schools.[28]

Schwung, Schwung, Wärme, Wärme

Steiner saw the practical anchoring of theories as a principal issue in education. For his own part he continued to gather practical experience of teaching and of people of all ages throughout his life. As we have seen, he financed his own school studies from the age of fourteen by giving private lessons to classmates and other children. Later, he also worked as private tutor in various families alongside his studies. Of particular importance to him was the human knowledge which he felt he had gained when as a young man he had worked with a seriously mentally retarded boy over a period of several years, who gradually, with his help, achieved astounding results in his studies. And throughout his life, Steiner continued to give a great number of lectures to the most diverse audiences.

Perhaps above all, he himself led the work in starting up the new school, which grew quickly and enrolled many hundreds of pupils. He was responsible for training the teachers, he led teaching-staff meetings each week, received teachers for consultation when they had problems of varying kinds, and also made constant visits to the children in the classrooms.

It is characteristic of Steiner that the impressions he made on different people differ so sharply. The eye-witness accounts of his work together with teachers and children in the school show sides of him which many people would not have expected. He seems to have been appreciated not only by the adults, but also to a high degree by the children. Someone relates how they flocked around him when he turned up in the schoolyard — they would hang on his arms and legs until he was barely visible because of all the children surrounding him. When he himself taught, he often sat perched on the teacher's desk, something that was probably not exactly standard procedure in the German school of the day. It is told how he again and again delivered surprises in his teaching and how he had an unusual sense of humour and imagination in making exciting and daring associations. He could do so because of the wide learning he possessed. He himself says that as a teacher one should endeavour to give the children images which can act as seeds — a matter of cunning in a rational manner, that is, always trying to have something up one's sleeve which can give the children something to think about.[29]

There are many examples of his inventiveness. Steiner, who highly appreciated the metaphysical and humoristic poems of Christian Morgenstern, who once at a dinner-party where the guests recited various poems by this poet. No one however, had managed to recite the poem 'Lullaby of the Fishes' *(Fisches Nachtgesang).* As the guests were leaving, Steiner is supposed to have then made his contribution with this poem, which he 'recited' by opening and closing his eyelids following the rhythm of the poem exactly, thereby inducing great laughter amongst the assembled guests.[30]

It is said that Steiner's frequent entreaty was that teaching must contain *'Schwung, Schwung, Wärme, Wärme!'* (warmth and liveliness). He always tried, they say, to bring out the positive side of each teacher, and his advice to them never consisted of persuasion or force. He tried rather to accomplish a sense of liberation in them. If, for instance, a teacher wanted advice from him concerning some pupil who was causing trouble — and there appear to have been quite a few such pupils in the school — he would try to get the teacher to be grateful for such a pupil. He would try to get the teacher to feel that these children were interesting persons and really an enrichment to the work of instruction. He would try to accentuate for him how very boring it would be to teach if nothing happened at school and if these pupils were not also part of the class.

Steiner himself was acutely aware of how difficult it is to explain the business of art and its connection with the spiritual to people of Western civilization. He prepared his teachers to be aware that they would meet with stiff opposition, but that trying to create something new and showing resistance is an act of culture which had to be done. All those taking part in this venture would be constantly obliged to make compromises because of various external demands. He under-

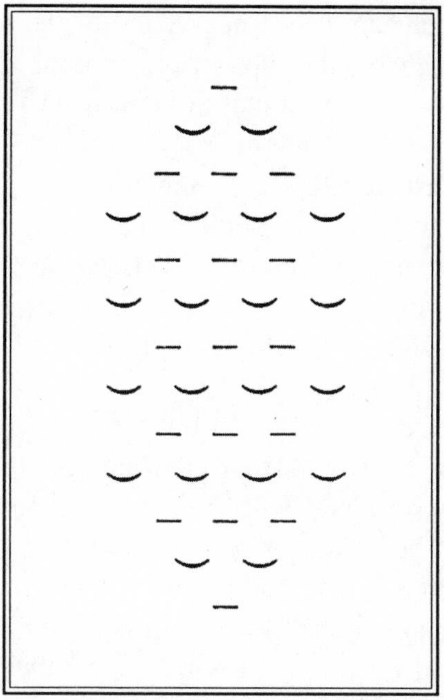

'Lullaby of the Fishes' by Christian Morgenstern.

lined that they could only become good teachers if they were aware all the time of how their ideals relate to the compromises they may be forced to make.

The issues Steiner addresses in his lectures for teachers, are not easy to assimilate all at once. It is not a matter of concrete formulas for teachers to take up and imitate. It is about a different approach to life and therefore also a different approach to pedagogy, methodology and subject theory.

Steiner saw it as a central cultural mission for educationalists in post-War Germany to try to work for a new kind of school. He attacked 'the thundering against the trespassing of the imagination into the educational system,' as he puts it. After the War a new way of thinking was called for, in his view, which started out from a different kind of human knowledge, unlike that embraced by the mechanistic view of knowledge. In that perspective, people had been treated like stencilled patterns. Standardized and formalized methods of teaching, an increasingly comprehensive school legislation and a multitude of inflexibly determinative exams, which were amongst other things a prerequisite for the centralized supervision of the teachers — all this had obstructed teachers and pupils from training their own personal creative abilities — the things that in point of fact made them human beings.

The teacher must develop a feeling for each individual pupil in order to be able to give that pupil in particular the opportunity to freely train and develop his aptitudes. The same thing applies to the teacher-trainer in regard to his students. But this is precisely one of the most difficult things to achieve in a centrally supervized educational system.

In conclusion, there is reason to link up once again with Schiller. His poem *'An die Freude'* (To Joy), which is sung in Beethoven's Choral Symphony, was originally called 'To Freedom,' but this title was censored.[31] The issues of freedom were what lay closest to Steiner's heart, and they also had for him a strong connection with joy as well as with music in man. Perhaps it is this that the young people of today the world over have discovered on their own, and which makes music such an important part of their lives — *out of* school. In the Waldorf educational system they are attempting to create room for this also *in* school.

Epilogue

The anthroposophical way of schooling seeks its path in the borders between art and science. Its object is to find a possible way of supplementing the mechanistic view of the world which has come to pervade our lives over a period of several hundred years. One basis for the Waldorf method of education concerns the enhancement of our knowledge of *humanity* and our part in the indivisible whole which we and the world together comprise in the universe. Neither the world nor human life is seen *merely* as a functioning mechanism. Above all there is a desire to see each person as a consciously active subject and to make room for art in us as well as enabling our own judgments, sense of responsibility and an active creative role in the world — for better or for worse.

The free, creating and playing human being is seen as the necessary link between, on the one hand, everything that is arranged in accordance with laws, the logical side of life, and, on the other hand, all the disordered, chaotic and spontaneous aspects which are, to an equally high degree, a part of life. Walking the tightrope between these extremes — and also between other polarities and paradoxes in our existence — is a difficult feat, but it must be undertaken. A different kind of educational method is called for if we are to be better suited to accomplish this than we have proven ourselves to be up to now. The goal here is a method of science and a method of education which do not only revolve around 'grey theory' but which *at the same time* embrace 'the green tree of life.'

The Waldorf teacher's conviction is that we distance ourselves from what life is by avoiding too much the inner visible, spiritual qualities in our existence — qualities which we can get at through art, and experience through our own acts of creativity and our own forms of expression. By this avoidance, we become 'mechanized in our minds.' In this way, teaching threatens to become trite, routine and dead, instead of being a vital force in the development of the student. By training our sensitivity to the arts of the Muses — for colours, shapes, rhythms and sounds — we can introduce movement and drama and also warmth, aspiration and energy into the process of acquiring knowledge.

By means of a more artistic form of training such as this, humankind could progress and achieve the synthesis necessary to understand all the tremendously admirable, but disjointed and specialized knowledge which we possess today. Teaching would then be able to take on a more artistically pictorial nature, and the teacher who was more artistically trained would have a greater feeling for what is musical and balanced and would then also be able to disseminate knowledge that won the approval of the students. It is a matter of training people to be more open so that they can also experience the pulse of life — so that they can see the interplay between those things which we instead have had to accustom ourselves to seeing as disconnected contrasts, such as body-soul, spirit-matter, light-dark, life-death, science-humanities, technology-humanity, theory-practice, male-female, and so on and so forth.

It is only the creating, interpreting human being as the active subject — who can create such an overall picture and achieve such methods of breaking through barriers in practice. But in order to achieve this a form of training is necessary which our methods of education neglect, and even, counteract. It is a question of an educational method which does not teach us to such a high degree to divide things and look at separate parts, but which *also and simultaneously* teaches us to see the whole aspect — in the same way that the warp and the weft constitute the prerequisites for each other in a piece of fabric.

As I understand it, it is such a way of seeing things that underlies the Waldorf method of education placing such weight on practical skills and artistic exercises — not to train people to become artists, but to develop the artistic aptitudes inherent in *each and every* person.

Can it perhaps be something of this that more and more children, young people and adults the world over lack in our educational institutions? Is it perhaps a greater understanding for art in us which is called for if we are to be able to develop to a higher degree the sort of knowledge that promotes life?

This kind of boundary-crossing offers many pitfalls. Completely distancing oneself from the problems and avoiding having to deal with them was, however, something Steiner regarded as being even more dangerous, as far as I understand it. Many people supported his endeavours. But he was also subjected to an extremely fierce and solid resistance from established circles in modern social life — from within the Church, the University and the Art world.

The anthroposophical path to knowledge can be said to be about trying to recover the unity between art, science and religion which formerly existed, but which had been lost in the so-called highly-developed countries of the West. Here, it really is a shift of paradigm or an about-turn of views in theoretical terms. But for the anthroposophists it meant *at the same time* that theories and methods were to be tried out in practical contexts.

There are of course great questions which anthroposophically based activities deal with. There are also large areas which I have not been able to concern myself with here. But the things I have found to be particularly overlooked have proved to be connected to issues to which later research within widely diverse fields has begun more and more to attach importance.

At the beginning of the twentieth century science was forced into a revolutionary kind of rethinking. Human experience of phenomena and our role as an active subject in the process of research proved to be of decisive importance precisely within physics, where one least of all would have believed it! The human being — the subject — had qualities which neither mathematical findings nor apparatus seemed to be able to replace.

The Danish physicist and Nobel Laureate Niels Bohr, during the last thirty years of his life, placed great importance on trying to unite apparently antithetical points of view, in what he called the 'principle of complementarity.' He believed that the study of the interaction between subject and object can also have significance for a better understanding of the mutual interaction between scientific and humanistic traditions.

Bohr wished to see the principle of complementarity as a cornerstone in a new epistemology which did not only apply to physics, but would also be applicable universally. Nevertheless, he noticed that even if most physicists accepted this principle within physics, it was difficult in any case both for them and for people from other disciplines to incorporate and understand this idea. He felt that people seemed to have difficulty accepting basic dualisms without striving after their mutual dissolution or reduction. He thought that it was perhaps primarily a matter of time — more time to assimilate a new theme in a sufficiently widely embracing manner.

What Steiner especially focused on in Goethe was how the latter's view of humanity and Nature came to constitute the basis for the whole of his world-view and attitude to life. Inner experience and outer observations interplayed in him in a rare and radical way. The human being as the subject, and external visible Nature, comprised for him an indivisible unity, where the whole was something other and more than merely the sum of the parts. Goethe felt intuitively a profound unease about the direction he feared that science would lead towards as a result of the mechanistic aspects of Newton's findings regarding the order of things in the universe. It was this apprehension which drove him to a systematic experimenting with the purpose of finding a method of research which could *supplement* the mechanistic point of view which in his day pervaded science and the system of education. He wished to accord *conscious humanity* greater importance. 'He wished to defend the sensuous world of perception from the assault of the mathematical abstractions of the research of physics,' as Werner Heisenberg expressed it.

Goethe was, as far as I understand, the first person to worry deeply about the dangers inherent in the scientific ideals of his time and who also ventured to formulate and try out new scientific methods. And Steiner was the first person from the scientific side who felt he was able to understand what Goethe meant with his criticism of Newton. Steiner believed that it was impossible to understand completely Goethe's poetry on Nature and his literary works — perhaps especially *Faust* — without also making a study of his research on Nature, in the same way as it was impossible to understand really what he intended with his scientific research without *at the same time* knowing about his artistic authorship. For Steiner, Goethe represents the example of a person in whom the artistic and the scientific have chimed together. It was his artistic method of observation which gave him the ability to see complementary and necessary connections between polarities in life. But in spite of the fact that Goethe's great authority in the artistic field was recognized, there were few people who could see anything other than dilettantism in the scientific part of his life's work.

When people working within the Waldorf system of education and anthroposophy seek to develop Goethe's natural scientific method further, it is the human element in the research process that they take hold of. It is our own close, direct experience of the phenomena, the subject-object relationship and our human power of judgment *(anschauende Urteilskraft),* to which they wish to bring attention and make more room for in education and research. It is thereby regarded as essential to extend the boundaries of science to encompass immaterial, invisible, more immeasurable inner qualities which exist in humanity and in Nature and which *also* have to do with life in its *fullest* sense.

According to Steiner's way of seeing things, neither the social issue nor any other of our time's most urgent issues can be solved unless we in the West open our eyes to the importance of this in our lives and begin to practise more experiencing of ourselves and to act in accordance with such realities in our lives.

For Steiner, it was this completeness or harmony in Goethe that had captured Schiller's interest and which also became the point of departure for the ideas on the aesthetic education of Man which Schiller formulated. A comparison of Steiner's interpretation of Schiller's ideas in this respect — as well as how these ideas today are taken up in the training of Waldorf teachers — with the latest findings of brain research, is quite astounding. During the very last weeks in which I worked on this book, I happened to read a recent book on the resources of the brain written by the physiologist Matti Bergström. In it he summarizes ideas based on a whole life of strict scientific research, which are of direct interest in this connection and which open exciting panoramas for continued research around the significance of art for humanity and human actions.

The post-modern image of the world, according to Stephen Toulmin, can be said to be 'an image of the world where the practical and the theoretical, the contemplative and the active, can no longer be separated from one another: it is an image of the world which gives us back that sense of unity, of order and of proportion — all those qualities which are encompassed by the Greek term *kosmos* — which the ancient philosophers insisted on and which the Renaissance destroyed.'[1] It could be claimed that it was a path such as this that Steiner — prior to later physicists, cerebral physiologists and postmodernists — tried to enter upon. He was himself highly educated both in the fields of science, technology and the humanities and he lived in the middle of the cultural debate and the cultural life of his time. At the same time it is palpable how he went his own ways and made his own interpretations.

When the Waldorf system of education, using as its point of departure Steiner and his interpretation of Goethe and Schiller, places especially great importance on art and artistic exercises in contexts of knowledge and of the development of one's identity, it is following a line in a living tradition of ideas. The idea that art should have a central role in human development and, it follows, for all education, has roots far back in time and was already emphasized by Plato. This idea can later be found again, for example in John Ruskin, William Morris and Herbert Read in England, in Frank Oppenheimer and his Science Museum 'Exploratorium' in San Francisco, in Loris Malaguzzi and Gianni Rodari in Reggio Emilia in Italy, as well as in Ellen Key, Carl Malmsten and Marita Lindgren-Fridell in Sweden, amongst others.

In Steiner's Germany, too, such ideas were a reflection of the age, for instance in people like Gottfried Semper and Alfred Lichtwark, and in the Bauhaus Movement. Steiner takes up the questions in his own way and develops them in relation to the vast amount of knowledge he possesses in very differing fields. His theories came to be an inspiration to many of the *avant garde* artists of the time, but they also — and this is perhaps the most remarkable aspect — come to provide the impulse for many alternative *practical experiments* within completely different sectors of society, possessing a strong vitality which continues today in various parts of the world.

Steiner's life and work give rise to unusually many and differing interpretations. Many people see in this the hope of something new. Other people see the tragedy in something which has a tendency to be misinterpreted. Much appears here to be incomprehensible. But as I see it, it would be unfortunate if this were to hinder more people from seriously attempting to make a decision for themselves. Unless science with a greater degree of boldness opens itself to different ways of seeing things in a more non-prejudicial way than has been the case to date, I believe there is a serious risk that science itself may come to be an instigational factor in giving anti-intellectualism free room to play.

I do not claim to have succeeded in this study in presenting a comprehensive picture of the complex issues concerned here. That the extensive material published in Steiner's name — but which in the majority of cases was never intended for anything other than oral presentation, and of which Steiner himself never had the chance to correct the faults in the transcripts — also encompasses ambiguities and, for our time, peculiar aspects, is impossible to ignore. But in order to make as fair a judgment as possible it has been necessary to bring forward previously overlooked points of departure for the Waldorf system of education. My hope is that a more all-round and scientific judgment will make it possible to establish a more open and constructive exchange of ideas. There are no simple answers to the questions raised here. This is inherent in the nature of the subject. But since the Waldorf method of education, as is also true of other practical activities based on anthroposophy, strives towards a different and theoretically constructed view of problems which are central to us all, it must be an urgent matter to establish as good a climate for discussion as is possible within this area.

Some people who have read my manuscript have felt that the subject-matter is too great — and I can assure the reader that I have myself many a time found this to be true, and have been close to shelving the whole project! But at the same time, it is precisely this wider view which has caught my interest, because I have so often felt the absence of such a view in the discussion on the theory of knowledge. This is why, in spite of everything, I have felt the need to present the results of my research. I hope that others will be motivated by some of this work to continue interpretation and study along their own paths.

Notes

Introduction

1. Lindberg, S.G., 1977.
2. Eppinger, 1985.
3. Bergström, 1990. See also Sperry, 1983.
4. Tranströmer, 1984.

Chapter 1

1. Read, 1953 and 1956. See also Arnheim, 1969; Langer, 1953; Nobel, 1979 and 1990.
2. Nobel, 1979.
3. Karlsson & Ruth, 1983.
4. Mumford, 1978.
5. Eliot, 1944, p.386.
6. Hägerstrand, 1986.
7. Fries, 1964.
8. Von Wright, 1979 and 1986.
9. Wilenius, 1981 and 1986.
10. See, for example, articles in *Dagens Nyheter* by the physicist K.-E. Eriksson, 1987.
11. Larsson, 1966.
12. The film 'Dead Poets Society' by Peter Weir.
13. Sperry, 1983, Nobel Laureate. See also Bergström, 1990.
14. Bohr, 1954, and Holton, 1988.
15. SOU 1981:29 p.194 and p.50.
16. Darwin, 1959. See also Beer, 1983.
17. Steiner, *Goethean Science,* 1988.
18. Sällström, 1979.
19. Sundén, 1962.
20. Ahlström *et al.,* 1977.

Chapter 2

1. Bohr, 1954; Holton, 1988; Bronowski, 1951 and 1956. Granit, 1983; Sperry, 1983. See also Toulmin, 1982; and the *American Journal of Physics,* July 1990, which contains an appeal for joint commitment between Science and Religion, written by Carl Sagan and signed by 32 scientists and 270 religious leaders and academics.
2. Steiner, *The Course of my Life,* p.272.
3. See Liedman's anthology *Humaniora på undantag — Humanistiska*

forskningstraditioner i Sverige (The Humanities neglected — Humanist traditions of research in Sweden) 1977, p.11ff and p.20ff.

4. Steiner, *Theosophy,* (GA 9) Preface.
5. Steiner, *Occult Science: an outline,* (GA 13) p.10.
6. See Lars Gyllensten in *Dagens Nyheter,* 15 March 1987. Also Inge Jonsson and Elisabet Hermodsson, 1977, on Swedenborg, in *Författarnas litteraturhistoria (Authors' History of Literature).*
7. Walter Ljungqvist's preface to a Swedish edition of Rudof Steiner's papers, *Antroposofi i teori och praktik (Anthroposophy in Theory and Practice),* Orion/Bonniers, 1963.
8. Schiller, 1915.
9. Rudolf Steiner's collected works, the *Gesamtausgabe* (GA). A summary can be found in the three volumes published by Rudolf Steiner Verlag, Dornach (see Bibliography).
10. Steiner is richly represented in several Swedish university libraries, mainly in special catalogues. In the 'Carolina' University Library in Uppsala, there is a large collection of works by and on Steiner, originating from a private donation in 1945. The Royal Library in Stockholm also has a specialized collection of around three hundred and fifty books resulting from a donation in 1951.

    The most complete and up-to-date collection in Scandinavia is at the Åbo Academy in Finland which, using funds donated in 1956, founded the Steiner Library at the Donner Institute. The founder donation also provided for the upkeep of the library, as well as funds for research scholarships.
11. See Magnus Ljunggren, 1982 and 1985. The author Saul Bellow also expressed views on this in an interview in the German magazine *INFO3,* 6/1987 pp.3–9.
12. See Hagar Olsson, 1965 and Gunnar Tideström, 1960.
13. This paper is included in *Kunst und Kunsterkenntnis. Grundlagen einer neuen Ästhetik,* (GA 271), p.45.
14. Zweig, S. pp.103–5.
15. Hjalmar Branting, the Swedish Prime Minister between 1920–23, is said to have spent two weeks at the Goetheanum (the Free University for Spiritual Science) founded by Steiner in Dornach, Switzerland, which is still the world-centre of anthroposophy today.
16. Hjalmar Sundén's *Rudolf Steiner — a Book on Anthroposophy* touches on the influence of Steiner far beyond anthroposophical circles, including amongst Social Democrats in Sweden (see Hagar Olsson's commentary, p.196ff).
17. See Steiner's lectures at the Anthroposophical Movement's Second International Congress in Vienna, June 1–12, 1922 (published as *West and East — Contrasting Worlds).*
18. See Holton, 1988.

Chapter 3

1. Steiner, *The Course of my Life,* p.3f.
2. *ibid.* p.5.
3. *ibid.* p.6.
4. *ibid.* p.10.
5. Steiner, 'Skizze eines Lebensabrisses.' Lecture of 4 February 1913 in Berlin. See also Poeppig, 1960, p.21.
6. Steiner, *The Course of my Life,* p.11f.
7. *ibid.* p.52f.
8. *ibid.* p.16f.
9. *ibid.* p.15.
10. *ibid.* p.18.
11. *ibid.* p.18.
12. *ibid.* p.24.
13. *ibid.* p.28.
14. *ibid.* p.25f.
15. *ibid.* p.29.
16. *ibid.* p.36.
17. *ibid.* p.27.
18. *ibid.* p.52.
19. Janik and Toulmin, 1973.
20. Steiner, *The Course of my Life,* p.38f.
21. *ibid.* p.41.
22. See Hemleben, 1975.
23. *The Course of my Life,* p.58.
24. *ibid.* p.59.
25. *ibid.* p.41.
26. *ibid.* p.42f.
27. *ibid.* p.43.
28. *ibid.* p.174.
29. *ibid.* p.277f.
30. *ibid.* p.46.
31. *ibid.* p.44.
32. *ibid.* p.47.
33. *ibid.* p.48.
34. See, for example, Steiner's *Goethe as the Founder of a New Science of Aesthetics* (GA 271) and *The Art of Education.*
35. Steiner, *The Course of my Life,* p.29.
36. *ibid.* p.141.
37. *ibid.* p.75ff.
38. Poeppig, 1960 p.60.
39. Steiner, *The Course of my Life,* p.78.
40. *ibid.* p.80.
41. The article 'Über das Komische und seinen Zusammenhang mit Kunst und

Leben,' is found in *Kunst und Kunsterkenntnis — Grundlagen einer neuen Ästhetik* (GA 271).

42. See for instance, Johannessen and Rolf, 1989.
43. Von Heydebrand, C., *Rudolf Steiner in der Waldorfschule,* 1927.

Chapter 4

1. See Eckermann, 1925, p.261.
2. See Steiner, *A Theory of Knowledge based on Goethe's World Conception,* note on p.120.
3. Steiner, *Goethes naturwissenschaftliche Schriften Weimarer Sophienausgabe,* Volumes 6–12, 1891–96.
4. Steiner, *The Course of my Life,* p.152f.
5. Steiner, *A Theory of Knowledge,* preface to first edition 1886.
6. Steiner, *The Course of my Life,* p.80.
7. *ibid.* p.85.
8. Steiner, *A Theory of Knowledge,* preface to second edition, p.xviii.
9. Steiner, *Goethe as the Founder of a new Science of Aesthetics,* (GA 271) preface to the second edition.
10. Steiner, *Goethe's World View,* epilogue to the new edition.
11. *Goethes färglära (Goethe's Theory of Colour).* With introduction, commentaries and appendix by Pehr Sällström, p.33. Other writers who have written about Goethe's research on nature are: Cottrell, 1982 (with a comprehensive bibliography; Capra, 1986; Eliot, 1957; Hegge, 1967 and 1987; Heisenberg, 1948, 1952, 1967; Heitler, 1968; Jaki, 1969; Lehrs, 1952; Uberoi, 1984; Walter, 1930; Wells, 1978; Vasco, 1978; Holbaeck-Hanssen, 1976.
12. Steiner, *A Theory of Knowledge,* p.1ff. See also *Goethean Science.*
13. Steiner, *A Theory of Knowledge,* notes to the new edition, 1924.
14. *ibid.* p.8.
15. Steiner, *Goethe's World-View,* p.32.
16. *ibid.* p.11.
17. See Steiner, *Goethean Science,* p.76f.
18. Steiner, *The Course of my Life,* p.128.
19. Steiner, 'Schiller and Our Times' (lecture of 4 May 1905 in Berlin). In *Uhrsprung und Ziel des Menschen — Grundbegriffe des Geisteswissenschaft* (GA 53).
20. Herbert Read in Ziegfield (ed.), 1953. Read is termed 'the No.1 art promoter of the world' by Marita Lindgren-Fridell in an article about him in *Vi,* no.22, 1960 (see Johannesson, L., 1986). Among others for whom Schiller's *Letters* were significant is the writer Michael Ende. John Dewey writes briefly on the letters in his book *Art as experience.*
21. See Read's lecture above. Of interest here, too, is the fact that three years before Schiller's *Letters* were published, Mozart first performed *The Magic Flute* (1791), which touched on the art-science relationship in a way that also links up with Steiner's interpretation of Schiller and Goethe.

22. See Steiner, *The Course of my Life,* pp.49f, 72f, 132ff.
23. Steiner, *Goethe as Founder,* p.24ff. (See further on Kandinsky in Chapter 5.)
24. *A Theory of Knowledge,* p.111.
25. Steiner, *Goethe as Founder,* p.28.
26. *ibid.* p.22f.
27. Steiner, *The Philosophy of Spiritual Activity,* Chapter 9.
28. *ibid.*, foreword to the first edition p.175f.
29. *ibid.* p.177f.
30. See Steiner's *Practical Advice to Teachers,* a lecture course in the first Waldorf School, 21 August–5 September 1919.
31. Steiner, *The Course of my Life,* p.81f.
32. Steiner, *A Theory of Knowledge,* Chapter 1. See also the whole passage on Organic Nature in *The Course of my Life,* p.81f.
33. Steiner, *A Theory of Knowledge,* Chapter 16, p.93ff.
34. Steiner, *Goethean Science,* p.13f. See also *The Essentials of Education,* lectures given in Stuttgart, 7–13 April 1924.
35. Steiner, *A Theory of Knowledge,* preface to the new edition, p.xiii.
36. Steiner, *Goethean Science,* Introduction and Chapter 1.
37. Lukacs p.48.
38. Von Wright, 1965 p.176.
39. The philosopher Reijo Wilenius discusses the deep relationship with Goethe's research method apparent in Wittgenstein's later thinking, in *Bildningens villkor (The Conditions of Culture) p.49.* See also Ingela Josefson's *Kunskapens former. Det reflekterade yrkeskunnandet (The Forms of Knowledge. The Reflected Expertise),* Carlsson Bokförlag 1991.
40. Steiner, *Goethean Science,* p.4f. The German text is:

    Man wird dann gewahr, dass er die in die *Idee* übersetzte Natur der Pflanze selbst ist, die in unserem Geiste ebenso lebt, wie im Objekt; man bemerkt auch, dass man sich einen Organismus bis in die kleinsten Teile hinein belebt, wenn man ihn nicht als toten, abgeschlossenen Gegenstand, sondern als sich Entwickelndes, Werdendes, als die stetige Unruhe in sich selbst vorstellt.

    ... die ihn [Goethe] später zu jener fruchtbaren Naturauffassung führten, in welcher Idee und Erfahrung in allseitiger Durchdringung sich gegenseitig beleben und zu einem Ganzen werden.
41. *ibid.* p.69f.
42. *ibid.* p.22.
43. *ibid.* p.12.
44. Steiner, *A Theory of Knowledge,* p.58.
45. Steiner, *Goethe's World-View,* p.80ff.
46. Steiner, *Goethean Science,* p.14. In a letter written by Goethe in 1816 (and cited by Steiner), he reveals Linnaeus' importance for him, saying: 'Apart from Shakespeare and Spinoza I knew of no person, no longer living, who had exercised such an influence on me as Linnaeus.'

47. Steiner, *Goethe's World-View,* p.81f.
48. Steiner, *Goethean Science,* p.12.
49. *ibid.* p.7f.
50. Darwin, *Autobiographical and other writings,* (Swedish edition) 1959 p.101ff. See also Gillian Beer's interesting book, *Darwin's Plots* (1983).
51. Liedman 1966, preface.
52. Eriksson, 1969, introduction pp.12, 17.
53. *ibid.* p.43.
54. Elias Fries in his essay 'Äro naturvetenskaperna något bildningsmedel?' (Are the natural sciences a means of culture?) See also Agnes Nobel's *Hur får kunskap liv? (How can knowledge gain life?),* especially the section *Behjärta vetenskapen* (Take science 'to heart') p.89.
55. Steiner, *A Theory of Knowledge,* p.95f.
56. Steiner, *Goethean Science,* p.59f. See also Steiner, 'Haeckel und seine Gegner' (1900).
57. *ibid.* p.53ff.
58. For this and the following quotations, see Steiner, *A Theory of Knowledge,* p.51ff.
59. Steiner, *Goethean Science,* Chapter 9, p.104ff.
60. *ibid.*
61. In Sällström, *Goethe's Theory of Colour,* p.373.
62. Bellow said this in a TV interview on Swedish Radio/TV, 11 December 1976.
63. Steiner, *Goethean Science,* p.93.
64. *ibid.* p.152ff.
65. See Elisabet Hermodsson's ecological oratorio *'Skapelse utlämnad'* (Creation Deserted), in particular the last stanzas, in the 1988 edition of her collected poems *Skapelsen utlämnad,* pp.209–22.
66. Steiner, *Goethean Science,* p.246.
67. *ibid.* p.248ff.
68. Granit, 1983, p.161.
69. *ibid.* p.216ff.
70. See Steiner, *The Karma of Vocation,* (lecture series 4–27 November 1916 in Dornach), p.25f.
71. Nilsson, 1975.
72. Sällström, *Goethe's Theory of Colour,* p.33ff.
73. *ibid.* p.203.
74. *ibid.* p.41.
75. *ibid.* p.397.
76. Steiner, *Goethean Science,* p.183ff.
77. Sällström, 1987 p.202. See also Nilsson, 1975.
78. See 'Goethe and Mathematics' (p.183ff) in Steiner's *Goethean Science.* See also Goethe's own comments on mathematics in Sällström's *Goethe's Theory of Colour,* p.298ff.

79. *Goethe's Theory of Colour,* p.177.
80. *ibid.* Goethe's own introduction to the *Theory of Colour,* p.51.
81. *ibid.* p.311.
82. *ibid.* p.296. Compare Elisabet Hermodsson's *'Att ge namn'* (Giving names) in *Ord i kvinnotid (Words in Time of Woman).*
83. *Goethe's Theory of Colour,* p.458.
84. *ibid.* p.473.
85. Heisenberg, 1952 p.60–76.
86. See Jaki, 1969, p.195–203.
87. See Strindberg's *En blå bok (A Blue Book).*
88. Larsson, 1910, p.9ff.
89. *ibid.* p.20.
90. *ibid.* p.76. See also a later commentary on Hans Larsson in Gunnar Aspelin's preface to his *Poesins Logik (The Logic of Poesy)* 1966.
91. Hermodsson, 1968.
92. Hermodsson, 1976.
93. Steiner, *Goethean Science,* p.236.
94. *ibid.* p.241.
95. Sällström, 1987 p.208. See also *Goethes Werke* (Beck, Munich), Vol.13, p.626.
96. See *Dagens Nyheter,* February, March 1987.
97. Steiner develops these thoughts in *The Philosophy of Spiritual Activity,* and elsewhere. He speaks of the need to develop an 'intuitive thinking,' a 'moral imagination,' and 'social confidence.' See further for example in the book *Rudolf Steiner om sin bok* Frihetens filosofi *(Rudolf Steiner on his book* The Philosophy of Freedom), an anthology with introduction and commentary by Otto Palmer.
98. See Sperry, *Science and moral priority: merging mind, brain and human values* (1983). See also Bergström, 1990 and Holton, 1988, on Niels Bohr and the roots of complementarity.
99. In Elisabet Hermodsson's collected poems *Skapelsen utlämnad (Creation Deserted)* 1988, p.95.

Chapter 5

1. See Steiner, *The Course of my Life,* Chapters 13 and 14.
2. *ibid.* p.256.
3. *ibid.* Chapter 28f.
4. Poeppig, 1960 p.117.
5. Steiner, *The Course of my Life,* p.284.
6. Mücke, Rudolph, 1979, p.66.
7. Steiner, *Gesammelte Aufsätze zur Kultur- und Zeitgeschichte 1887–1901* (GA 31); *Gesammelte Aufsätze zur Literatur 1884–1902* (GA 32).
8. *ibid.* See also Poeppig p.124.
9. Steiner, *The Course of my Life,* p.299ff, p.312ff. See also Marie Steiner-von Sivers, by Marie Savitch, 1965.

10. *ibid.* p.332.
11. Fant, 1977 p.120.
12. Ringbom, 1970, 1982, 1986 in *The Spiritual in Art.*
13. Kandinsky, 1969 p.35.
14. Steiner, *Theosophy* (1936), Preface, p.*v.*
15. Kandinsky, 1969, p.77.
16. Ringbom, p.68. Perhaps it is this elusive idea of 'life' which Edvard Munch in 1911 was communicating to us with his sun and its vibrating rays of colour, which the artist chose — to the irritation of many — as the central image of his monumental triptych for the Main Hall in Oslo University.
17. *ibid.* p.147
18. Steiner, *Goethean Science.* See also Theodor Schwenk's *Sensitive Chaos.*
19. Bronowski 1951, 1956.
20. Kandinsky pp.79–83 and p.106.
21. See Steiner, *West and East — Contrasting Worlds,* Chapter 1: 'Anthroposophy and Natural Science.'
22. Steiner, *The Philosophy of Spiritual Activity,* p.92.
23. Steiner, *The Course of my Life,* Chapter 11.
24. Steiner, *West and East — Contrasting Worlds,* Chapter 5: 'Anthroposophy and Cosmology.'
25. Lindborg, 1983 p.18.
26. *ibid.* p.19.
27. Johannisson, 1984 p.4ff.
28. *ibid.*
29. See Steiner, *Mysticism at the Dawn of the Modern Age* (also published as *Eleven European Mystics).*
30. Steiner, *The Gospel according to St. John,* see Chapter 1: 'The Doctrine of the Logos.'
31. Heitler, 1968, p.78. The lectures have been published under the title *Science and Man (Naturvetenskapen och människan).*
32. Von Wright, 1978.
33. Steiner, *The Course of my Life,* p.81.
34. Steiner, *West and East — Contrasting Worlds,* chapter on 'The Present Age and its Social Demands.'
35. *ibid.* p.21.
36. *ibid.* p.41f.
37. Steiner, *The Course of my Life,* p.271f.
38. Harry Martinson, Swedish Nobel Laureate in literature, was perhaps alluding to something like this in his poetical works, where he often speaks of things that 'lock man to the cogs and wheels of precision.' Ingvar Holm discusses this theme in his book on myths, paintings, motifs in the work of Harry Martinson. Holm writes:

> At the same time as the phenomena that Martinson attacks in his polemic are rationally definable, intangibility in his books on Nature

becomes itself a measuring-rod of value. In *Reality to the Death*, ... the matter is stated unequivocally. There the theme is from beginning to end 'the value of the vague in the world': When the existence of approximation in all areas is threatened by the tyrannical exactness in all areas, then the great war between poet and engineer has begun. A sense of *free approximation is the highest human aspect.* Take this away and man has become a termite in a termite hill without a soul, for approximation is soul. Theoretically, such a stand is naturally difficult to defend, but the attitude is, in Martinson's case, consistent. It is there already from the first moment when the author enters the scene, undecided, unsure and difficult to bring into line with the strict disciplines of society, ideologies and the art schools. In his period-criticizing authorship he allows softness to equip itself for battle. (Holm, 1965 p.245ff.)

39. Steiner, *The Course of my Life,* p.272.
40. *ibid.* Chapter 10.
41. *ibid.* See also Rudolf Steiner's article 'The sensual-supersensible. Spiritual knowledge and artistic creativity' as well as the Norwegian lyricist Alf Larsen's article *'Konstens helgedom'* (The Sanctuary of Art) in *Antropos* no.8, 1980.
42. On Saul Bellow's interest in Rudolf Steiner, see *Saul Bellow and History,* by Judie Newman, as well as *Rudolf Steiner — Life, work, inner path and social initiatives,* by Rudi Lissau.
43. Steiner, *The Younger Generation,* Chapter 1. On Steiner's attitude towards Theosophy, see *The Course of my Life,* Chapter 32.

Chapter 6

1. Steiner's *The Threefold Social Order* is available in English as *Towards Social Renewal. Basic Issues of the Social Question.* See Chapter 2.
2. *ibid.* p.75f.
3. For a broad discussion on teaching mathematics and social development, see *Daedalus,* Journal of the American Academy of Arts and Sciences, special issue on 'Literacy in America,' Spring 1990. See also Chapter 8 here for more on Waldorf approaches to children's development of mathematical knowledge.
4. See, for example, Steiner *Women and Society,* lecture of 17 November, Hamburg. Rudolf Steiner Press, London 1985.
5. Steiner, *Towards Social Renewal,* p.87f.
6. *ibid.* p.93f.
7. *ibid.* p.124f.
8. *ibid.* p.139.
9. See for example the Norwegian philosopher Hjalmar Hegge in *Frihet individualitet og samfunn (Freedom, individuality and society),* p.493.
10. Huber 1979, 'Astral-Marx. Über Anthroposophie, einer gewißen Marxismus

und andere Alternatiefen,' (Astral-Marx. On Anthroposophy, a certain Marxism and other Alternatives) in *Kursbuch* (no.55), the German magazine started by Hans-Magnus Enzensberger in 1979.

11. Strawe, C. 1986, *Marxismus und Anthroposophie (Marxism and Anthroposophy),* p.59 and p.295ff.
12. *ibid.* p.291ff.
13. *ibid.* p.297–303.
14. On later thinking in Russian pedagogy, see for example N.K. Goncharov, 'The pedagogical ideas and practice of L.N. Tolstoy' in *Soviet Education: Selected articles from Soviet education journals in English translation,* 4 (1961/62), No.12.
15. Railing, P.R. 1989, *From science to systems of art: On Russian abstract art and language 1910–20; and other essays.*
16. Ljunggren 1982, *The dream of rebirth. A Study of Andrei Belyi's novel* Petersburg.
17. Ljunggren 1985, *'Antroposofins decennium i Ryssland'* (The Decade of Anthroposophy in Russia), in *Antropos* No.2/3.
18. *ibid.*
19. See also in Savitch, 1965, *Marie Steiner-von Sivers.*
20. Ljunggren 1985, p.33ff. Compare here Belyi's description of his own experience of Steiner: 'An infinity of human suffering, tenderness and 'mad' recklessness, was reflected in his face,' according to Ljunggren 1982, p.61.
21. Ljunggren 1982, p.107.
22. See *Night-thoughts of a classical physicist,* by R. McCormmach.
23. Compare for example, Salvador Dali, Paul Klee.
24. In Russia there are also fruitful stimuli and projects for future research in regard to these complex connections. See in particular Michail Bakhtin and his research on Dostoevsky, on 'Rabelais and the history of laughter' and also 'The Dialogic Word.'
25. See Ljunggren 1985. For more on Russian orthodox spiritual tradition see, for example, Per-Arne Bodin, *Världen som ikon (The World as Icon),* Artos bokförlag 1988.

Chapter 7

1. Liljevalch Art Hall Exhibition Catalogue *Joseph Beuys och hans krets: Brännpunkt Düsseldorf 1987 (Joseph Beuys and his Circle: Focus on Düsseldorf 1987)*
2. Harlan V. 1986, 'Was ist Kunst? — Werkstattsgespräch mit Joseph Beuys' (What is art? — Workshop discussion with Joseph Beuys), p.29.
3. *ibid.* p.15.
4. Adriani, G., Konnertz, W., Thomas, K., 1981, pp.278ff, 313–23; see also Tisdall C. 1979, p.265.
5. See the magazines *Info3* and *Balder.* A biography called *Joseph Beuys* by Heiner Stachelhus also came out in 1988.

6. Adriani *et al.* pp.371–73 and Tisdall, p.254ff.
7. This statement comes from an interview with Beuys in the magazine *Balder,* No.23, 1982, previously published in German in *Info3* (2/1982).
8. Adriani *et al.* p.286 and 267.
9. Tisdall p.265.
10. The magazines *Info3* and *Balder.*
11. Adriani *et al.* p.329.
12. Harlan p.21.
13. Adriani *et al.* p.253.
14. *ibid.* p.267.
15. *ibid.* p.80. See also Agneta Hallgren's paper *'Jag är haren — Joseph Beuys som en personifiering av arketypen trickster'* (I am the hare — Joseph Beuys as a personification of the trickster archetype), Stockholm University 1987. Here, Beuys' actions are interpreted starting out from the shamanistic code of conduct. The shaman as archaic archetype 'is the principle of disorder, metamorphosis and creativity, and thereby also of going beyond limits. In his contradictory nature can be distinguished characteristic aspects of the trickster, the hero, the guide and the saviour. He is portrayed as divine, man and animal. This can be found in Beuys, who, in addition, acknowledges the original code of conduct, which was alien to the differentiation between matter and the supersensual.'

    Similarly, it is emphasized here, in connection with the strongly divergent opinions on Beuys, that 'there are several well-known figures in our literature who give us the same ambivalent feelings as Beuys — for example, Dostoevsky's Idiot and Cervantes' Don Quijote. Like Beuys, they are controversial, heroic, touching and seem at times quite mad.'

    For more on Beuys, see also Ulmer 1985.

Chapter 8

1. See *The Curriculum of the First Waldorf School* assembled by Caroline von Heydebrand and first published shortly after Steiner's death. Also the more detailed *Rudolf Steiner's Curriculum for Waldorf Schools* by Karl Stockmeyer. Both these writers were themselves teachers at the first Waldorf School. Also see, in particular, Frans Carlgren and Arne Klingborg *Education towards Freedom.*
2. See Steiner *Study of Man;* also *Practical Advice to Teachers* and *Discussions with Teachers.* These three courses comprise the preparation that Steiner arranged for the teachers of the first Waldorf School in Stuttgart.
3. Steiner, *The Education of the Child in the Light of Anthroposophy,* p.8.
4. *ibid.* p.12f.
5. *ibid.* p.10ff.
6. *ibid.* p.35f.
7. Steiner, *Study of Man,* p.16f.
8. See Steiner *Practical Advice to Teachers,* p.15f.

9. Werner Heisenberg (1967) quoted by Sällström, 1979 p.499.
10. Kandinsky 1969.
11. Steiner, *The Education of the Child,* pp.25-27.
12. Steiner, *Waldorf Education for Adolescence,* Lecture 1.
13. Steiner, *The Essentials of Education,* Lecture 1. Five lectures in Stuttgart 7–13 April 1924.
14. Steiner, *Discussions with Teachers,* see Discussions 10–13.
15. Steiner, *The Education of the Child,* p.37f.
16. *ibid.* p.42.
17. Steiner 1924, p.39ff. This quotation originates from a lecture which I have not succeeded in identifying from my notes. The same theme recurs with some variation in different lectures.
18. Steiner, *The Education of the Child,* p.45f.
19. Steiner, *The Essentials of Education,* p.29f.
20. Steiner *Practical Advice to Teachers,* p.79f. Steiner often returns to Goethe's spelling mistakes when addressing teachers.
21. Steiner, *Study of Man,* p.24.
22. Rudolf Grosse, who was himself a pupil at the first Waldorf School and who later became a Waldorf teacher, says this in his book *Erlebte Pädagogik,* p.59. Two other books which show how adults have worked with pen and brush in order to get the feel of and learn the configurative language of architecture and nature, are *Gardens for Pleasure and Profit (Trädgård till nöje och nytta)* (Klingborg and Fant, 1985) and *Trends in the Architecture of our Time (Tendenser i vår tids arkitektur)* (Klingborg 1983). Both these books discuss work done at the Rudolf Steiner Teacher-Training College in Järna primarily under the guidance of Arne Klingborg, and later shown to the public in exhibitions at the Liljevalch Art Hall in Stockholm.
23. See Steiner, *Practical Advice to Teachers,* p.59f.
24. Hauck, *Handarbeit und Kunstgewerbe,* pp.30, 126, 226.
25. *ibid.* pp.90, 199, 200.
26. Steiner often takes up this theme in his education lectures. See *The Education of the Child,* p.46.
27. Andersen, H. 1983, 1984, 1985.
28. Baravelle, H. *The Teaching of Arithmetic in the Waldorf Schools; Geometry; Perspective;* and other titles. See also what Steiner says on teaching mathematics in Hauck, pp.91 and 299.
29. Steiner, *Practical Advice to Teachers,* p.71.
30. Eppinger, p.283
31. Knight, p.168.

Epilogue

1. Toulmin, 1982.

Bibliography

Adler-Karlsson, G. 1990: *Lärobok för 90-talet. Om vår överlevnads villkor (Textbook for the Nineties. On the conditions for our survival),* Prisma.

Ahlström, K.-G. *et al.*, 1977: *Kristofferskolan som pedagogiskt experiment (The Kristoffer School as Pedagogical Experiment),* Pedagogiska institutionen, Lärarhögskolan i Uppsala (stencil).

Andersen, H. 1983: *Regn og Hop! (Count and Hop!),* Brage.

Andersen, H. 1984: *Del og hel! Fra Rudolf Steinerskolans regneundervisning i de mindre klasser (Part and whole! From the Rudolf Steiner School's arithmetic course for the younger classes).* Brage.

———, 1985: *Vej og mål! (Path and goal),* Brage.

Anér, K. 1990: 'Former ur kaos. Ett försök till samtal mellan antroposofin och den nya kaosforskningen' (Forms out of chaos. An attempt at a discussion between anthroposophy and the new research into chaos) in *Balder* No.1.

Antropos (anthroposophical journal), c/o Sahlberg, Karlbergsvägen 40, S-113 27 Stockholm.

Arkitektur (Swedish Review of Architecture), 1984, No.6. Special issue on the architect Erik Asmussen.

Arnheim, R. 1969: *Visual Thinking,* University of California Press.

Asplund, J. 1987: *Det sociala livets elementära former (The elementary form of social life),* Bokförlaget Korpen.

Bakhtin, M. 1986: *Rabelais och skrattets historia. François Rabelais' verk och den folkliga kulturen under medeltiden och renässansen* Anthropos. Published in English as *Rabelais and his world,* MIT Press 1968.

Balder (Magazine for Anthroposophy and Social Threefolding), Järna.

Biodynamisk tidskrift (Bio-dynamic magazine), S-153 00 Järna.

Bellow, S., 1976: *Humboldt's Gift,* Penguin Books. Also in TV interview on 11 December 1976.

Bergström, M. 1990: *Hjärnans resurser — en bok om idéernas uppkomst (The resources of the brain — a book on the genesis of ideas),* Bokförlaget Seminarium.

Beuys, Joseph 1982: 'Joseph Beuys — at home.' Interview in German magazine *INFO3,* 1982 in Brull, 1985, also in the Swedish magazine *Balder* No.23, 1982.

Björklund, S. 1989: 'Att bygga på vetenskaplig grund' (Building on scientific grounds), in *Universitet och samhälle,* publication dedicated to Martin Holmdahl.

Bjørkvold, J-R. 1989: *Det musiske menneske. Barnet og sangen, lek og læring gjennom livets faser (The man of arts. The child and the song, play and learning through the phases of life),* Freidig Forlag. Oslo.

Bodin, P-A. 1988: *Världen som ikon: Åtta föredrag om den ryskortodoxa andliga traditionen (The world as icon: Eight lectures on the Russian Orthodox spiritual tradition),* Artos bokförlag.

Bohr, N. 1954: 'Kunskapens enhet' (The unity of knowledge) in *Atomfysik och mänskligt vetande.*

Borgman-Hansen, O. 1979: *Antroposofi: Rudolf Steiners bidrag till videnskap, kunst og religion (Anthroposophy: Rudolf Steiner's contribution to science, art and religion),* Berlingske Leksikon bibliotek.

Bronowski, J. 1951: *The Common Sense of Science,* Penguin.

———, 1956: *Science and Human Values,* Harper & Row.

Brusewitz, G. 1989: *Guldörnen och duvorna: Fågelmotiv hos Strindberg (The golden eagle and the doves: Bird motifs in Strindberg),* Wahlström & Widstrand.

Capra, F. 1986: 'Den helhetlig-okologiske tenkning i den tyske åndshistorie' (The holistic-ecological way of thinking in German spiritual history), *Arken* No.4.

Carlgren, Frans & Klingborg, Arne 1976: *Education towards Freedom,* Lanthorn Press, East Grinstead.

Carlgren, Frans 1980: *Den antroposofiska kunskapsvägen (The Anthroposophic path to knowledge),* Larson.

———, 1985: *Den antroposofiska rörelsen: verksamheter, bakgrunder, framtidsperspektiv (The Anthroposophical movement: activities, background, future perspectives),* Larson.

Cornell, P. 1979: *Inside and outside modernism,* Gidlunds.

———, 1981: *Den hemliga källan. Om initiationsmönster i konst, litteratur och politik (The secret spring. On patterns of initiation in art, literature and politics.),* Gidlunds bokförlag.

Cottrell, A.P. 1982: *Goethe's View of Evil,* Floris Books, Edinburgh.

Dahlin, B. 1990: 'Konsten att uppfatta världen. Mot en fenomenologisk konstpedagogik' (The art of comprehending the world. Towards a phenomenological art-pedagogy). In the Swedish magazine *Paletten* No.3.

Dale, E.D. 1990: *Kunskapens tre og kunstens skjønnhet. Om den estetiske oppdragelse i det moderna samfunn (The tree of knowledge and the beauty of art. On aesthetic education in modern society),* Gyldendal Norsk Forlag, Oslo.

Darwin, C. 1959: *Självbiografi och andra skrifter (Autobiographical and other writings),* selections by Knut Hagberg. Natur och Kultur.

Det alternativa Järna. Presentation of activities inspired by Anthroposophy. Special issue of *Biodynamisk tidskrift,* No.5, 1986.

Dewey, J. 1958: *Art as Experience,* Capricorn Books.

Eckermann, J.P. 1925: *Gespräche mit Goethe in der letzten Jahren seines Lebens,* H.H. Hoeben (ed), Leipzig.

Edwards, Betty 1983: *Drawing on the Right Side of the Brain,* Fontana, UK.

———, 1988: *Drawing on the artist inside you,* Fontana, UK.

Ekman, B. & Nobel, A. 1982: 'Om humaniora för naturvetare in gymnasieskolan' (On the Humanities for science pupils in the secondary school), *Pedagogisk Forskning i Uppsala* No.39. Uppsala University.

Eliot, T.S. 1944: 'The man of letters and the future of Europe.' In *Horizon: a review of literature and art.* Vol.X. No.60.

———, 1957: 'Goethe and the sage.' In *On Poetry and Poets,* Faber & Faber.

Eppinger, H. 1985: *Humor und Heiterkeit im Leben und Werk Rudolf Steiners.* Goetheanum, 1985.

Eriksson, G. 1962: *Elias Fries och den romantiska biologin (Elias Fries and Romantic Biology),* Almqvist & Wiksell.

———, 1969: *Romantikens värld speglad i 1800-talets svenska vetenskap (The world of Romanticism mirrored in nineteenth century Swedish science),* Wahlström & Widstrand.

———, 1981: 'Från Galilei till Gamow.' *Institutionen för idéhistoria. Umeå universitet.* No. 16.

———, 1984: 'Om stilens betydelse i humaniora' (On the importance of style in the Humanities), *Tvärsnitt* No.1.

———, and Svensson, Lena 1986: *Vetenskapen i underlandet (Science in Wonderland),* Norstedts.

Eriksson, K.-E. 1987: series of articles in *Dagens Nyheter:* 'Farväl till Newton' (Farewell to Newton), 1 March and 4 February 1987.

Eurythmie in Kunst, Pädagogik, Medizin. Collection of articles from magazine *Erziehungskunst,* 1975, booklet No.6. Freies Geistesleben, Stuttgart. See also the magazine *Balder* No. 16/17, 1980, on Eurythmy.

Fant, Å. 1977: *Framtidens byggnad, 1913–23 (Architecture of the future).* A study comparing Rudolf Steiner's architecture in Dornach with the group of architects around Bruno Taut in Berlin. Akademilitteratur.

———, 1989: *Hilma af Klint — Ockult målarinna och abstrakt pionjär. (Hilma af Klint. Occult painter and pioneer of abstract art),* exhibition catalogue of Stockholm's Moderna museet, No.232. Raster förlag.

Forman, P. 1985: 'Weimarkultur, kausalitet och kvantteori, 1918–27.' In *Häften för kritiska studier* 3/85.

Forser, T. 1977: *Humaniora på undantag — Humanistiska forskningstraditioner i Sverige (The Humanities put to one side. Humanist research traditions in Sweden),* an anthology. Pan/Norstedts.

Forum Järna (a cultural magazine). First issue January 1991. Address: Pl.1800, 153 00 Järna.

Frängsmyr, T. 1984: *Vetenskapsmannen som hjälte (The scientist as hero).* (see the chapter on *The Death of Nature-Women, Ecology and the Scientific Revolution* by C. Merchant, 1980), Norstedts.

Fries, E. 1964: 'Äro naturvetenskaperna något bildningsmedel?' (Are the natural sciences a means of culture?). In *Botaniska utflykter. Natur och Kultur.*

Gardner, H. 1985: *Frames of Mind— the Theory of Multiple Intelligences,* Basic Books.

Goethe, J.W. von 1979: *The Tale of the Green Snake and the Beautiful Lily.* Floris Books; Rudolf Steiner Publications, NY.

———, *Faust* (Part One/Part Two) Trans. Philip Wayne, 1949. Penguin, UK.

Goethes färglära (Goethe's Theory of Colour), with introduction, commentaries and appendix by Pehr Sällström, 1976. Kosmos Förlag.

Goethes Werke. Hamburgerausgabe (14 vols). Published by E.Trunz. Verlag C.H. Beck, Munich.

Granit, R. 1983: *Hur kom det sig? — Forskarminnen och motiveringar (How did it happen? — Reminiscences from research, and motivations),* Norstedts.

Grimen, H. 1989: 'Handling, differensiering og rasjonalitet' (Action, differentiation and rationality), Centre for Theory of Science, publication series No.10, Bergen University.

Hägerstrand, T. 1986: in Swedish Council report *Kulturvetenskaperna i framtiden.* Humanistisk-samhällsvetenskapliga forskningsrådet. (See below.)

Hall, T. 1981: *Naturvetenskap och poesi (Science and Poetry),* Bonniers.

Hallgren, A. 1987: 'Jag är haren' — Joseph Beuys som en personifiering av arketypen trickster (I am the hare — Joseph Beuys as a personification of the trickster archetype), Konstvetenskapliga institutionen, Stockholms universitet.

Harding, S. 1986: *The Science Question in Feminism,* Cornell University Press.

Harlan, V. 1986: *Was ist Kunst? Werkstattsgespräch mit Joseph Beuys.* Urachhaus, Stuttgart.

Hauck, H. 1981: *Handarbeit und Kunstgewerbe. Angaben von Rudolf Steiner,* Freies Geistesleben, Stuttgart.

Hecht, W. 1982: *Goethe als Zeichner,* C.H. Beck, Munich.

Hegge, H. 1967: 'Noen vitenskapsteoretiske sporsmål belyst ved Goethes naturvitenskap' (Some questions on the theory of science elucidated by Goethe's science), *Norsk filosofisk tidskrift,* vol 2.

———, 1987: *Frihet, individualitet og samfunn — En moralfilosofisk, erkjennelseteoretisk og socialfilosofisk studie i menneskelig eksistens (Freedom, individuality and society — a moral philosophical, theory of knowledge and social philosophical study on human existence),* Oslo University.

Heisenberg, W. 1948: *Wandlungen in den Grundlagen der Naturwissenschaft.* Lecture on 'Die Goethesche und die Newtonische Farbenlehre im Lichte der modernen Physik,' 1941.

———, 1962: *Philosophic Problems of Nuclear Science,* Faber, London.

———, 1967: 'Das naturbild Goethes und die technisch-naturwissenschaftliche Welt.' In *Neue Folge des Jahrbuchs der Goethe Gesellschaft,* No.29. See also *Frankfurter Allgemeine Zeitung,* 23 May 1967.

Heitler, W. 1968: *Naturvetenskapen och människan (Science and man),* Verbum. (German ed. 1961.)

Hellström, E. (ed) 1986: *Växa för livet. Waldorfpedagogik — en fortbildningsmodell (Grow for life. The Waldorf approach — a model for further education),* Norstedts.

Hemleben, J. 1963: *Rudolf Steiner.* Rowohlt, Hamburg (original German edition). English trans. Leo Twyman 1975. Henry Goulden, East Grinstead, UK.

Hermodsson, E. 1968: *Rit och revolution (Rite and revolution),* Verbum.

———, 1975: *Synvända (Turn-sight) Essays and polemics.* Rabén & Sjögren.

———, 1976: *Att ge namn (Giving names),* From publication dedicated to Georg Landberg. Later in *Ord i kvinnotid,* (1979). Rabén & Sjögren.

———, 1988: *Skapelse utlämnad: samlade dikter (Creation deserted: collected poems),* Rabén & Sjögren.

Holbaeck-Hanssen, L. 1976: *Metoder og Modeller i markedsföringen. Bind 3: Planleggning, budsjettering og styringssystemer (Methods and models in marketing. Volume 3: Planning, budgeting and management systems),* Oslo: Tanum-Nordli.

Holm, I. 1965: *Harry Martinson — Myter, Målningar, Motiv (Harry Martinson Myths, Paintings, Motifs),* Aldus.

Holton, G. 1988: 'The roots of complementarity.' In *Daedalus — Journal of the American Academy of Arts and Sciences.* Summer 1988.

Huber, J. 1979: 'Astral-Marx.' In *Kursbuch,* Rotbuch. No.55.

Humanistisk-samhällsvetenskapliga forskningsrådet (Swedish Council for Research in the Humanities and Social Sciences), 1986: Report on *Kulturvetenskapen i framtiden (The Humanities in the Future).*

INFO3 (Journal of anthroposophical initiatives), Frankfurt.

Jaki, S.L. 1969: 'Goethe and the Physicists,' *American Journal of Physics,* 37.

Janik, A. and Toulmin, S. 1973: *Wittgenstein's Vienna,* Touchstone, Simon & Schuster, NY.

Johannessen, K. & Rolf, B. 1989: *Om tyst kunskap (On hidden knowledge),* Centrum för didaktik, Uppsala universitet. No.7.

Johannesson, L. (ed) 1986: Marita Lindgren-Fridells festskrift, 'Konstpedagogiskt avantgarde.' (Publication dedicated to Marita Lindgren-Fridell 'Art-pedagogical avant garde'). Acta Universitatis Upsaliensis. Ars Suetica 9.

Johannisson, K. 1984: *Magic, Science and Institutionalization in the Seventeenth and Eighteenth Centuries,* (stencil). Swedish translation in *Lychnos,* year-book of Lärdomshistoriska samfundet, 1984.

Josefson, I. 1991: *Kunskapens former. Det reflekterande yrkeskunnandet (The forms of knowledge. The reflecting professional expertise),* Carlsson Bokförlag.

Kandinsky, V. 1969: *Om det andliga i konsten.* No.1 of series of publications by Royal Swedish Academy of Arts. Stockholm.

Karlsson, I. and Ruth, A. 1983: *Samhället som teater (Society as theatre),* Liber.

Klingborg, A. 1962: 'Konsten och viljan' (Art and will). Article in magazine *På Väg,* No.4.

———, 1971: 'Ur arkitekturens historia i klass tolv' (From the history of architecture in class twelve). In *På Väg,* No. 4.

———, 1975: 'Konstnärligt skapande' (Artistic creativity), *På Väg,* No.1.

———, 1988: 'Reformpedagogen' (The reformist teacher). In *Inspiration och förnyelse. Carl Malmsten 100 år.* Nordiska museet *et al.,* Wiken.

———, 1983: *Trädgård till nöje och nytta (Gardens for pleasure and purpose),* Kosmos.

———, and Fant, Å. 1985: *Tendenser i vår tids arkitektur (Trends in the architecture of our time),* Kosmos.

———, and Carlgren, F. *(see* Carlgren, F.)

Knight, F. 1974: *Beethoven and the Age of Revolution,* International, NY.

Langer, S. 1953: *Feeling and Form,* Routledge and Kegan Paul, London.

Larsen, A. 1980: 'Konstens helgedom' (The temple of art), in *Antropos* No.8, 1980.

Larsson, H. 1910: *Intuition. Några ord om diktning och vetenskap (Intuition. A few words on writing poetry and on science),* Bonniers. Stockholm

———, 1966: *Poesins logik (The logic of poesy),* Aldus/Bonniers.

Lehrs, E. 1952: *Man or Matter. Introduction to a spiritual understanding of nature on the basis of Goethe's method of training and thought.* Faber, London.

Liebendörfer, W. 1987: 'Erfahrung in der Geographie und ihre Vertiefung zu gestigen Verstehen — dargestellt an Beispielen aus Skandinavien.' In *Erziehungskunst — Monatsschrift zur Pädagogik Rudolf Steiners.* Publication No.5.

Liedman, S.-E. 1966: *Det organiska livet i tysk debatt 1795–1845 (The German debate on organic life, 1795–1845),* Gothenburg University

———, 1977: 'Humanistiska forskningstraditioner i Sverige. Kritiska och historiska perspektiv' (Humanist research traditions in Sweden. Critical and historical perspectives). In Forser, T. (ed.) 1977 *(op.cit.)*

Lievegoed, B. 1979: *Phases. The spiritual rhythms of adult life.* Rudolf Steiner Press, London.

Liljevalchs Art Hall 1987: *Brännpunkt Düsseldorf. Joseph Beuys och hans krets (Focus on Düsseldorf. Joseph Beuys and his circle),* Liljevachs exhibition catalogue.

Lindberg, A.-L. 1988: *Konstpedagogikens dilemma (The Dilemma of Teaching Art),* Lund University Press.

Lindberg, S.G. 1977: 'Terrae filius och hans bröder. Lärda narrar, kloka tokar och tredjeopponenten' (Terrae filius and his brothers. Learned buffoons, wise fools and the Third Opponent.) Year-book 1977/78 Collegium Curiosorum Novum, Uppsala.

Lindborg, R. 1983: 'Vetenskap contra mystik.' (Science versus mysticism). In *Insikt och handling. Humanistiskt debattforum,* Vol.2, No.1 and 2.

Lindenberg, C. 1977: *Waldorfskolan. Lära utan fruktan, handla medvetet och med ansvar (The Waldorf School. Learn without fear, act consciously and with responsibility),* Bonniers.

Lindgren-Fridell, M. 1960: Bildsymbolernas kraft (The power of pictorial symbols), *See* No.22. *See also* Johannesson, L. 1986.

Lindholm, S. 1985: *Kunskap — från fragment till helhetssyn (Knowledge — from fragment to holism),* Kontenta.

Lissau, R. 1987: *Rudolf Steiner — Life, work, inner path and social initiatives,* Hawthorn Press, UK.

Ljunggren, M. 1985: 'Antroposofins decennium i Ryssland.' (The decade of Anthroposophy in Russia). In *Antropos,* Nos.2–3, 1985.

Ljungquist, W. 1963: Preface in *Antroposofi i teori och praktik.* Orion/Bonniers.

Lukacs, G. 1949: *Goethes Faust,* Ljus.

Lunggren, M. 1982: 'The Dream of Rebirth — a study of Andrej Belyi's novel *Peterburg,'* doctoral thesis, Institute for Slavonic and Baltic languages. Stockholm University.

McCormmach, R. 1982: *Night Thoughts of a Classical Physicist,* Harvard University Press.

May, R. 1975: *Modet att skapa (Courage to be creative),* Aldus.

Mees-Christeller, Eva 1988: *Kunsttherapie in der Praxis,* Urachhaus, Stuttgart.

Morgenstern, C. 1947: *Alle Galgenlieder,* Insel.

Mücke, J. and Rudolph, A.A. 1979: *Erinnerungen an Rudolf Steiner und seine Wirksamkeit an der Arbeiterbildungsschule in Berlin 1899–1904,* Zbinden, Basel.

Mumford, L. 1978: *Kunskapens automatisering (The automatization of knowledge),* Delegationen för lånsiktsmotiverad forskning, Stockholm.

Newman, Judie 1984: *Saul Bellow and History,* St Martin's Press, NY.

Nietzsche, F. 1987: *Den glada vetenskapen (The glad science),* Korpen.

Nilsson, P. 1975: 'Goethe, Newton och färgerna.' (Goethe, Newton and the colours.) In *Upptäckten av universum. Essäer om människor och världsbilder (Discovery of the universe. Essays on people and pictures of the world),* Rabén & Sjögren.

Nobel, A. 1979: 'Boken i skolan' (The book in school — a study with special reference to the function of the library in the elementary school), Ph.D. thesis. Acta Universitatis Upsaliensis. Uppsala Studies in Education 10. Stockholm: Almqvist & Wiksell International.

———, 1982: 'Pedagogik, konst och vetenskap' (Pedagogy, art and science), *Tvärsnitt* No.1.

———, and Sjöstedt, B. 1982: *Konst och konstnärer i skolans arbete (Art and artists in the work of the school),* Sektionen för läromedelsfrågor. Stockholm: Skolöverstyrelsen.

———, and Ekman, B. *see* Ekman, B.

———, 1982: *Forskningsinformation för barn och ungdom — ett utredningsuppdrag (Research information for children and young people — an investigation),* Arbetsrapporter från Pedagogiska institutionen, Uppsala universitet No.48.

———, 1990 (first printed 1984): *Hur får kunskap liv? Om konst och eget skapande i undervisning (How does knowledge achieve life? On art and one's own creativity in teaching),* Allmänna förlaget. Stockholm.

———, 1986: 'Datorer och kunskapsutveckling' (Computers and the development of knowledge), *Forskning om utbildning,* No.1.

———, 1990: 'Waldorfpedagogikens okända bakgrund' (The unknown background to Waldorf Education), *Tiden,* No.9/19.

Nordin-Lönner, Ulla 1987: *C.J.L. Almqvists Målaren — En strukturanalys (C.J.L. Almqvist's 'The Painter' — a structural analysis),* Almqvist & Wiksell.

Norlin, E. 1986: *I fantasins och arbets skola. Bilder och berättelser ur ett gymnasieprojekt (In the school of the imagination and work. Pictures and tales from a secondary school project),* Carlssons.

Olsson, Hagar 1965: *Ediths brev (Edith's letters),* Letters from Edith Södergran to Hagar Olsson, with commentaries by Hagar Olsson, Schildts.

Oppenheimer, F. 1972: 'The Exploratorium. A playful museum combines perception and art in science education.' *American Journal of Physics,* Vol.40.

———, 1977: In *Coming to our senses.* A report by the American Council for the Arts in Education.

På Väg. Magazine for the Waldorf educational system. See *På Väg* subject index and list of authors, October 1960–October 1990. Address: *På Väg,* Box 78, 161 26 Bromma.

Palmer, O. 1986: *Rudolf Steiner om* Frihetens filosofi *(Rudolf Steiner on* The Philosophy of Freedom), Bokarbeten, Järna.

Poeppig, F. 1960: *Rudolf Steiner — der grosse Unbekannte. Leben und Werk.* Bettina Woiczik OHG.

Railing, Patricia 1989: *From Science to Sytems of Art — On Russian Art and Language 1910–20,* Artists Bookworks, East Sussex, UK.

Read, H. 1950: Lectures in *Education and art: a symposium.* E. Ziegfield (ed). UNESCO 1953.

———, 1953: *Art and personality.*

———, 1956: *Education through art,* Faber, London.

———, 1963: *To Hell with Culture,* Routledge & Kegan Paul.

———, 1967: *Art and Alienation. The role of the artist in society.* Thames & Hudson.

Richards, M.C. 1989: *Centering — in Pottery, Poetry and the Person.* Wesleyan University Press, USA.

Richardson, G. 1987: *Tekniken, människan och samhället. — Humanistiska inslag i 1940– och 50–talens tekniska utbildning (Technology, man and society. Humanist elements in the technological education of the 1940s and 1950s),* Föreningen för svensk utbildningshistoria 160.

Ringbom, S. 1970: *The Sounding of the Cosmos.* A study of the spiritualism of Kandinsky and the genesis of abstract painting. Åbo. Acta Academica Aboensis.

———, 1982: 'Kandinsky und das Okkulte.' In *Kandinsky und München. Begegnungen und Wandlungen 1896–1914.*

———, 1986: 'Transcending the visible: The generation of the abstract pioneers.' In *The spiritual in art: Abstract painting 1890–1985.* Los Angeles County Museum of Art, Abbeville Press, NY.

Robygge. Catalogue of literature with anthroposophic orientation. 1990.

Rodari, G. 1988: *Fantasins grammatik (The grammar of the imagination),* Bokförlaget Korpen.

Rydén, L. (ed) 1990: *Etik för forskare (Ethics for researchers),* an anthology around work on the Uppsala Codex. UHÄ/FoU 1990:1.

Sällström, P.(ed) 1976: *Goethes färglära (Goethe's Theory of Colour),* Kosmos.

———, 1987: 'Goethes färglära och Newtons teori om ljuset' (Goethe's Theory of Colour and Newton's Theory of Light.) In *Kosmos Fysikhistoria,* annual publication of Svenska fysikersamfundet, Vol. 64.

———, 1980: 'Goethe och naturvetenskapen' (Goethe and science). In *Balder* No.18/19, special issue on alternative research.

———, 1982. 'Goethe som naturforskare' (Goethe as scientific researcher). *På Väg,* No.2.

Sandqvist, Mona 1989: *Alkemins tecken i Göran Sonnevis* Det omöjliga *(Alchemical symbols in Göran Sonnevi's* The Impossible). Literature, theatre, film. Nya serien 4. Lund University Press.

Sandström, S. 1986: *Redon. Darwinistisk symbolism. (Redon. Darwinian symbolism),* Scripta Sancti Petri. Symposion.

———, 1989: 'De sinnliga konceptens konst och tänkandet' (The art and thinking of the sensual concept), *Paletten,* No.1.

———, 1990: 'Bildkonsten och den tysta mångdimensionalitetens tänkande.' (Pictorial art and the tacit thinking of multiple dimensionality), *Paletten,* No.2.

Savitch, Marie 1965: *Marie Steiner-von Sivers — Mitarbeiterin von Rudolf Steiner,* Philosophisch-Anthroposophischer Verlag, Dornach.

Schiller, F. 1967: *On the Aesthetic Education of Man in a Series of Letters,* Clarendon, Oxford.

Schneider, P. 1985: *Einführung in die Waldorfpädagogik,* Klett-Cotta.

Schwenk, T. 1965 rep. 1996: *Sensitive chaos. The creation of flowing forms in water and air,* Rudolf Steiner Press, London.

SOU 1981: *Forskningens framtid (The future of Research.)* (29)

Sperry, R. 1983: *Science and Moral Priority,* Basil Blackwell, Oxford.

Stachelhaus, H. 1989: *Joseph Beuys,* Wilhelm Heyne, Munich.

Steiner, Rudolf. **Principal titles.** GA = Gesamtausgabe (Collected edition of Steiner's complete works. Rudolf Steiner Verlag, Dornach, Switzerland.)

———, *Briefe,* Vol.1 (GA 38).

———, *The Course of My Life* (1923–25), Anthroposophic Press, NY, 1986.

———, *The Education of the Child in the Light of Anthroposophy* (1907), Rudolf Steiner Press, London, 1981.

———, *Gesammelte Aufsätze zur Kultur- und Zeitgeschichte, 1887–1901* (GA 31).

———, *Gesammelte Aufsätze sur Literatur 1884–1902* (GA 32).

———, *Goethe as the Founder of a New Science of Aesthetics* (1888), Anthroposophical Publishing Company, London, 1922.

———, *Goethean Science,* Mercury Press, Spring Valley, 1988. Also published as *Goethe the Scientist,* Anthroposophic Press, NY, 1950.

———, 'Haeckel and his Opponents,' in *Three Essays on Haeckel and Karma* (1914), Theosophical Publishing Society, London 1914.

———, *The Karma of Vocation* (1916), Anthroposophic Press, NY, 1984.

———, *Kunst und Kunsterkenntnis* (GA 271).

———, *Mysticism at the Dawn of the Modern Age* (1901), (also published as *Eleven European Mystics),* Steiner Books, New Jersey, 198O.

———, *The Philosophy of Spiritual Activity — A Philosophy of Freedom* (1894), Rudolf Steiner Press, Bristol, 1992.

———, *Schiller and our Times* (May 4, 1905), Anthroposophical Publishing Company, London, 1933. From *Ursprung und Ziel des Menschen — Grundbegriffe des Geisteswissenschaft* (GA 53).

———, *A Theory of Knowledge based on Goethe's World Conception* (1886), Anthroposophic Press, NY, 1968.

———, *Theosophy — An introduction to the supersensible knowledge of the world and the destination of Man* (1904), Rudolf Steiner Press, London, 1989.

———, *Towards Social Renewal* (1919), Rudolf Steiner Press, Bristol, 1992.

———, *Truth and Knowledge* (1892), Steiner Books, NY, 1981.

Steiner, Rudolf. **Lectures**

———, *The Child's Changing Consciousness and Waldorf Education* (1923), Rudolf Steiner Press, London, 1988.

———, *Die Erneurerung der drei grossen Ideale der Menschheit Kunst, Wissenschaft und Religion* (Feb 22, 1923), Philosophisch-Anthroposophischer Verlag, Dornach, 1943.

Discussions with Teachers (1919), Rudolf Steiner Press, London, 1983.

———, *The Essentials of Education* (1924), Rudolf Steiner Press, London, 1982.

———, *The Gospel of St John* (1908), Anthroposophic Press, NY, 1984.

———, *Human Values in Education* (1924), Rudolf Steiner Press, London, 1971.

———, *The Kingdom of Childhood* (1924), Rudolf Steiner Press, London, 1988.

———, *A Modern Art of Education* (1923), Rudolf Steiner Press, London, 1981.

———, *Practical Advice to Teachers* (1919), Rudolf Steiner Press, London, 1988.

———, *A Social Basis for Primary and Secondary Education* (1919), Steiner Schools Fellowship, Forest Row, 1994.

———, *Study of Man* (1919), Rudolf Steiner Press, London, 198l.

———, *Waldorf Education for Adolescence* (June 1921), Kolisko Archive Publications, 1980.

———, *West and East — Contrasting Worlds* (June 1922), Rudolf Steiner Publishing Company, London (no date).

———, *The Younger Generation* (1922), Anthroposophic Press, NY, 1967.

Steiner, Rudolf. **Summary reference volumes.** Rudolf Steiner Verlag, Dornach.

———, I. (1984). *Bibliographische Übersicht (Bibliographical overview).*

———, II. (1990). *Sachwort- und Namenregister der Inhaltsangaben (Subject and name index of contents).*

———, III. (1982). *Inhaltsangaben aus 291 Bänden der Gesamtausgabe (Summary contents of 291 volumes of the complete works).*

Stockmeyer, Karl 1991: *Rudolf Steiner's Curriculum for Waldorf Schools,* Steiner School Fellowship Publications, Forest Row, East Sussex, UK.

Strindberg, A. 1976: *En blå bok 1 (A blue book 1),* Wahlström & Widstrand, Stockholm.

Sundén, H. 1962: *Rudolf Steiner: en bok om antroposofi (Rudolf Steiner: a book on anthroposophy).* An SKDB book.

Sundin, B. 1982: *Barnen och de sköna konsterna (Children and the fine arts),* Statens kulturråd.

———, 1982: *Musiken i människan. Om tradition och förnyelse inom det estetiska områdets pedagogik (Music in man. On tradition and renewal in aesthetic education),* Natur och Kultur.

Tranströmer, T. 1984: *Dikter (Poems),* Månpocket.

Uberoi, J.P.S. 1984: *The Other Mind of Europe. Goethe as a Scientist.* Oxford University Press.

Ulin, B. 1982: *Att finna ett spår (Finding a way).* Motives and methods in mathematics teaching. Experiences from Waldorf Pedagogy. Robygge.

Vasco, G.M. 1978: *Diderot and Goethe. A study in science and humanism.* Librairie Slatkine, Geneva.

Walter, J. 1940: *Goethe als Seher und Erforscher der Natur.* Dedicated special publication from the Leopold Academy in Halle.

Wells, G.A. 1978: *Goethe and the Development of Science, 1750–1900,* Sijthoff & Noordhoff, Netherlands.

Wilenius, R. 1981: *Bildningens villkor. Ett utkast till fostrans filosofi (The conditions of culture. A draft for a philosophy of education),* AB Svenska Läromedel.

———, 1986: 'Utveckling och utbildning för ett rikare liv' (Development and education for a richer life), lecture addressed to the seminar on the future of the Nordic welfare society, arranged by the Nordic Council's Social and Environmental Committee in Uppsala 2–4 April, 1986.

Wright, G.H. von 1964: *Tanke och förkunnelse (Thought and Promulgation),* Gleerups.

———, 1978: *Humanismen som livshållning och andra essayer (Humanism as attitude to life, and other essays),* Rabén & Sjögren.

———, 1986: *Vetenskapen och förnuftet: ett försök till orientering (Science and reason: an attempt to orient the reader),* Bonniers.

Zajonc, A.G. 1983: *Facts as theory: Aspects of Goethe's Philosophy of Science.* Teacher's College Record. USA.

———, 1973: 'Goethe's Theory of Colors and Scientific Intuition' in *American Journal of Physics,* 44, No.4 (April 1976).

———, 1984: 'The Wearer of Shapes. Goethe's study of clouds and weather.' *Orion.*

Ziegfield, E. (ed.) *Education and art — a symposium.* UNESCO 1953.

Zweig, S. 1945: *Die Welt von Gestern,* Fischer.

Appendix 1: On the publication of Steiner's lectures

An extract from Rudolf Steiner's autobiography The Course of My Life *(Chapter 35) translated by Otto Wannamaker.*

Two results are available from my anthroposophical work: first, my books issued for the general public; secondly, a great number of courses of lectures which were at first to be considered as privately printed and to be sold only to members of the Theosophical (later the Anthroposophical) Society. These were really reports on lectures, more or less accurate, which, for lack of time, I could not correct. It would have pleased me best if spoken words had remained spoken words. But the members wished the courses privately printed, so this came about. If I had then had time to correct the reports, the restriction 'for members only' would from the beginning have been unnecessary. For more than a year now this restriction has been dropped.

At this point in this 'course of my life' it is most of all necessary to say how the two things — my published works and the privately printed material — combine into what I elaborated as anthroposophy.

Whoever wishes to trace my own inner struggle and labour to set anthroposophy before the consciousness of the present age must do this on the basis of the writings published for general circulation. Moreover, in these writings I make my position clear with respect to everything in the nature of a striving for knowledge which exists in the present age. Here is presented that which took form for me more and more in 'spiritual beholding,' what became the edifice of anthroposophy — in a form incomplete, to be sure, from many points of view.

Along with this requirement, however, of building up anthroposophy and thereby meeting only the situation resulting from the need to impart information from the world of spirit to the contemporary cultural world in general, the other requirement now appeared — to meet fully whatever became manifest in the membership as the needs of their minds and the craving of their spirits.

Strongest of all was the inclination to hear the Gospels and the content of the Biblical writings in general placed in what had appeared as the anthroposophical light. The desire existed to attend lecture cycles on these revelations given to mankind.

While internal lecture cycles were delivered in accordance with this requirement, something else came about in addition. Only members attended these courses. They were acquainted with the elementary communications out of anthroposophy. It was possible to speak to them as to persons advanced in the realm of anthroposophy. These internal lectures were conducted as they could not have been if they had been writings for the general public.

In internal groups I could rightly speak about things in a form which I should have been obliged to modify for a public presentation if from the first these things had been intended for such an audience.

Thus in the two things, the public and the private publications, something really exists which springs out of two different backgrounds. The entirely public writings are the result of what struggled and laboured in me; in the privately printed material the Society itself shares in this struggle and labour. I listen to the pulsations in the soul-life of the membership, and out of my sharing in what I thus hear the form of the lecture course is determined.

Nothing has ever been said that is not in utmost degree the purest result of the developing anthroposophy. There can be no question of any concession whatever to the preconceived opinions or sentiments of the members. Whoever reads this privately printed material can take it in the fullest sense as containing what anthroposophy has to say. Therefore, it was possible without hesitation — when complaints became too insistent in this direction — to depart from the plan of circulating this printed matter among members alone. Only, it will be necessary to put up with the fact that erroneous matter is included in the lecture reports which I did not revise.

The right to a judgment about the content of such privately printed material can naturally be conceded only to one who knows what is taken for granted as the prerequisite basis of this judgment. And for most of this printed matter prerequisite will be *at least* the anthroposophical knowledge of the human being, and of the cosmos, to the extent that their nature is set forth in anthroposophy, and of what exists in the form of 'anthroposophical history' in the communications from the world of spirit.

Appendix 2: Waldorf Schools around the world

Contact addresses in English-speaking countries:

Australia. Association of Rudolf Steiner Schools in Australia, 213 Wonga Road, Warranwood, Vic 3134.

Canada. See United States of America

Ireland. See United Kingdom

New Zealand. Federation of Rudolf Steiner Schools, P O Box 888, Hastings, Hawkes Bay.

South Africa. Southern African Federation of Waldorf Schools, P O Box 67587, Bryanston, 2021.

United Kingdom. Steiner Schools Fellowship, Kidbrooke Park, Forest Row, East Sussex, RH18 5JB.

United States of America. Association of Waldorf Schools of North America. 3750 Bannister Road, Fair Oaks, CA 95628.

General list of countries with number of Steiner/Waldorf schools:

EUROPE: Austria (10); Belgium (17); Croatia (3); Czech Republic (7); Denmark (16); Estonia (6); Finland (17); France (11); Germany (162); Hungary (7); Ireland (2); Italy (13); Latvia (2); Liechtenstein (1); Luxembourg (1); Netherlands (91); Norway (24); Poland (1); Portugal (1); Romania (5); Russia (2); Slovenia (1); Spain (2); Sweden (24); Switzerland (38); United Kingdom (31)

AFRICA: Kenya (1); South Africa (7)

MIDDLE EAST: Egypt (1); Israel (3)

NORTH AMERICA: Canada (12 in Alberta, British Columbia, Ontario, Quebec); United States of America (87 in California, Colorado, Florida, Georgia, Hawaii, Idaho, Illinois, Maine, Maryland, Massachusetts, Michigan, Minnesota, New Hampshire, New Jersey, New Mexico, New York, North Carolina, Ohio, Oregon, Pennsylvania, Rhode Island, Texas, Vermont, Virginia, Washington, Wisconsin)

LATIN AMERICA: Argentinia (2); Brazil (7); Chile (2); Colombia (3); Ecuador (2); Mexico (2); Peru (2); Uruguay (1)

ASIA: Japan (1)

AUSTRALASIA: Australia (29); New Zealand (7)

Index